BEYOND DESOLATE TACKLES A VERY TOUGH AND VERY PRESENT ISSUE IN the world today, and it does so in a way that gives hope to those that have experienced abuse of any form. It speaks directly to anyone who might be too scared or too scarred to find their own voice anymore. This book will be one that I use as a reference and would also recommend to anyone who feels hopeless.

Melissa Brock, Superchick

SEXUAL ABUSE IS A PROBLEM THAT IS MUCH MORE PREVALENT THAN most would like to admit. Many adults who presently experience broken lives have childhood sexual abuse as a common denominator. It is refreshing to read a book that deals with this subject with compassion, rich insight and a strong biblical framework. It will be a help to those who counsel and to those who have experienced sexual trauma.

Tim Fletcher, Finding Freedom *Founder and Educator, Winnipeg, Canada*

I AM DEEPLY STRUCK BY THE ILLUMINATING AND PERCEPTIVE APproach Hannah and Tammy have taken to the delicate combination of spirituality, counseling and the ramifications of sexual abuse and exploitation. Hannah and Tammy have truly and gently touched the deepest insults inflicted upon the victims of sexual abuse and sex trafficking. Their writing not only relieves the chronic torment, it unlocks the shackles of the continued abuse inflicted upon ourselves in the aftermath of sexual exploitation, sexual abuse and sex trafficking (formerly and pejoratively referred to as prostitution).

Susan Munsey, LCSW, Executive Director of Generate Hope

THROUGHOUT MY EDUCATION, COUNSELING, AND TEACHING, I HAVE never encountered a book on abuse that cultivates empathy and healing comparable to *Beyond Desolate*. It provides encouragement to abuse survivors, as well as education to loved ones and professionals

by reflecting on personal journeys through scripture, life experiences, and God's love. My spirit rejoiced as the authors inspired hope and opened my eyes to the true healing and joy that only God can provide.

Angelia D. H. Dickens, Ph.D., Capella University

BEYOND DESOLATE IS NOT DESENSITIZED OR CLICHE BUT RATHER POW-erful, authentic and moving. The journey allows readers to present our haunting questions by anticipating our wrestling and honoring our pain. And yet, we are not left there but rather gently ushered into the hope and love of God where only He can resurrect our suffering into a new song that goes "beyond the desolation." I recommend this book as a must-read for those who have experienced abuse or care for those who have.

Shannon Rants, M.A., Licensed Professional Counselor

BEYOND DESOLATE ISN'T JUST FOR WOMEN OR JUST FOR MEN OR JUST for those who have been abused or just for Americans. It speaks to the pain of humanity suffering since the Fall and it brings hope to the hurting of the world, a world where too many are hurting and too few can see any hope at all.

Robert Andrews, Central Asian Church leader and Culture Advisor

WHILE READING THIS DEEPLY MOVING, EXCEPTIONAL BOOK, I KEPT thinking of how many copies I want to purchase and give away to bring instruction, encouragement and hope. Tammy and Hannah employ careful boldness to describe sexual abuse from the vantage point of survivors, each of whom may processes their trauma differently. Though written by two women abused by men, both of whom I count as dear friends, it is refreshing to find no hint of global disdain for the male gender, rather an inclusive study of the issue from both perspectives. *Beyond Desolate* presents a thoroughly scriptural viewpoint, while disagreeing with differing positions using kind professionalism and outstanding scientific and biblical research. I was often moved to tears to read the agony of the suffering, the what others are saying about

Beyond Desolate

WE HUMAN BEINGS TEND NOT TO SEE THE UGLY BECAUSE IT HURTS. It's disturbing. And it calls you to do something. But nothing is hidden from the eyes of the sovereign and tender hearted God. He is brave to talk about Tamar and her sad story in His Holy Book, as we call it here in Turkey. *Beyond Desolate* invites us to see the ugly, to understand the sadness, and to rejoice in the redeeming work of the Lord while it equips us to be a part of the solution.

Cigdem Özbek, Pastor, Ankara Foursquare Church

MY HEART SOARED AS I READ *BEYOND DESOLATE*.
It is not a workbook, but it is a sure guide to survivors.
It is not a psalter, but it continually praises God.
It is not a commentary, but it opens the Scripture.
It is not a biography, but it is life stories of two Christ followers in formation.
It is not a wisdom book, but the quotes sparkle like gems.
It is not a romance novel, but it is the story of love.
What is *Beyond Desolate?* It is one of the most well-balanced books I have read on abuse. It hits just the right level by avoiding the equal and opposite dangers of psychobabble and over spiritualization. It unblinkingly faces the horror of abuse and unashamedly insists that our great Father can exchange the desolation of abuse for a life of beauty.

Charles D. Dolph, Ph.D., Cedarville University

BEYOND DESOLATE IS A BRILLIANT INTERPLAY BETWEEN THE WAY IT is and the way it ought to be. The authors have not spared the reader the gruesome details. These stories will break your heart, stir your passion for justice and maybe even reprimand your complacency as a leader in the church. The bigger story that is masterfully weaved throughout will draw your heart and your mind to the core truth of everyone's story, the truth that each of us will need to wrestle through to get beyond desolate and that is: He was there. Tammy and Hannah have masterfully weaved an incredible testimony of theirs and others' stories of abuse and survival from around the globe, yet it is really the story of the all-consuming love of God. I will be recommending this book to pastors, counselors and leaders in the church. It ought to be required reading for church board members, school teachers and anyone else who works with children.

Rod Buxton D.Min., Chair, Department of Counselling, Providence Theological Seminary, Otterburne, MB, Canada

To read *Beyond Desolate* is to get a taste of the all-consuming fire of God. The authors invite its readers to nuzzle into our Savior's warmth, a soothing balm that envelops all who enter into the embrace of His inscrutable peace. This same peace permeates the pages of *Beyond Desolate*, and so allows its readers to experience the healing salve of His Spirit who groans on our behalf in ultrasonic tones. Tammy and Hannah have ripped the lock off of Pandora's Box of helplessness that imprisons the oppressed, the abused, the hopeless, giving voice to the silenced, liberating the songbird from its cage so that it may be free sing the Master's melody once more.

Sarah Campbell, Therapist, Nicaraguan Resource Network Leader

If you work with hurting people, this book is for you—it is a must-read. The authors share deep insights that will help you care for those that are suffering. Each chapter is full of wise, theological, psychological, personal knowledge, and rich examples that will help you in your practice and ministry.

Jamie D. Aten, Ph.D., Director, Humanitarian Disaster Institute, Wheaton College gut-wrenching struggle and genuine healing of God experienced by many survivors. This profound message of hope should be read by every Christian worker, every parent, everyone who has suffered any form of injustice or abuse, or knows someone who has.

Roger Peugh, D. Min., Grace College & Theological Seminary

Beyond
desolate

TAMMY SCHULTZ, Ph.D.
and HANNAH ESTABROOK, M.A.

Beyond desolate

HOPE VERSUS HATE
in the RUBBLE *of*
SEXUAL ABUSE

BMH Books
bmhbooks.com
P.O. Box 544
Winona Lake, IN 46590

Dedication

To my Dad who instilled in me a love for words
and an even greater love for THE Word (1931-2012);

Mukhabbat, who is realizing that LOVE permits pain.
She inspires me daily to live in the land beyond;

Michelle, who has made praying for me and
the writing of *Beyond Desolate* her precious privilege; and

My clients and Grace graduate students who are by far,
the best teachers.

Tammy

To my dad and two brothers, Matthew and Daniel:
You taught me how a girl is supposed to be treated.
This world wasn't a kind one to grow up in,
but I always found safety in your hugs;

Ashley and Laura: You've prayed faithfully for me
and this project. Thanks for being willing characters in
the death-to-life chapters of my *Beyond* story;

My husband: Your love and faithfulness heals
my heart a little more each day. Thanks for always
being the best guy I couldn't just get over;

(Thank You, Father. Wow.)

Hannah

Table of Contents

Birth

a beginning or commencement;
to deliver; to bear.[1]

JUST AS EVERY SURVIVOR HAS A STORY, *BEYOND DESOLATE* WAS ALSO birthed in narrative. Several years ago, the two of us, Hannah and Tammy, took a trip to South Korea to speak at a sexual abuse conference. At the end of the conference a poised and beautiful young woman lingered, waiting until the line-up of folks ran dry. With hesitation, she looked around to ensure that no one could hear and then with her gaze fastened to the floor, she spoke in a hushed tone. A trusted and much-loved leader in her church had sexually violated her when she was teenager. She explained that she would never confront this loved elder as that would bring dishonor to the church. With the aid of trusted translators, we were deluged with many more sad stories of abuse by Korean women.

On that long flight from South Korea to Germany, Hannah scribbled a downpour of ideas in a soft, red leather journal as we talked, dreamed, and prayed while the writing journey of *Beyond Desolate* was born. During our travels across the globe, we have listened to brave male and female survivors share their stories. Sadly, sexual violence is a worldwide phenomenon. More recently, we have become aware of sexual violence that is epidemic in many Muslim countries,[2] regions where counselors are few and far between and settings in which victims are frequently blamed for bringing shame on their families when abuse is revealed.[3] Sexual violations are flavored and affected by cul-

1

tural contexts. Thus, we decided that *Beyond Desolate* would include a call to caregivers to become attuned to the ways that culture shapes and is shaped by trauma. The sullied story of an Israeli princess who was raped would begin the tapestry of *Beyond Desolate* and threads of her narrative would be interwoven throughout its fabric. When we first read Tamar's story in 2 Samuel, we were undone—at the way God so astutely understood and described the way abuse impacted every aspect of her being. Without an excess of words, Scripture reveals that He sees and understands the imprint of sexual violation that crosses culture and class. As a result, we were moved and directed to share the message of God's deep understanding of sexual violence with the myriad of individuals who were living in desolation and the caregivers who journey with them. Simultaneously, Tamar's story invites the reader to contend with the God who permits such violence. Against the backdrop of Tamar's torment, the stage would be set for Jesus, a fellow-sufferer, to speak into the sorrow of survivors and pave the road toward a life beyond desolation.

Along the flight path over Russia we agreed it was imperative that chapter portions should be drawn from the reservoir of our own stories. The bittersweet waters that we have swallowed remind us that *Beyond Desolate* was set in motion long before we met. Two women conceived in different decades, both experienced personally in the ways of abuse. Coincidence? Hardly. We were being prepared in advance by God for what He wanted us to do.[4] It would be of paramount importance to share sips of God's grace poured out in our lives with our readers.

Still, despite all of our combined experiences, personal opinions alone would be insufficient as we intended this to be a research-informed book for veteran caregivers and counselors-in-training who bear witness to stories of traumatized individuals. Thus, we would sift through the river of research, panning for flecks of gold.

As we hiked through the Frankfurt, Germany, airport, we dragged duffle-bag-sized stories stuffed with heartache shared by numerous Korean women at the conference we just left. The heaviness reminded us that we could *not* be immersed in the wrathful waters of sexual abuse without leaning into Him. We would drown if we continued to be saturated in evil via reading stacks of books, watching trauma videos, listening to survivors, and writing about abuse. He must be the air in our life raft, the bell clanging on stormy nights, the shaft of light leading us home. Thus each chapter would be drenched in "God stories" for the benefit of the reader and for the sake of us as writers. Still, the tender voice of the One who searches for the broken and bruised is not always what survivors hear when they read Scripture. Sometimes the degrading taunts of abusers drown out His gentle, persistent call. Thus, our prayer would be that the authentic voice of the One who penned love letters to His people would ring loud and clear.

The five years since that plane ride from South Korea has grown our tattered trust in our good God. We have journeyed through forests of gloom as we heard *one more* story about a famous Christian leader molesting a trusting teenager. We have begged our Abba for His perspective when our own understanding lacked. Each week, we researched, wrote, and then got together over bowls of chicken and rice soup or a cup of chai to read chapters and pray. We challenged each other to dig deeper, to add descriptions of ladders out of the pit, and to look to Him as certain topics felt pitch-black.

Beyond Desolate was written for all who are concerned for survivors of abuse: therapists, medical professionals, family members, and friends. This book is also for survivors. We knew we had hope to offer victims of abuse: that they are not alone and that God *gets* abuse. As we struggled to find the right words for difficult topics, we dreamed about how survivors could be encouraged to share their stories even when words were lacking. We prayed desperately that when survivors bravely dove into the content of a book like this, they might shed the rags of being defined by their perpetrator's evil deeds and instead be clothed in God's power, perspective, and love. To the caregivers who are hearers of evil, this book is a signpost to becoming increasingly grounded in the character of God and wise forms of self-care.

3

Alienating male therapists or male survivors was the last thing on earth we wanted but we realized that two women writing might lend the book a feminine slant. And while survivors of abuse are primarily female,[5] abuse is not respectful of gender and redemption is a gift from a good God desired for daughters and sons alike. Therefore, we received feedback from those who scanned *Beyond Desolate* for "girly" words and analogies that by their usage might create silence or distance.[6]

Just as our writing flight plan was not a straight line from Point A to Point B, neither is the trek of survivors. Rather, this non-linear journey is marked by sharp turns, steep valleys, unexpected detours, and mountains beckoning us onward. Many pages are raw and disturbing, bereft of the neat and tidy. Over the years, we have found that the wreckage of abuse in our own lives and the lives of survivors is not so easily pressed, absent of wrinkles. Perhaps God does not want the mysteries of suffering so easily jettisoned. Instead, the theme that runs like a bright red thread through these pages is that survivors need to speak about their suffering before they can sing the song of hope. *Beyond Desolate* is an invitation onward to the land of Beyond where the kindest of all Kings reigns.

GIVE SORROW WORDS. THE GRIEF THAT DOES NOT SPEAK
WHISPERS THE O'ER-FRAUGHT HEART, AND BIDS IT BREAK.

Malcom in William Shakespeare's Macbeth

CHILD SEXUAL ABUSE [IS] LIKE GETTING BITTEN BY A
RATTLESNAKE: SOME KIDS RECOVER COMPLETELY,
AND SOME [DON'T], BUT IT [ISN'T] GOOD FOR ANYBODY.

Anna Salter

...MY WAY IS HIDDEN FROM THE LORD AND THE JUSTICE
DUE ME ESCAPES THE NOTICE OF MY GOD.

Isaiah 40:27

JUST AS ICEBERGS SHOW ONLY A FRACTION OF THEMSELVES
ABOVE THE SURFACE, SO EVENTS ARE ALWAYS MORE
THAN THEY APPEAR TO BE AT FIRST GLANCE.

John R. Claypool

MYSTERY IS NOT THE ABSENCE OF MEANING,
IT IS THE PRESENCE OF MORE MEANING
THAN WE CAN FULLY COMPREHEND.

Dennis Covington

SOMEONE WAS HURT BEFORE YOU.....BEATEN BEFORE YOU;
HUMILIATED BEFORE YOU; RAPED BEFORE YOU;
YET SOMEONE SURVIVED.

Maya Angelou

Tamar

a desolate woman

Listen closely. It's a story about a rape. Except this one doesn't take place in a poorly lit alley in the inner city hood. This one is tucked away in the pages of Scripture, somewhere between that David and Goliath story and the one about the guy swallowed by a whale.

Few have heard a sermon or Sunday school lesson based on Tamar. But it's there, inspired by the Holy Spirit and recorded in the Word of God.[1]

Once upon a time in a faraway land, a long, long time ago, a beautiful girl lived in a royal palace. As many daughters of kings do, she waited for the day when her Prince Charming would arrive on the scene, recognize her beauty, and fall in love with her.

Prince Charming never came. She didn't live happily ever after. Something devastating happened instead.

Her brother raped her.

Her *brother.*[2]

"Amnon was so frustrated because of his sister Tamar that he made himself ill, for she was a *virgin* and it seemed hard to Amnon to do anything *to* her."[3]

She was a *virgin*. And she was his sister. So she was closed off to him. He wasn't thinking of things he could do *with* her. "It seemed hard to Amnon to do anything *to* her." Notice the word "to." It is absent of any relational emphasis; "to" is about Amnon, not about Tamar.

In his frustration, he consulted a family member. Enter a man named Jonadab.

Listen to Jonadab's words of *wisdom*.

Jonadab: "What's wrong with you? Talk to me."

Amnon: "I am in love with Tamar, the sister of my brother Absalom."[4]

In love.

Strong's concordance offers sundry definitions of love. Understanding the definition of a word in Scripture requires an understanding of the context. As later events in this story show, the brand of "love" Amnon was experiencing was plain old *lust*. In contrast, the variety of love discussed in 1 Corinthians is patient and kind, is not proud, rude, self-seeking, or easily angered, does not delight in evil, and always protects.

Amnon was in lust with Tamar.

"Then Jonadab said to him, 'lie down on your bed and pretend to be ill; when your father comes to see you, say to him, "please let my sister Tamar come and give me some food to eat, and let her prepare the food in my sight, that I may see it and eat from her hand."'"[5]

Is it just us or does it bother anyone else that there was no hesitation in the way Jonadab dispensed this advice? We would have preferred to see: "Then Jonadab warned Amnon that Tamar was not property. He was not entitled to take at will. His uncle was concerned that Amnon's feelings could lead to violation and to violence. Then, having prayed about what Amnon had told him, he shared words of wisdom with him three days later…"

But the Bible doesn't say that.

It says that Jonadab shared his advice with unwavering bravado. In a condensed moment, an entire underhanded and violent scheme was devised and Jonadab doled out a helping hand so the prince could get what he wanted.

Was Jonadab experienced in the ways of manipulation and evil seduction? Our knowledge is lean and spare, but one thing is evident: he connived, colluded, and conspired in the plot against Tamar.

Imagine for a moment that you were watching this incident take place on a stage. The mastermind of the upcoming act (Jonadab) has just exited stage right. Entering stage left is David, and somewhere in the distance we see Tamar hard at work. The scene is absent of any advanced warning, but danger is coming.

We notice that she is beautiful.[6]

Amnon, on center stage, is feigning the kind of groans we would make on our deathbed. The wriggling worm on the hook was set. He solicited King David: could Tamar care for him in his bed-ridden condition? Reeled in. The King didn't hesitate. Royal catch at sea that day. King David fell for it hook, line, and sinker—yet he was a wise king, one of the best.[7]

How did the King miss this?

Simply put, rapists are adept at lying.[8] Perpetrators use outsiders as pawns in their chess game, moving them one or two spaces at a time until a victim is trapped in checkmate. The pawn didn't see it coming.[9] At the same time, this is a **like-father-like-son scene**. Years earlier, David also pilfered what was not his.[10]

Imagine in your mind the point when the King, her father, entreated Tamar to go to Amnon and take care of him. You saw the last scene; you know what's coming. She has no idea. It's tantamount to witnessing a horror movie in which you see a woman racing through a house to escape a nefarious villain. She enters a room and pauses to gulp for air. Meanwhile, the camera is zooming in on the evildoer hiding behind the door. This is the moment when you want to stand up and scream, "He's behind the door! Check behind you! Look!" Unaware of the ambush that awaited her, Tamar obeyed her father; not to mention that she was likely worried about her brother's illness.

Tamar finished baking the cakes and walked to Amnon to feed him. He refused to eat what she had made him. Then the Crown Prince ordered everyone else who was in the room to leave and they complied. Perhaps Tamar began to feel uneasy, but we're not sure. Scripture doesn't specify. In response to his request, she followed him into the bedroom so that Amnon could "eat from her hand."[11]

She drew near to feed him—to care for him and meet his needs. And when she began to feed him, he smelled her scent, heard her voice, and saw what she looked like up close. She was beautiful. How could she have known what would happen next?

Then he grabbed her, and she pleaded with Amnon to stop. Tamar was not silent. She was well-acquainted with the law.[12] She knew that this thing that Amnon was trying to pull, *this* was disgraceful, this was wicked.

She

said

NO.

But Tamar's "no" was spurned. In her own home, she was brutally violated by someone she knew. This is an all-too-common tale.[13]

Tamar said "no" but not every victim is able to voice that word.

Some are scared speechless.
Some don't have enough understanding to know that they could say no.
Some have a hand covering their mouth.
Others were too young to even speak an intelligible sound.

But somehow Tamar uttered something peculiar to twenty-first century, North American culture:

"As for me, where could I get rid of my disgrace? And as for you, you will be like one of the fools in Israel. Now therefore, please speak to the king, for he will not withhold me from you." [14]

What is Tamar saying here? Is she bargaining with her rapist?

As she stares into her attacker's lust-filled eyes it doesn't take her too long to think of what the cost would be. She would be blamed, cast aside as a damaged woman, used, soiled, and tattered. [15]

Tamar stated accurately that Amnon would be seen as a wicked fool. In the Old Testament, rape was considered as serious as murder. Rape warranted death. The Bible takes the penalty of rape more seriously than most justice systems. Perhaps we could take a lesson about the seriousness of sexual assault from the Word of God. [16]

Finally, to his forced offer, she provided a sort of counteroffer.

She asked him to wait
and then

She
Proposed
Marriage

Can you imagine committing your life to a person who looks at you the way Amnon looked at Tamar? She was a thing, an object, his playground. But Tamar knew in her culture, there was nothing worse than being cast aside—reputation beyond repair, alone. She lived in a time and culture when a woman's worth was gauged by the number of sons she could bear. Who would want her now? [17]

Tamar's petition was both a bargaining tool with her raping brother and a cultural reality. There were no rape crisis hotlines for her to call. [18] There were no shelters for her to turn to. If Amnon followed through with his plan, she would be empty. Alone. Desolate. Who would take her side, plead her case, or fight for her innocence?

Presently in Muslim countries around the world, rape is an issue of dishonor toward the family. Sadly, the responsibility for the tarnishing of the family often lies with the victim of the assault. The central goal becomes wiping the family honor clean. Since the woman is no longer a virgin, the solution may involve marrying the rapist. However, often the only man that will accept marrying a woman who is not a virgin is "usually old, handicapped, divorced, or already married."[19] Even when the marriage suitor *is* the rapist.

In Tamar's mind, there was one way out: "If he wants me this badly, then maybe he'll marry me." She also knew the Jewish law. She knew that if her brother raped her, she would be off limits for anyone else to marry—Amnon, her rapist, would be her one and only suitor.[20] But to her pleas, Amnon responded in the way he had been scheming all along: "… He would not listen to her; since he was stronger than she, he violated her and lay with her."[21]

Amnon wanted to own and possess Tamar. He wanted to envelope her, swallow her dignity, and spit out her innocence. He wanted to steal her beauty. So he **RAVAGED** her.

"Then Amnon hated her with a very great hatred; for the hatred with which he hated her was greater than the love with which he had loved her…"[22]

Wait a second: Amnon just got what he wanted, and now he… hates her? How could this be? During the rape, the alarm, distress, and disgust on Tamar's face mirrored his malicious heart, but the reflection was unsettling, too revealing. So he smashed the mirror and his servant swept up the royal pieces and dumped them in the trash.

"This woman" was disposable.[23] *This woman.*

He couldn't even whisper her name. She was barely human, scarcely a woman with mind and soul. She was not family. She was not "sister." She was *this woman*, a woman discarded and forgotten. He completely ignored her cries before, during, and after the rape.

Tamar, who had been wearing the fine robes that a virgin daughter of the king would wear, walked out of that place and did what Jews did when they were grieving. She put ashes on her head and she tore her beautiful robes. She wept and wept.

The robes symbolized that she was a virgin, but according to her culture, she could no longer make that claim.

Yet, with great courage, she made public what Amnon did surreptitiously. She begged for justice with each moan and wail until someone noticed.

And someone did notice. Brother #2, Absalom.

His advice was pointed, clipped, curt: "But now keep silent, my sister, he is your brother; do not take this matter to heart. "[24]

Do not take this matter to heart.
Don't let it get to you.
It could have been worse. You should be grateful.
Protect the family image.

Yes, in looking ahead we see that Absalom was plotting revenge against Amnon, the Crown Prince,[25] but this is not the first time that these words had been spoken in this family. Not too far in the past, King David spoke similar words after he had Uriah eliminated.

"... Your servant Uriah the Hittite is dead." David told the messenger, "Say this to Joab: '*Don't let this upset you; the sword devours one as well as another.*'"[26]

Don't take this matter to heart. The sins of the father are passed on to the next generation. David endeavored to cover up his sin, and from the second generation's sin, we learn a very important fact: The way families respond to abuse matters. When survivors disclose and their disclosure is greeted with admonitions to put the secret back under wraps, devastating repercussions occur.[27]

In this case, one brother raped, and another brother silenced. And that's not all.

Their father, King David, found out about what had happened, and Scripture tells us that "he was very angry." [28] At this point you might be expecting some harsh discipline meted out from David. But the truth is that he did nothing. *Nothing.* Not even a lecture or harsh warning that we know of. The truth is he did nothing in the same way that he did nothing when Uriah was killed in response to his command.

The plot thickens. Revenge happened when Absalom conspired for two years to have Amnon killed for what he had done to their sister. Sin begets sin. Absalom's plan was fulfilled, and David got word. Now David mourned. He tore his clothes and wept and wept. His servants and all his men wept and tore their clothes. Amnon's death elicited a widespread response—a group of men mourning. [29]

But what about what happened to Tamar? Who mourned for her? Who wiped the tears from her eyes?

"So Tamar remained and was *desolate* in her brother Absalom's house." [30]

Desolate. A poignant word. The Hebrew word is *Shamenm,* and means to be deflowered, deserted, appalled, devastated, *ravaged.* It is a word that literally means "barren." This is remarkably significant because the name Tamar means "palm tree," signifying fruitfulness, the opposite of barren. [31] Tamar was designed to bear fruit. Perhaps she could have been a mom with lots of kids or maybe she could have been a spiritual parent who led many to Yahweh. Instead, Tamar lived as a desolate woman.

Forsaken.
Abandoned.
Shamed.
Empty.
Vacant.
Lonely.
Despondent.

Broken-hearted.
Grief-stricken.
Downcast.
Cast down.
Dejected.
Crushed.

This solitary evil act and the responses of those around her crushed her to the point that she no longer lived the life for which she was designed.

In this story, words of hope are in short supply. There is no happily ever after. Tamar lived a desolate life. Period.

This unsavory story begs an important question: *Why would God include this passage in Scripture?*
There are no uncomplicated answers to this question.

This question breaks into a kindergarten classroom, the back seat of a Volkswagen bug, near a swing set at the local playground, in a bathtub where brightly-colored toys are floating, or any other place where abuse happens. It arouses another question in us, as well: *Where is God?*

Tamar's life begs for there to be something more. Someone more.

Who wipes Tamar's tears? Psalm 56:8 says that "you... put my tears in Your bottle." God saw Tamar, her rape, and her life of desolation.[32] He saw her weeping night after night. He heard the responses of others, and knew of the ache in her life. He walked all the way down to the deepest pit in her soul. He knew. He remembered.

He has taken this matter to heart.

Perhaps a more personal question is this: For what reason would God include stories like this one in chapters of the lives of our clients?
Our loved ones?
Our own lives?

And who cares if He saw or if He knows? Why didn't He stop Amnon? Why didn't He stop my abuser? Does He care or is He passive like David? These are worthy questions explored in the pages of *Beyond Desolate*. For now, we conclude this chapter with the emphatic statement that survivors of abuse were not designed to live a desolate life. They were made for something far greater. Survivors of abuse were made for what is beyond desolate. Way beyond.

We invite you, the reader, to dig deep into the difficult questions that Tamar's story brings to light. There are many Tamars living in desolation, thirsting for a life beyond.

Tamar was silenced.

We are breaking her silence.

...YOU HAVE SEEN, O LORD, THE WRONG DONE TO ME...

Lamentations 3:59

Tamar

a desolate woman

DISCUSSION STARTERS

1. What do you think is significant about the fact that Tamar was beautiful? Since every word in Scripture is there for a reason, why might God have included it?

2. What do you think Tamar was feeling when her "no" was not respected? Can you think of a time when your "no" was not respected? What did that feel like?

3. What would you have liked King David to do when he found out about the rape of his daughter?

4. Can you think of clients/family members/friends you know who you would describe as living a "desolate" life? What makes their life desolate?

5. Take a stab at answering that heart-wrenching question: *Why does God allow chapters like this in our lives?*

Aftermath

of abuse

IN THE POIGNANT VIDEO, *SPEAK*, MELINDA IS DATE-RAPED, STRIPPED of friends and voice.[1] *Desolate.* Not long afterward, the fall semester begins and an out-of-the-box high school art teacher assigns the class a task—to draw a tree. And Melinda's eyes roll. The assignment is *too* elementary, but over time she embraces the art project *and* her journey of healing. Near the end of the school year, Melinda guides her beaten-down-by-administration art teacher into a roomful of trees she has created. There are

Painted trees,
Sculpted trees,
Penciled trees.
Trees with leaves.
Trees in barren lands.
No two trees alike.

At the close of the scene, art teacher and student say farewell and both leave lightened of their loads. The kindness of a teacher plus an imaginative assignment became the path to a re-captured voice and kindled passion.

The tree episode is telling in more ways than one. The draw-a-tree homework resulted in one damaged high school girl drawing a cluster of trees. All di*ff*Eren*t*.

If you asked a men's lacrosse team, bunch of boy scouts, quilting bee, or roomful of mechanical engineers to draw a tree, there would be scads of trees, with varying shapes, heights, textures, hues.

The same goes for victims of abuse. An attorney once asked me (Tammy) why a client in question didn't fit several of the post-traumatic stress disorder (PTSD) symptomatology. His question reflected a one-size-fits-all model; however, people who are sexually abused do not react in carbon copy ways. They are a heterogeneous group. This means no two survivors are exactly alike. Diversity of abuse ensures diversity of aftermath effects of abuse.[2] As psychiatrist Frank Putnam explains,

> Childhood sexual abuse is a complex life experience... This diversity alone ensures that there will be a range of outcomes... Thus sexually abused children constitute a very heterogeneous group with many degrees of abuse about whom few simple generalizations hold.[3]

Open any textbook on childhood sexual abuse (CSA) and you will see consistency among trauma clinicians and researchers regarding the most common negative aftereffects. Yet differences are apparent as well. This is due, in part, because victims of sexual abuse resemble a collage.

A collage is a work of visual art concocted from an assemblage of
magazine clippings,
torn photographs,
scraps of thread,
jarring words.
Each item attached to a canvas.
No *2* alike.

The age of the victim, severity of abuse, nature of the relationship with the perpetrator, response of caregivers and significant others, personality factors, support system, relationship with God, family dynamics, use of force and aggression, number of perpetrators, culture, and other types of trauma experience, all contribute to differing symptoms, dissimilar collages. In addition, specific symptoms may dominate at one point along the journey while other effects may preside during a different phase.[4]

Christine Courtois explained the differences among incest survivors in this way:

> ...experiences are tremendously variable, occurring for numerous reasons under a wide variety of circumstances. Aftereffects are similarly variable in their development, range, and severity.[5]

Clinician and researcher Lenore Terr lets us know that "Type I" single-event or limited traumas (e.g., natural disaster, single episode of abuse or assault) and "Type II" complex or repetitive traumas (e.g., repeated abuse, war, genocide) can impact people very differently.[6] Typically, there is a profound betrayal involved with Type II traumas because the abuse is perpetrated by someone known to the victim. Another word for Type II trauma is complex trauma which often entails additional aftermath effects compared to Type I traumas.[7]

Thus, the way abuse leaves its imprint on people varies. Yet there are a sundry of aftermath commonalities. There are *themes*. We give description of these themes in the first half of *Beyond Desolate*.

Goal of Healing

Many self-help books offer sure fire steps to healing. The linear nature and certainty of the ABC steps appear helpful at first and second glance. They seem full of possibility but are often devoid of substance.

Like a convoluted illness that cannot be treated with a single vaccine, healing paths are varied for survivors of abuse. However, there is a trend, in the mental health arena, to approach the therapy of clients with a one-size-fits-all mentality. Like cans of corn with the same no-name yellow jacket label, clients are approached with a proliferation of treatment manuals that embrace a step 1, 2, and 3 to healing.

Hearing the steps others have taken can be helpful as they can provide pictures of what others have done in similar situations. Steps can provide hope (i.e., *If he could face it, I can too.*). Steps can provide a visual and concrete picture of what healing could look like. Still, formulaic approaches sometimes offer the illusion of certainty and control when godliness is not always measured in three simple steps or three stages…The goal of healing in *Beyond Desolate* is not simply the cessation of symptoms. The purpose of healing is to thrive, to be freed up to love others, and to be freed up to love Him. Those who are marred by tragedy are designed for triumph.

A Few Caveats: Counseling by its very nature, is a private profession and ministry. We typically sit with clients in rooms where no one else can hear what is being said. However, when we write, we share stories to illumine the darkness of others. Therefore, we have shared stories only when we have received permission. We do not use real names, and we change the details to protect the brave souls who have shared with us.

You will notice that the first half of *Beyond Desolate* includes pictures that contain dark hues and rough edges and not every portrait contains *happily ever after* shades. While we crave these endings, many of us must get back on the proverbial wagon again and again. The getting back on part of the stories of our lives must be expressed as well. Still, as the paint has spilled and splattered, leaving the art room in seeming disarray, one resounding airtight truth remains. The Master Artist intended the aftermath of abuse to be transformed, and even redeemed.

Due to the darker hues used, we did not intend *Beyond Desolate* to be a single-sitting book. When athletes exercise too long and too hard their muscles do not have sufficient recovery time. Overtraining can lead to poor performance and injuries. So too, whether you work with individuals who have been abused and/or you have been abused, it is important to read at the tempo that fits who you are and where you are presently. It is our hope that you will allow the Master Story Teller to use the message of *Beyond Desolate* to reveal, redeem, and restore according to His timing.

A Note about Names: POWs, Holocaust survivors, and other groups of folks who have lived through evil experiences identify themselves in certain ways. When it comes to a fitting name to refer to individuals who have lived through abuse, there are varying opinions. The term "victim" connotes the truth of being sexually violated, raped, abused, molested, pawed, exploited, ravaged, powerless, and betrayed. This word allocates placing responsibility for the abuse with the perpetrator and underscores that abuse was something done *to* the person who was violated. Authors Hunter and Gerber recommend using the term "victim" in the early stages of treatment for men who have experienced sexual violations as youth.[8] However, some reject the usage of "victim" because people who have been abused are not only victims. They are also agents who make choices, not about the abuse but about ways to respond to the abuse.

Others embrace the identification with the word "survivor" because it honors the fact that while a person did not escape the evil of abuse, that person lived through it. Nevertheless, Hunter and Gerber explain that for men, using the term "survivor" in the initial stages of wrestling with abuse can bolster denial and the often deeply-imbedded stance that victimization did not occur.

Neither word by itself captures the person who has been abused. No label does. People who have been abused are so much more than their abuse. However, both terms suggest a portion of the picture. For the same person, on one day, the term victim may more adequately express her feelings about the abuse and her experience of it. On another day, the designation of survivor is preferable. More descriptive. More appropriate. As Harvard clinical instructor Jim Hopper wisely expresses, "No matter how much abuse someone has experienced, or how complete her or his memories are, there is always much more to that person than 'abuse victim' or 'abuse survivor.'"[9]

When I (Tammy) asked my trauma class to gather in groups to discuss the most fitting term for individuals who have experienced abuse, the first student to speak was a woman whose husband had died in the Iraq war. She shared a story about filling out papers when she was asked to check off one of three boxes: Single, Married, or Widowed. We felt her angst as she told our class that the years she was married to her husband and his death could never be captured in checking one little box on a piece of paper. She was right. Another student queried, "What do people who have been abused call themselves?" My students are so wise.

On the pages of *Beyond Desolate,* we use both "victim" and "survivor" when we speak of individuals who have experienced sexual violatioe. We realize however, these terms will never capture the magnificence of image bearers.

We invite caregivers to ask individuals who know abuse first hand, how they want to be known. We invite people who have been abused to select the word that depicts their experience and identity best at their present juncture of the healing journey. And over time, the word may change.[10] Over time, they may shed these names like winter attire in a tropical forest as they no longer allow themselves to be defined by what happened to them. Over time, they may step into His sentiments about how He feels about them and ask God to share the name that He picked out just for them.[11]

PEOPLE INVENT MANY WAYS TO ESCAPE THEIR SHAME.
NONE OF THEM WORK. THEY ONLY PUSH THE SHAME OUT OF
THE FRONT DOOR OF THEIR FEELINGS AND LET IT IN AGAIN
THROUGH THE BACK DOOR. THE BETTER WAY TO DEAL
WITH SHAME IS NOT TO ESCAPE IT BUT TO HEAL IT.

Lewis Smedes

TO HIM WHO IS ABLE TO KEEP YOU FROM FALLING AND TO PRESENT
YOU BEFORE HIS GLORIOUS PRESENCE WITHOUT FAULT AND WITH
GREAT JOY – TO THE ONLY GOD OUR SAVIOR BE GLORY, MAJESTY,
POWER AND AUTHORITY, THROUGH JESUS CHRIST OUR LORD,
BEFORE ALL AGES, NOW AND FOREVERMORE! AMEN.

Jude 1:24-25

INSTEAD OF THEIR SHAME MY PEOPLE WILL RECEIVE A DOUBLE
PORTION, & INSTEAD OF THEIR DISGRACE THEY WILL REJOICE IN
THEIR INHERITANCE; & SO THEY WILL INHERIT A DOUBLE PORTION
IN THEIR LAND, & EVERLASTING JOY WILL BE THEIRS.

Isaiah 61:7

Cesspools
of shame

Sin Meets Savior

Sometimes it's difficult to get a grip on shame because not all shame is soul damaging. There is the kind of shame that emerges as a result of our sin revealed. It reminds us that we are cracked pots, broken mirrors. For example, when we pick someone apart with our words, we need to feel shame.

Healthy shame is found in the story of *Les Miserables* when Jean Valjean's sinful state sinks in. He realizes that he is unable to make himself an honest and kind man and he physically collapses under the weight of his wrongdoing. However, it is because of this crucial awareness and calling out to God that he becomes a changed man:

> His knees suddenly bent under him, as if an invisible pow-er overwhelmed him at a blow, with the weight of his bad conscience; he fell exhausted upon a great stone, his hands clenched in his hair, and his face on his knees, and exclaimed: "What a wretch I am!..." How long did he weep thus? What did he do after weeping? Where did he go? Nobody ever knew. It is known simply that on that very night, the stage driver who drove at that time on the Grenoble route...saw,

as he passed through the bishop's street a man in the attitude of prayer, kneel upon the pavement in the shadow.[1]

Second Corinthians 7:8-11 spells out the design for healthy shame. We were made to feel shame so that we would eventually arrive at a scene of sorrow over wrong we have done to others, ourselves, and our God, leading us to repentance. Like Jean Valjean, the awareness of our sinful state is designed to lead us to *kneel upon the pavement* and pour out our words of sorrow to God. But there is something more. Paul explains, "Godly sorrow brings repentance that leads to salvation and leaves no regret, but worldly sorrow brings death."[2]

No regret. Free. *Free.*

Healthy shame unfetters us from our enslavement and ushers us into the arms of our forgiving Savior.

If your shame has not allowed you to experience repentance, forgiveness, and *freedom,* He has a gift waiting for you. Or perchance your clients' or your own sack of shame carried day after day is a different kind of shame ...

"My Fault" Kind of Shame

HUMAN BEINGS STAND IN THE RUBBLE OF FORMER BELIEFS.
WE FINGER THROUGH THE SHARDS OF MEANING TRYING TO
IMAGINE WHAT THE WHOLE MIGHT HAVE BEEN LIKE.

K.E. Helminski

In this chapter, we center on the strain of shame shackled to abuse. We consider why someone blames him or herself for the abuse done *to* him, *to* her. We grapple with the question *why me?* that looms with traumatic memories.

Wrapping your mind around shame is central to understanding the aftermath of abuse.[3] For example, a few years ago some researchers interviewed 147 child and adolescent victims who were assessed subsequent to their abuse and then one year later. They found that one of the most important factors that paved the way toward this group adjusting after the abuse was related to how they dealt with their shame. The researchers found that when shame diminished, the children and adolescents coped better.[4] Author Christiane Sanderson states that shame is the most common emotional effect of child sexual abuse[5] and professor Lisa Fontes explains that understanding shame is central to understanding the impact of abuse, particularly when working with cultural minority groups.[6]

The "my fault" kind of shame is the sense of being

Stained,
Soiled,
Infected,
Flawed,
Marked,
Defective,
Dirty,
Damaged.

Researchers David Finklehor and Angela Browne call this stigmatization.[7] Trauma expert Bessel van der Kolk refers to the misguided perspective survivors tightly clench as "trauma-based internal schemes."[8]

It is the deep-seated belief that when I was a ten-year-old child, if only I hadn't gone to my elementary school on that Saturday, then the janitor wouldn't have touched me, molested me.

It is the I-should-have-known-better kind of mortification.

This shame impels us to hang our head, lower our eyes, and dash for cover. It prods us to take up less space. To be unnoticeable.

It is the brand of under-our-breath put-downs that are deployed like stealth weapons.

This variety of shame involves ousting comments of praise because the person praising me doesn't really know me. It includes cutting the loneliness, insecurities, and despair from the body through razor blades, knives.

It's the felt need to wear layers of clothing to veil the hatred we have for our body.

This breed of shame is horizontal, not wanting to be "found out" by those around us. It pummels us before the day really even gets started. It screams the lie, "you're not good enough."

Never amount to anything. Better luck next time… maybe.

This shame drives us like a subway we can't exit. It steers us into sinful behaviors and ruinous relationships because *No one would want me now. This is what I deserve. This is as good as it gets.*

This batch of shame is the result of staring at ourselves through a human lens; especially the spectacles worn by those we care about most: If my husband beats me, I must be worth bruises and black eyes. If my boss fires me, I must not be worthy or capable of a good job. If my fiancé is unfaithful, I must not deserve to wear a wedding dress. If my dad uses me for sex, I must only be good for that.

This kind of shame is a hulking weight like the tonnage of the world Atlas carried on his shoulders.

This kind of shame is carried by the majority of people who have been sexually violated.

I'm So Sorry…

In the movie *Good Will Hunting*, there is a poignant scene where Will (Matt Damon), a young man who raced ahead of the pack in intelligence, converses with Shaun (Robin Williams), his therapist. Shaun cradles Will's counseling file—a file jammed with gruesome pictures of injuries Will experienced at the hands of his alcoholic dad. Shaun gently declares to Will that the stuff he was looking at in the file – the pictures of bruises from beatings – this stuff wasn't his fault. Will brushes off the statement by responding that he knew this already. Shaun doesn't buy it that Will actually believes the abuse wasn't his fault. So, he continues to repeat himself, telling Will over and over again that it wasn't his fault. Will begins to get angry, taking steps back as Shaun continues. Finally, Will allows Shaun's words to come near, touch his soul, and he begins to weep as Shaun embraces him. Will's response is different this time. This time, Will says, I'm so sorry.[9] What incited Will's words? Why was **HE** sorry?

Why are people who are manhandled, mishandled, molested *so sorry* about what was done *to* them?

Explanations about behaviors are complicated. "Some things are too complex to suffer reduction to a simple equation of why/because."[10]

Molesters Who Maul

ARE THEY ASHAMED OF THEIR LOATHSOME CONDUCT?
NO, THEY HAVE NO SHAME AT ALL;
THEY DO NOT EVEN KNOW HOW TO BLUSH.

Jeremiah 6:15

Perhaps one of the reasons Will wore his dad's shame is because individuals who abuse are adept at flicking humiliation on their victims. That is their cup of tea, their trademark. As a result, abused kids internalize the noxious labels doled out by offenders.[11] Author Anna Salter explains, "Survivors often internalize the sex offender's version of the abuse, partly because he is the only person who knows about it at the time, and therefore is in a unique position to define her reality."[12]

I (Tammy) learned a lot about shame from my work with perpetrators. Offenders routinely elicit sympathy from their victims. One perpetrator threw light on the way he groomed his daughter. After his wife moved out, he regularly unloaded his loneliness and loss on his ten-year-old. She became his surrogate wife. One specific time he sat reciting an onslaught of his woes as his daughter sat next to him, listening, feeling a gnawing despair for her dad. During the moment she felt an ardent angst for him, her dad fondled her. Eyes wide, she charged back. He attempted to assuage her agitation with words—"you're my special helper." He added, "Please don't tell. Others wouldn't understand our relationship."

Eventually she told. His actions landed him in jail.

I asked this father what he thought his daughter might struggle with as a result of what he did *to* her. With certainty, he said she would think it was her fault. The question of "Why?" was countered with the explanation that he had quizzed her several times if she minded his touch. He'd asked her if she was all right with what he was doing. His apparent concern fused with fondling left her in knots. She felt complicit. Added to the mix, her mom was missing-in-action and she was thirsty for love.

Perpetrators deploy other tactics that sully victim identities.[13] He may dispense accolades over her developing body.

She may "gently" caress her victim, providing the appearance of care, and relationship. Abuse and relationship may be offered only via a package deal. All these ruses leave victims languishing in a confusing, shameful state.

Lisa Fontes throws light on the matter:

> Most children seek affection. If they receive sexual abuse instead, they may come to believe it was their desire for closeness that brought about the sexual acts.[14]

A particular and significant shame should be mentioned briefly here for victims of sex trafficking, a global industry reality. [15] For many people, the topic of trafficking elicits images of faraway places and different-looking people groups, but this is also a reality that is taking place in our own backyard: Some 90 percent of victims are domestically trafficked as opposed to internationally trafficked. When I (Hannah) asked a group of girls who had been trafficked what they would want others to know: It could happen to anyone. Girls could be kidnapped or they could be "tricked" into thinking that a man is in love with them and wants to be their boyfriend. For a lot of vulnerable girls, the interest of a man is enough of a reason to keep them hoping that the nightmare will end. But the nightmare continues, and there is quite a profit being made: Last year, traffickers made somewhere around $32 billion, which is more money than Google, Nike, and Starbucks made combined.[16]

Similar to survivors of incest and other types of child sexual abuse, many victims of sex trafficking are vulnerable to their perpetrator: In this case, it is the allure of a pimp. A "typical" scenario might go something like this: A 12-year-old girl named Madison is caught up in the foster system because her father abandoned her and her mom can't seem to get over her drug habit. Madison has not been well-loved in her short life, and she is struggling to stay focused in school. She feels awkward around other kids her age who seem to come mostly from "put together" homes, and those other kids aren't very accepting of her either. One day, after a particularly awful argument with her foster father, she skips school and walks around the mall just to be in a different setting and to get away from all the hardship at home and school. Little does she know that malls are a hot spot for pimps to look for young girls in her type of situation. A man notices her looking at a way-too-expensive pair of shoes and approaches her, offering to buy her the fancy shoes. Thinking that these shoes might help her to fit in better at school, she accepts the offer, and secretly admits that she is enjoying this man's attention and smiles. Delighted with his praises of her beauty and "potential," she spends the rest of the afternoon with this man as he buys her a nice meal and a scarf and earrings too. Before she knows it, this man asks Madison if she would like to see his place, and remembering the fight from the night before, she agrees to go with the man. Within hours, she is feeling more at home than she has ever felt, and decides she's not looking back. Having sex with the man a few nights later seems like a small price to pay for a home. And so the slow descent into the abyss begins, as she is offered security, clothes, and plenty of special attention. All she has to do is perform a few sexual favors each night.

If you were to meet Madison years after this nightmare was behind her and you asked about her story, she would likely express shame. Shame for enjoying the attention of a seemingly kind man. Shame for skipping school and being a "bad kid." Shame for falling for a trap. Shame for not having anyone to reach out to. Shame for being sexually connected to a host of men. Shame for carrying an STD, or for having multiple abortions in order to stay active in the trade. Shame for not trying to run away from this man. Shame for going home to a pimp night after night, handing over money, and actually thinking that maybe he would be pleased, that maybe she might get some sort of special treatment, or even ... *love.*

The reality for Madison and millions of other victims is that when they stop blaming themselves, they have to acknowledge a tremendous amount of evil in the world: parents that don't care for their children, pimps that allure and coerce young vulnerable girls into the sex trade, thousands of clients who pay for sex with a child. Blaming herself is how Madison maintains a sense of control.

To be abused means to feel helpless, powerless, out-of-control. Shame over the abuse stems, in part, from this place without power. It is a grim moment when we come to grips with our vulnerability and powerlessness. Shame staves off helpless feelings. We want to believe we really can make sense of the evil things that happen to us. Author and speaker Allender explains,

> Fallen man works tenaciously, at times to psychotic lengths, to gain magical control over life by generating reasons that explain the why and what for of that which seems beyond his understanding.[17]

Abuse Dichotomy

A child exposed to sexual violations is saddled with a dilemma: My brother, uncle, neighbor, youth pastor, grandmother was sexual with me because she or he is bad or

I am being hurt because

I am B A D.

Especially if I enjoyed the attention. And without a doubt, my badness is confirmed because my body responded. Christiane Sanderson explains,

> If the child's body responds to the sexual contact with pleasure, sexual arousal, or orgasm, he may feel doubly ashamed that his body responded and 'betrayed' him. This is particularly true for the older child, who may know that CSA is wrong and yet derive some pleasure from the sexual acts.[18]

Trauma expert John Briere calls this dilemma the "abuse dichotomy." Commonly, the only tenable solution is—*I am bad.*[19] As vile as this option is, at least the abuse can be decoded. It's my fault. Shame short circuits that out-of-control feeling. And since it is my fault, I can do something about it. I can become a better kid, better woman, better man.

If it's my fault, I can change myself to make it better. If it's someone else's fault, I am out of control. I can't do anything. I can annihilate my masculinity, because being male is what got me in trouble in the first place. Or I will spend the rest of my days proving there was nothing about my maleness that made him do that to me.

I can wreak havoc on hope—never let myself need again because needing is what got me in this mess. *I* climbed up on my daddy's lap. *I* nestled my head on his chest. It was my entreaty that brought his rapt attention. I will put the lid on longing so I will never be hurt like that again.

Shame padlocks Pandora's Box of helplessness. It gives us the mistaken impression that we really are in control.

Purging Perpetrator Shame

For survivors, relinquishing the lie *It was my fault* is, in fact, a journey. It's a process. It involves receiving and embracing the truth that just because the perpetrator said you wanted it doesn't make it so. Just because she was "kind," doesn't mean the sex signified a relationship, an affair. And just because you may have loved or do love the perpetrator, it doesn't mean he or she had a right to do that to you. Seizing this truth is a step of monumental proportions and it takes time.

Healing the shame that suffocates, smothers, and silences involves relinquishing control. Self-hate is a formidable diversion.

One spring morning, a hanging basket of red begonias swayed on a light post in my (Tammy's) front yard. Peering out the window, I witnessed the one-bird construction crew assemble her new digs. The official move-in date ensued and thereafter, whenever I opened my front door that was within fifteen feet of the new nest, mother bird flew the coop. It seemed mom tried to lead me away from her nest to distract me from the three azure-colored eggs that she had deposited.

In a similar way, blaming myself for the abuse functions as a distraction. Rather than focusing on the anguish over being violated, I focus my attention on all the things that I could have done differently to stop the abuse. I focus on ways I could have said something, done something, and thought something different. When I blame myself for the abuse, my attention is diverted and I maintain an illusory sense of control over the uncontrollable. However, blaming myself for the abuse is a ball chained to my leg that weighs heavy on my soul and prevents me from running free.

If my-fault-kind-of-shame is a distraction from entering helpless feelings and weeping over the sin done against us, it follows that healing involves entering into the mess of helplessness. The old saying *You got to feel it to heal it* is true. And the seismic step toward giving up the self-hate and refusing to be chained to the lies of responsibility over the violation is only wisely undertaken with the awareness that God saw what happened to you. He knows and He waits to enter the ache with you. And He is enough.

Drenched in the Aroma of Jesus

Quia amasti me, fecisti me amabilem.
IN LOVING ME, YOU MADE ME LOVABLE.

St. Augustine

There is a story about a woman with a bottle of perfume in the New Testament. Jesus was invited to a dinner party at the home of a Pharisee named Simon (Luke 7: 36-50). The sizable dinner gathering necessitated a home of considerable dimensions and disposable cash for the spread of food for his guests.

Verse 36 tells us that Jesus "reclined at the table." Picture the last time you sat at the dinner table. A good bet would be that you perched on a chair while your feet were positioned under the table. But that is not how it was at Simon's gathering. Guests reclined on couches with feet extended away from the table. Visitors leaned on one side and stretched for the meal with their other hand. This posture made it possible for what was about to happen next.

A notable sinner brought an alabaster vial of perfume and began weeping at Jesus' feet. This woman lived in a shame and honor society. An Arab proverb explains that "a concealed shame is two thirds forgiven." However, this story reveals that this woman's shame was known. Was it a sexual sin? We do not know. However, we do know that her tears over her sin were so profuse the feet of Jesus got wet. That's a lot of tears. Tears that left her vulnerable and exposed. Tears poured out on Jesus, the Son of God.

After all the sinful woman's weeping, she began kissing His feet. The Greek indicates that she began to tenderly kiss this respected teacher again and again. *He did not recoil or rebuke her.*

She clutched her alabaster jar and the perfume cascaded on Jesus' feet. In the background, Simon stood tall and watched this scene take place. He was appalled. Doesn't Jesus know who she is? She was "one of them." Today, in our pews, *she* might be an unkempt woman who drinks her troubles away, a lesbian, or a woman knee-deep in porn…

37

How did she get to such a miserable existence? Were her formative years marked by pagan parents who valued their sons and not their daughter? Was she sexually abused by a trusted someone? Or did she simply rebel against her godly parents? We don't know. We only know that later in verse 47 Jesus said her sins were many, much, large. They were huge.

Scripture tells us that Simon mulled over his disgust to himself. But Jesus knew what he was thinking. Perhaps Simon's aversion to this woman was smeared all over his face. Perhaps there was a roomful of people thinking the same thing.

This part of the story hit us like a **Mack Truck.**

How on earth was this uninvited woman able to enter this home when almost everybody didn't want her there? Why didn't she stay hidden like a rodent in the dark? How was she able to come close to Jesus, even *touch* Him?

There's only one way: "Let us then approach the throne of grace with confidence, so that we may receive *mercy* and find *grace* to help us in our time of need" (Hebrews 4:16).

Somewhere, somehow, this notorious sinner had heard about Jesus and His grace blanketed her, gave her confidence, allowed her to enter a room and worship Him as if no one else was there. His grace defined her. Simon's contemptible sneer was unimportant. Jesus was all that mattered.

Sexual abuse often elicits mammoth amounts of anguish and grief but one thing it does not have the power to do: Determine someone's worth. Child sexual abuse, rape, or other types of sexual violations are deceitful weigh scales regarding the value of victims. Abuse opens someone's eyes to experiences they were never meant to see, feel, or taste. Yet the prison of lies the Enemy builds for us is of even greater damage.

In God's eyes, this unnamed sinful woman was forgiven (Luke 7:48). Free. Defined and delighted in by God.

And in the case of abuse, where the perpetrator is always **100%** responsible,

God defines.

Tamar, who said, "What about me? Where could I get rid of my disgrace?"[20] was no less a princess after the rape than she was before it happened. In God's eyes, she was always His beautiful girl, worthy of wearing her royal garments. Through the eyes of her culture, she would have been seen by many as filthy rags and worth little in a marriage deal. She would have been deemed less of a princess. But not to Jesus. And He is who matters.

Jesus was despised and rejected by men, a man of sorrows, and familiar with suffering (Isaiah 53:3). But He did not allow the contempt of man to determine Him.

Healing the shame of abuse that belongs to the perpetrator necessitates an encounter with Jesus. *So let Jesus define you.* Allow Him to share the news of how He feels about you and how He felt about you precisely when you were being abused. Ask Him about it. Go ahead. He would love to tell you.

Sisters & Shame

THOUGH THE SEX TO WHICH I BELONG IS CONSIDERED WEAK
YOU WILL NEVERTHELESS FIND ME A ROCK THAT BENDS TO NO WIND.

Queen Elizabeth I

It is common for women who have been abused to feel shame specifically in the area of their femininity—that something about me *as a girl* caused the abuse. A woman who has been abused often feels like it was the fact that she wanted to be loved that caused the abuse. So she must numb her femininity and anesthetize her craving to be loved in this very specific way. She must, like Tamar, rip her princess garments to shreds.

39

Maybe you have tried to tear your royal attire to pieces. Maybe your Cinderella dreams faded so long ago that the rags you've been wearing have started to feel like home.

What we crave for the Tamars of this world is to experience what that sinful woman experienced that afternoon with Jesus: The ability to *bask in His presence until no one else's opinion matters.*

And there is more.

Isaiah 61:10 says, "I will rejoice in the Lord, my soul will exult in my God; for He has *clothed me* with garments of salvation, He has *wrapped me with a robe of righteousness*, as a bridegroom decks himself with a garland, and as a bride adorns herself with her jewels."

Imagine, if you can, the most beautiful gown you have ever seen. Maybe it's your wedding dress or a dress you saw in a store, magazine, or movie. Picture it. But you should know that the outfit He's making for you is even more beautiful.

This is not the first time in Scripture that we learn that the God of this universe is the original fashion designer. In the Garden of Eden, God made clothing for Adam and Eve after they sinned, because they were immediately aware of their nakedness and felt shame (Genesis 3:21). From the time of the fall of man, clothing and shame have been married. In a perfect world, free of shame, Adam and Eve walked around naked, and didn't even comprehend this. In the same way, it didn't matter who forked out disapproving glances to the sinful woman with the perfume. She was walking "naked" before her Lord.

God knows the barricades you lurk behind and He knows that from which you are hiding. To the part of you that buries yourself under your bed, to the part that curls up in the fetal position in your closet, to the part of you that scans every room you enter for the vacant corner, God extends an invitation to emerge out of hiding and to listen to Him as He tells you what you mean to Him. He will repeat Himself over and over again until you realize you're already wearing the dress He clothed you with—the dress He paid for.

Brothers & Shame

HE RAISES THE POOR FROM THE DUST & LIFTS THE NEEDY
FROM THE ASH HEAP; HE SEATS THEM WITH
PRINCES & HAS THEM INHERIT A THRONE OF HONOR.

1 Samuel 2:8

It is easy for men to believe that there is something lacking about their *maleness* that caused the abuse. "Real men" don't let this happen to them. As a result, scores of boys becoming men are left with a fierce desire to conceal that part of them that feels like a run-down shack. They can try to present mansions of glory, all the time thinking, *If you only knew the real me—the faulty foundation, the cracks in the windows and holes in the floor. If only you knew that my house is sinking into the ground and the ceiling is caving in.* And to this awareness, a vow is made: *No one must ever know.*

Are you tired of all the hard work you've put into striving to be enough ? All the labor into building a mansion that is falling apart on the inside? It may be time to drop your tools and let someone else do the building. "Unless the Lord builds the house, they labor in vain who build it" (Psalm 127:1a).

Like Abraham, Peter, and Paul, who Jesus furnished with a new name, a man must ask the Lord what kind of son *He* sees. We need new vantage points.

Once upon a time, the Word became flesh and dwelt among us, and the Word had some buddies. These fellas needed some encouragement one night, and Jesus spoke: "In my father's house are many dwelling places; if it were not so, I would have told you; for I go to prepare a place for you. If I go and prepare a place for you, I will come again and receive you to myself, that where I am, there you may be also. And you know the way where I am going" (John 14:2-4).

Jesus was a carpenter during His time on this earth, limited then to earthly materials. Meanwhile, He was and is developing the blueprints for your mansion. He gave up His magnificent home to exist

41

and die so that you would be able to surrender your shack for His mansion. Whether you know it or not, Jesus wants to be *Home* to you. He wants to find a home in you, and He's not asking you to fix up the place before He drops in. He just knocks. He is preparing a place for you.

Living Out Our Daughter & Son-Ship

In the story of the *Lion King*, Simba spends his adult-lion life running from his painful past. Then one day the spirit of his father, Mufasa, rebukes him for forgetting his birthright, his responsibility, and his identity. Mufasa asks Simba to remember who he is – to remember *whose* he is.[21]

God speaks into the core of who we are in the same way in Romans 8:1 and 15:

> "Therefore, there is now no condemnation
> for those who are in Christ Jesus…
> For you did not receive a spirit that makes you a slave again
> to fear, but you received the Spirit of sonship.
> And by Him we cry, 'Abba, Father.'"

You are the spitting image of the true King, Abba Father. You are His son, His daughter. You are not what someone did to you. You are not what you did after the abuse. Your royal Father looks you in your eyes and asks you to remember who you are – to remember *whose* you are.

But there's one more important step involved in dealing with my-fault kind of shame.

When Simba realized *who he was* and *whose he was*, he went back to his homeland and ran into battle. He defeated his wicked uncle and embraced his royal position. It took king-sized resolve and boldness to return home and enter the fray. But it took even more courage for Simba to relinquish his shame-based orphan identity.

We too are called to realize who we are and whose we are. As we embrace our royal heritage, we are called to ride into the challenging battle of life, to look into the eyes of others knowing they cannot define us, to disallow the abuse the power to continue to determine our worth and identity, to face our deepest fears knowing we have received the spirit of sonship and daughtership.

So, what battle are you being asked to ride into?
As you enter the fray, remember who you are and whose you are.

When we fail to remember that we are HIS, we go back to our waste lands, we put on our old dresses again, and we leave the dance floor. Instead, let us cry with David, "I am Yours!"[22] Let us remember the battle for our sonship and daughtership has already been won.

> "I am the Lord your God,
> who brought you out of Egypt so that
> you would no longer be slaves to the Egyptians;
> I broke the bars of your yoke
> & enabled you to walk with
> heads held high."[23]

Cesspools
of shame

DISCUSSION STARTERS

1. What would it take for you to enter that room like the woman with the alabaster jar and lavish your Lord with your tears?

2. What do you think God thinks of YOU?

3. What battle are you, as a unique daughter or son of God, being called to ride into?

To live as a child of God is to live
with love & hope & growth,
but it is also to live with longing,
with aching for a fullness of love
that is never quite within our grasp.

Gerald May

You hear, O Lord, the desire of the afflicted;
You encourage them, and you listen to their cry,
defending the fatherless and the oppressed,
in order that man, who is of the earth,
may terrify no more.

Psalm 10:17-18

Allegiance
di/vided

Wading through biographies of evil dictators—yes, evil dictators—is a peculiar way to spend an afternoon. A careful study of these chilling life histories sheds light on ambivalence, a complex and common emotion among both people pillaged by nefarious oppressors _and_ survivors of child sexual abuse. For example, Joseph Stalin's narrative furnishes glaring clues regarding the ways oppressors ravage their victims and, perhaps surprisingly, leave many simultaneously _despising and drawn to_ the very one who wreaked devastation.

Throughout Stalin's reign of terror, he exterminated approximately 20 million people. His trail of liquidation included colleagues, peasants, and anyone who potentially stood in his way. Tales about his formative years are an intriguing read. His father's incessant drinking binges fueled repeated beatings of Joseph and his mother. His father's rage endowed Joseph with a rancor of his own, discharged later on his own son and second wife who both committed suicide. Stalin's conflict resolution skills consisted of ridding rivals by way of torture and execution.

Yet his overt ruthless actions were punctuated by conspicuous charity. For example, the story is told that in 1935, Stalin gathered his senior KGB and general staff officers before him in order to reprimand them for not being savage enough with the Russian people.

And then…

> …Stalin called for a live chicken and proceeded to use it
> to make an unforgettable point before some of his hench-
> men. Forcefully clutching the chicken in one hand, with the
> other he began to systematically pluck out its feathers. As
> the chicken struggled in vain to escape, he continued with
> the painful denuding until the bird was completely stripped.
> "Now you watch," Stalin said as he placed the chicken on the
> floor and walked away with some bread crumbs in his hand.
> Incredibly the fear-crazed chicken hobbled toward him and
> clung to the legs of his trousers. Stalin threw a handful of
> grain to the bird and it began to follow him around the
> room. He turned to his dumbfounded colleagues and said
> quietly, "This is the way to rule people. Did you see how that
> chicken followed me for food, even though I had caused it
> such torture? People are like that chicken. If you inflict in-
> ordinate pain on them they will follow you for food the rest
> of their lives." [1]

Stalin's words are chilling. Sadly, they accurately reflect the way many
perpetrators vacillate between dispensing vicious violations and apparent goodwill. In response, many children and adolescents who
experience abuse are like the little chicken—crushed by the evil done
to them and yet hobbling to the open hand of the abuser, clinging to
the legs of his trousers.

Ambivalence is defined as "the coexistence of opposing attitudes or
feelings, such as love and hate, toward a person, object, or idea."[2]

In other words, ambivalence leaves violated people feeling *confused.*

CRAZY.

Why isn't a victim of an evil oppressor or sexual perpetrator clear-
headed enough to simply loathe her abuser? Why would a teenager
not unambiguously despise the youth pastor who fondled him? Why
would a young lad defend the very teacher who hurt him?

Some victims are single-focused in their emotions. Their rage is clear. The confusion is absent. At the time of the abuse, there were no mixed feelings of wanting to be close to the perpetrator and at the same time, yearning to be far, far away. But for many, this was not the case. Ambivalence enveloped their soul and they were both drawn to and repulsed by the one who brought such damage.

Researcher Jennifer Freyd explains that, "the more the victim is dependent on the perpetrator, the more power the perpetrator has over the victim."[3] Children and adolescents will hold tightly to the one who offers time, relationship, candy, attention, and a kind word.

Ambivalence is a **COMPLICATED** and **CONFLICTING** emotion.

Sometimes the ambivalence survivors experience with the perpetrator is compounded by ambivalence experienced with the Creator of this world. A group of researchers conducted a large clinical sample of adult male substance abusers.[4] Ronald Lawson and his colleagues explained that among their sample who reported a history of child abuse, a significant number appeared to have conflicting religious responses.

Let's take a look at an oppressed people who felt conflicted with their oppressor and with their God.

Not Forgotten

The words on the pages of Exodus holler to the reader that Pharaoh was *not* a nice guy. In fact, he was downright **vicious**.

> "Then a new king, who did not know about Joseph, came to power in Egypt…They put slave masters over [the Israelites] to *oppress* them with forced labor…But the more they were *oppressed*, the more they multiplied and spread; so the Egyptians came to dread the Israelites and worked them *ruthlessly*. They made their lives *bitter* with hard labor in brick and mortar and with all kinds of work in the fields; in all their hard labor the Egyptians used them *ruthlessly*" (emphasis added).[5]

Pharaoh didn't stop there.

> "The king of Egypt said to the Hebrew midwives... 'When
> you help the Hebrew women in childbirth and observe
> them on the delivery stool, if it is a boy, kill him; but if it
> is a girl, let her live.'... Then Pharaoh gave this order to all
> his people: 'Every boy that is born you must throw into the
> Nile, but let every girl live.'"[6]

In the midst of Pharaoh's protracted and grinding cruelty, God had
not forgotten His people. Previously, God had told the Israelites that
He cared about them and He reminded them of this fact. And His
reminder came when their hearts were broken.

> "Moses and Aaron brought together all the elders of the
> Israelites and Aaron told them everything the Lord had said
> to Moses. He also performed the signs before the people,
> and they believed. And when they heard that the Lord was
> concerned about them and had seen their misery, *they bowed
> down and worshiped*" (emphasis added).[7]

Bowed Down and Worshiped

God's care moved the Israelites to lower themselves and praise the
Most High in the midst of their ache. That is God's ultimate
purpose of freeing people from bondage—not simply the deliverance
from the shackles of literal slavery, alcoholism, binging, or rage. He
desires those who are free to worship Him.[8]

The Exodus story doesn't end after the Israelites made a break out of
Egypt. God steers them smack-dab in front of the Red Sea. And then
"six hundred of the best chariots, along with all the other chariots of
Egypt, with the officers over all of them" pursued the fleeing Jews
(Exodus 14:6). "As Pharaoh approached, the Israelites *looked up,* and
there were the Egyptians, marching after them" (Exodus 14:10).[9]

With the Red Sea to their backs and the Egyptians at break-neck
speed surging toward them, the Israelites responded.

They said to Moses, "Was it because there were no graves in Egypt that you brought us to the desert to die? What have you done to us by bringing us out of Egypt? Didn't we say to you in Egypt, 'Leave us alone; let us serve the Egyptians'? It would have been better for us to serve the Egyptians than to die in the desert!"[10]

The Israelites were terrified and as the army drew within close range and their dream of freedom began to fade, they wondered if it wasn't better back in Egypt, under Pharaoh's thumb. At that moment, Pharaoh looked more appealing than death.

When the unknown looms before us, our previous pastimes like chemical addictions, a string of affairs, food binges and purges, or even slavery under wicked Pharaoh—can suddenly seem rather alluring... seductive. Maybe it wasn't so bad. All this pain incubates a desire to return to our Egypts.

The Israelites not only felt conflicting emotions toward Pharaoh and their Egyptian dwelling, but also toward their God. The God whom they recently bowed before and worshiped was now the God they doubted.

Ambivalence with God is not exclusive to the Israelites who escaped Egypt. It is the substance of Job's cries and the fabric of many of the Psalms.[11] Vacillating between trust and distrust when our circumstances do not make sense is familiar to many of us.

"I love you God. You are good... but I'm mad at you. Don't you CARE?"

Sexual Abuse & Ambivalence

When it comes to abuse victims, many experience the tangled and conflicting feelings of attachment.[12] This ambivalence is overheard in the words of an 11-year-old whose stepfather had oral sex and sodomized her, sometimes three times a week, for more than a year. She carried complex feelings toward her mother's husband. When asked if she missed her stepfather, she replied,

> I do miss him a little, cause he was there when I got glass in my hand and when I had to go to the hospital cause I was rollerblading. He took me to get ice cream, he bought me stuff and he was really nice.[13]

Richard Berendzen, former president of American University, resigned at the height of his career after bizarre and sexually suggestive phone calls to women were traced to his office. During the aftermath, without excuses for his adult actions, he described years of early childhood sexual and physical abuse by his mother in his memoir, *Come Here.*[14] Sentiments of both love and hate, pleasure and pain, jumbled together like the colors in a kaleidoscope when his mother began sexually violating him as an eight-year-old boy.

> I felt a deep revulsion, a revulsion buried under my skin. My body knew a secret, hidden from the world. Yet within this awful revulsion, I experienced momentary pleasure, ripples of tingling sensation. To experience pleasure and disgust for the same reason and almost simultaneously created overwhelming confusion and torment... In an instant, the most intimate connection one can have with another human became the most dehumanizing and degrading.[15]

In the case of sibling incest, ambivalence resounds. Diana Russell explains,

> [B]rother-sister incestuous abuse is the most discounted of all forms of sexual abuse by relatives. So strong is the myth of mutuality that many victims themselves internalize the discounting of their experiences, particularly if their brothers did not use force, if they themselves did not forcefully resist the abuse at the time, if they still continued to care about their brothers, or if they did not consider it abuse when it occurred.[16]

A noteworthy aspect among women reporting incest in Russell's study of 930 women is that there was a significant relationship between the identity of the perpetrator and how supportive the individual was who learned of the abuse. Russell found that the more distant the relationship, the more supportive the response tended to be.[17]

Ambivalence is the boy who passively "submits" to his father's sexual advances so that he is not beaten. It doesn't mean that he wants the abuse or is to blame. It means that the thing which is tearing him up inside looks more appealing than being totally cast aside.

Ambivalence takes center-stage in Hannah's story...

Yellow Pants

I learned early how to make men smile. I grew up in a neighborhood and school saturated with inappropriate expressions of sexuality. No matter how many times I heard from my mom or church leaders (when it was already too late) that sex was a gift from God, I was already covered with a shield of experience which did not allow their words to sink in. Sex had already become an unlocked mystery, dropping its clues all over my undeveloped body.

When I was only five, I was molested at school by a boy in my class who was a year or two older. I wore yellow pants that day. My teacher was reading a story to us, and I was sitting near the back of the room. The boy claimed this as a good time to reach into my pants and explore what was not his to explore. I was confused more than anything. *What is he doing? Is this ok? I doubt it. But then again... what do I know?*

Then someone noticed. She was another girl in my class who sat up tall, looked at me with pointed finger, and exclaimed, "Ewww, gross. Why are you letting him do that to you?" I had been confused before her comment, but even more so now. I missed the part where *I gave him permission.* I don't remember the name of the boy that molested me that day.

But I've never forgotten the name of that girl.

Eight-year-old Temptress

After being served a few more courses of sexual abuse by several others, I found myself a couple of years later "preparing" for a friend of my brother's who was coming over. It was an older neighborhood boy, four or five *years* older who was the "cool guy" in the neighborhood. He was coming to spend the night—a boy who had already pinned me against a wall and asked me to touch his penis, a boy who had asked to see me undressed, a boy who begged me for "real" kisses, a boy who was more acquainted with my body against his than I was with my own body standing alone. He was coming over, and I put on my charm. I wore a short pink t-shirt without shorts. I think it must have rained that night, because at some point I went to my brother's room and claimed to be scared, asking them to sleep in my room…

For the past sixteen years, I have thought about that night, and wondered how an eight-year-old girl could be such a… *slut*. Temptress. What little girl would act so seductive? How else could I explain that night? *I must have wanted what was to happen. Didn't I?*

The story of that night ended just short of physical violence. I had no noticeable bruises or physical scars, but the damage done to my body was fierce. This became the only instance when I ever said no to him. We wrestled. He gave up. *I'm such a tease.*

The story of my life that continues to be written has found me curious about some of these earlier chapters. So on a hot summer day not long ago, I mustered up the courage to flip through the earlier pages and read them out loud to a trusted friend. Let me tell you what I discovered.

On that night of my life, I always pictured God with a pointed finger and downcast expression. He was enraged with me. Disappointed that I was becoming such a *whore*. And pretty much every mistake I've made with a man since then, I've pictured *that* god. A god who would say, *This is who you are. Ever since you were five, you've been seducing men to make yourself feel good. Shame on you.*

Recently I decided to allow God to clarify if this was the case or not. I asked Him to show me His face on that night of my life—I asked Him what He was thinking of me then. Whore? Slut? Temptress? No.

Child.

If I told you a similar tale of a twenty-year-old, there's no doubt we'd have a discussion about my responsibility and sinful behavior. But I wasn't 20. I was 8, and he was 12 or 13. He was cool. He was my brother's older friend. And I wanted to be noticed, wanted to be beautiful to someone. But I didn't want to be sexually abused. For sixteen years, I thought about that night with an adult mind. Finally I gave myself permission to be EIGHT.

And what I saw was
the broken-hearted face of God –
not *at* me,
but *for* me.

As we've been working on this book, we continually come to a place of awareness that it is God's opinion that matters. What does He think of us?

The more and more acquainted we've allowed ourselves to get with His heart, we have watched our opinions fall to the wayside. It reminds us of the woman who brought her perfume to Jesus. She continues to stand out to us in so many ways; namely, when she sat at His feet, pouring perfume, it was only the opinion of Jesus that mattered to her. And it was this very fact that allowed her to WORSHIP Him freely. And oh, how we want to worship Him that way.

So that day I told my story and saw His broken heart for me. My surroundings (Borders bookstore in South Bend, Indiana) became irrelevant as I felt His opinion take its rightful throne. He loves His baby girl, me. And it grieves Him that I was violated.

This truth washed over me. I was freed up to pour out my perfume at His feet.

So… ambivalence.

I (Hannah) tell you all of this to say—ambivalence is not a chapter I've been looking forward to working on. It has felt so confusing. The task of putting words to something this bewildering has been daunting. Which is why I had to wrestle with my own ambivalence first. Some days I *feel* more to blame than others. Some days, when everything *feels* like my fault, the abuse gets inappropriately thrown onto my plate of shame. This is exactly why the entire issue of blame can't be based on how *I feel.* I go to Him. I ask Him. He reminds me what it was, how He feels about it, and how He feels about me now, in this very moment.

On the one hand, I wanted that older boy to come into my room that night. If he didn't, I would be unnoticed. Worthless. And yet to lay a hand on me was to reinforce a *lack of worth*—I became a devalued *object*. It became a *lose-lose* situation. One choice and I feel beautiful, but worthless in the long-run. The other choice causes me to feel unwanted and overlooked, but perhaps also allows me to believe more freely that I am worth protecting.

See? Confusing. And if you have felt this way, let me reinforce that you're not alone. There is hope. Ask a trusted and wise person their perspective about the time someone older, cooler, or more powerful was sexually involved with you. And then ask God what *He* thinks of your experience and allow God to show you how HE feels about YOU.

Back to Tamar

When Tamar was trying to bargain with her brother/rapist, she gave him an option that may seem like she… *wanted* it. She says, "Now therefore, please speak to the king, for he will not withhold me from you" (vs. 13c).

Translation: "I don't want your hands on me. But if you won't be derailed in your savage plot, I cannot bare your violation in addition to the penalty of our culture which will happen if you rob my body."

In other words, Tamar played the marriage card, not because she wanted to be raped, but because losing her virginity meant losing her value, her worth, her prospect of marriage during a time in history and culture where marriage was essential. And the loss of virginity, well, it was a

"go directly to desolate life" card.

Lisa Fontes' study of sexual abuse in a variety of cultures sheds light on the fact that since many cultures are highly organized around honor and shame, shame combined with ambivalence is a death-blow.[18] Fontes' interview with a Peruvian woman whose brother was discovered to be having sex with his nine-year-old stepdaughter illustrates this point.

> It wasn't his fault! The girl was right there with him and was very pretty. She wore short dresses. She sat on his lap. She asked him to tuck her in at night. Her mother was away for a month. He couldn't help himself![19]

This nine-year-old Peruvian girl was then banished to a convent.

Presently, in many Muslim cultures around the world, including Sudan, Iran, Saudi Arabia, Pakistan, Turkey, and Nigeria, a girl who is sexually abused is judged as guilty of having sex outside of marriage and is therefore severely penalized. For example, Yuksel explained,

> In many places the absence of virginity may mean that a young girl loses her chance for marriage. If the situation is known, she loses her prestige within the family [just] as the family loses it in their close neighborhood.[20]

Thus, females who are sexually abused in numerous places around the world are viewed as damaged goods, not only in their eyes but in the eyes of their culture. And this is in the 21st century. Imagine the intensity of consequences that pummeled Tamar when Amnon began his violation.

So where does one go with all these convoluted feelings?

Gutting it Through

In Caroline Kettlewell's journey away from her love-hate affair with cutting her body, she realized that surrendering her cutting paraphernalia involved facing her sorrows unvoiced. She explained,

> Choosing not to cut has meant that instead I have had to sit there with the awful agony of unhappiness when it comes—with loneliness, loss, anger, regret, disappointment—and **gut it through**. The first few times, when I had a fight with my husband, when my cat died, when free-range anxiety swallowed me up whole, it was like having unanesthetized surgery. I had to keep screaming to myself above my shrieking of my distress, "THIS WILL NOT KILL YOU!" [emphasis added][21]

Caroline has something here. Healing does require us to enter the voiceless ache of being violated by someone. Perhaps a trusted someone. A loved someone. This journey into the desert means facing the pain, loss, feelings of helplessness, ache. But we believe there must be something more than simply being able to "gut it through."

When God's people were freed from their bondage in Egypt, they experienced a ferocious thirst and pangs of hunger. He satisfied their yearning with sweet water and rained down manna for their hunger.[22] He did not blot out their desert but He did give His people an absolute guarantee beyond their thirst and hunger. He was *in* their desert.[23] And He is in our desert.

Allegiance divided

DISCUSSION STARTERS

1. Is there a "Pharaoh" or "Egypt" in your life—something that you know hurts you, but which you feel unable to resist?

2. Are there any memories that feel confusing for you in terms of placing appropriate blame? How are these memories sitting with you now? Is there a wise and safe person you can talk to about these memories?

3. What does God think about what happened to you when you were abused? How does HE feel about YOU?

4. What does "gutting it through" look like in your life? What does it mean for you to move beyond gutting it through?

5. Caregivers: What does it mean for you to help survivors move beyond "gutting it through" and instead, to be held by our weeping God?

To betray, you must first belong.

Harold Philby

If an enemy were insulting me, I could endure it;
If a foe were raising himself against me,
I could hide from him.
But it is you, a man like myself, my companion,
my close friend, with whom I once enjoyed
sweet fellowship as we walked with
the throng at the house of God.

Psalm 55:12-14[1]

Let us remember what hurts the victim most
is not the cruelty of the oppressor,
but the silence of the bystander.

Elie Wiesel

I believe in the sun even when it isn't shining.
I believe in love even when I'm alone.
And I believe in God even when He is silent.

Graffiti found on a cellar wall where Jews hid during WWII

God is not a man, that He should lie, nor a son of man,
that He should change His mind. Does He speak and not
act? Does He promise and not fulfill?

Numbers 23:19

Never

trust again

Paper, crayons, vanilla wafers and juice, toys, toys, and more toys, brightly-colored flannel-graph Adam and Eve figures hiding behind the bushes... these are necessary components of a typical toddler Sunday school room.

Banners hanging on the walls say things like "Scars of Love: He bore your pain," or "Jesus loves the little children." Stained glass windows show Jesus on the cross, Jesus in the garden, Jesus with His disciples, Jesus' birth. A towering cross is positioned central stage. A man wearing a robe with his Bible open speaks with passionate and persuasive words. Sense the aroma of lit candles, musical crescendos, quiet prayers, bread and wine, offering plates. Kneeling. Standing. Sitting. Reciting Scripture. Hands raised.

A young girl, dressed in a pleated skirt she hates and a top that does nothing for her, enters a Christian school where there are verses on the walls and plaques honoring people for being *servants*, for being *godly*. She hears announcements in the morning over the PA. A fifth grade teacher takes prayer requests before the day gets underway. *I pledge allegiance to the Christian flag...* Students all around her rattle on about going to youth group, looking forward to the next church retreat. Chapel. "Shout to the Lord." Talks of revival. Cleansing.

These religious items and experiences may
convey pleasing and comforting thoughts for many.
But for some individuals,
these are the haunting sights, sounds,
and smells indelibly wedded with being molested.

Disturbing Deception

Father John Porter's victims were legion. Eventually, 222 survivors disclosed that they had been molested by this priest.

Not 2.
Not 22.

Rather, 222 precious boys and girls. [2]

He began his unrestrained bout of molesting children in 1960, on the heels of best wishes and having his tassel turned at seminary graduation. Within a week of his arrival at St. Mary's Church in North Attleboro, Massachusetts, John Porter preyed on his first fifth-grade victim. He was not discriminatory in the selection of his victims. Both girls and boys were targets. In 1963, a mother lodged a complaint about Porter molesting her twelve-year-old boy. This priest was transferred to another parish.

There was a trail of victims wherever he went. A pattern ensued:

Molestation allegation.
Relocation to another parish.
Molestation allegation.
Relocation to another parish...

Porter was eventually sent for treatment in 1967, but upon release, his molesting spree continued unabated. Finally, after further complaints, Porter was advised to petition to leave the priesthood. He was granted his request by the Pope in 1974.

Years later, one of his victims hired a private detective who located Porter. After admitting to some of his abusing rampage, the former priest was finally arrested in September, 1992, after far too much time.[3]

Most of the global news regarding clergy molestation has centered on abuse by Catholic priests. But abuse is not exclusive to any religious denomination. The Catholic Church is more centralized, while many Protestant congregations are independent. Thus, the trail of bread crumbs leading to abuse has been easier to bury in Protestant circles. Despite this fact, three primary insurance companies for the majority of American Protestant churches reported that they yearly receive in the neighborhood of 260 allegations of child sexual abuse by Christian church leaders or volunteers.[4] Sadly, the epic tragedy of molestation appears to be coming to light in Protestant ministries.[5]

As we are editing this chapter, a renowned coach who allegedly molested scores of disadvantaged boys made the papers. Here the violation took place with boys craving to become skilled athletes; Boys hungry to look up to someone.

Callous Disregard

When it comes to child sexual abuse, Finkelhor and Browne explain that betrayal is

> the dynamic by which children discover that someone on whom they were vitally dependent has caused them harm... someone whom they loved or whose affection was important to them treated them with *callous disregard*. [emphasis added][6]

The lifeblood of betrayal is that the victim doesn't see it coming, like an unannounced tornado that touches down before unsuspecting city-dwellers have a chance to take cover. Deception blindsides victims in its wake.

Betrayal comes in a variety-pack of characters. There is the obvious betrayal by the perpetrator, but what can be equally damaging is the betrayal committed by the bystander, the non-offending parent or teacher who knows about the abuse and does nothing. There's the betrayal of those who seek to silence, the betrayal of those who distance themselves from the victim as a result of the abuse, the betrayal of church leaders who don't take it to heart and the assumed betrayal of God who seemingly doesn't care.

The victim of betrayal is like a field mouse caught in a glue-trap; like a fish fastened on a hook.

Bait on a Hook

THINGS ARE NOT ALWAYS WHAT THEY SEEM.
Phaedrus

He had pockets full of candy: red, green, yellow. Take your pick. At recess, the kids would clamor around Patrick and beg him for "One more!" Wheat-germ, powdered skim milk, and tiny cups of vitamins were daily routine in my (Tammy's) home, so anything with sugar was bait on a hook for this nine-year-old fish with freckles and strawberry blonde hair.

Patrick slipped me a handful of candies one particular afternoon when other kids were scarce. A personal invitation to come to the school the following Saturday was extended and the prize of "lots of candies" was an offer too hard to refuse. But, he cautioned, I shouldn't tell anyone because otherwise all the kids would want to come. This made sense to my little-girl logic.

Saturday came and I asked my mom for permission to play outside, carefully omitting the part about going to my school to collect my sugary jackpot. The expectation escalated over those few short blocks to Bedson Elementary School, a path trudged twice daily since the beginning of my kindergarten career. Patrick opened the school side door and led me down the hall into a classroom.

"Why …why are you showing me these rabbits
doing things to each other?"
"Um… where are the… candies… you promised me?"
"Why are you kissing me… touching me like that?"

These questions surged and spun inside me. There were no candies that day.

I told Patrick that I wasn't feeling well and I wanted, needed, to go home. There was no need for this elementary school janitor to urge me to keep the events of that day under wraps. I didn't have the vocabulary to describe a grown man pillaging the body of a little girl.

The walk home remains a blank spot in my memory but I do recall later, lying on my bed, feeling sick to my nine-year-old stomach.

As I reflect back to this event of several decades ago, I am alive to the fact that Patrick stole something from me that day that changed the course of history in my life. I am also aware I didn't go to meet Patrick because I was hungering for a relationship with an adult male. I had a dad who was deeply involved in my life.

Plain and simple, *I was a little girl who wanted candy.*

Individuals who abuse understand the desires of young people. Sexual abuse doesn't "just happen," despite the claims of many who molest. There tends to be a pattern to abuse. Perpetrators frequently prepare their victims. And they do this by:

Being helpful,
Offering a "special relationship,"
Invitations to excursions,
Gifts,
Tenderness,
Toys,
Time, and
Rough & tumble play.

Each of these gifts or involvements entices children deeper into the web. What seems like an act of kindness to many onlookers is in reality miles apart from something good-hearted. These acts pull kids in to a perpetrator's magnetic field.

With adolescent victims, this same "special relationship" takes place, but it is simply a more grown-up version. A perpetrator may seek to treat the adolescent as an adult (which most adolescents hunger after), dole out extra responsibility (i.e. being a coach's or teacher's assistant), expose personal information never designed for a young person (i.e., "I can talk to you so much better than to my wife"), and provide a listening ear to a street-hardened teen in need of a sheltering wing.

These calculated "acts of kindness" serve to form a relationship with someone less powerful in order to later have sexual involvement. This process is called **grooming**. This act of preparing victims for abuse is a common practice among perpetrators.[7] This carefully stage-managed, premeditated setup often takes weeks or even months to construct. At some point, the perpetrator may include seemingly innocuous tickling, wrestling, and hugging. All are forms of the indispensible ingredient of life: *Touch.*

The trap may also include creating an atmosphere where swearing, telling dirty jokes, and viewing pornography is acceptable, yet part of the special relationship that needs to be kept hush-hush. This component further serves to normalize a sexual element in the relationship, distance the child from loved ones, and entrap the child in the sense that he is a willing accomplice.

Step by step, boundary violations escalate, peaking in sexual activity.[8] Not only do offenders groom young people, they often work on the family and even set up organizational leaders who act as gatekeepers to places where children abound.

Clinician Mary Gail Frawley-O'Dea explains the careful grooming process through the story of a man who shares his experiences as an eight-year-old and the way his "favorite priest" changed his life forever:

Empty classrooms, the sacristy, the small school chapel, the nurse's office, the rectory—all become sexualized spaces. He (Fr. Bill) asks your parents if he can take you to his summer place at the beach and they are relieved not to have to worry about you. There, the abuse, during which you always are blindfolded, meshes with fishing expeditions, movies, riding the ocean waves, clam digging, and other activities a lonely child living in a city apartment building with drunk and arguing parents finds amazing. That fun and adventure fills your days. Your nights, on the other hand, find Fr. Bill rubbing his penis between your buttocks, caressing and sucking on your now erect penis, tongue kissing you, and pushing your blindfolded face on his penis.[9]

Words can't describe the impact this "favorite priest" had on this boy. The violent interjection of delight-filled-days preceding abuse-infused-nights is the landscape of grooming for some.

Sexual offending expert Anna Salter explains that the essential ingredient in the batter of grooming is trust.

The establishment (and eventual betrayal) of affection and trust occupies a central role in the child molester's interactions with children…It takes little to discover that *emotional seduction* is the most effective way to manipulate children. [emphasis added][10]

And yet we were created to trust. The way we open ourselves to God is through trust. Tragically, perpetrators use trust as their foot-in-the-door maneuver which often leaves victims enraged at themselves for opening the door.

God chronicles the elaborate grooming process in the story of Tamar. The trap was positioned, the scent of human deception covered; the trigger was set; and the victim was caught.

"Go to bed and pretend to be ill," Jonadab said. "When your father comes to see you, say to him, 'I would like my sister Tamar to come and give me something to eat. Let her prepare the food in my sight so I may watch her and then eat it from her hand.'"

So Amnon lay down and pretended to be ill. When the king came to see him, Amnon said to him, "I would like my sister Tamar to come and make some special bread in my sight, so I may eat from her hand."

So Tamar went...[11]

Grave Disenchantment: A Wolf in Shepherd's Clothing

AND FROM PROPHET TO PRIEST, EVERY ONE DEALS FALSELY.
THEY HAVE HEALED THE WOUNDS OF MY PEOPLE LIGHTLY,
SAYING, 'PEACE, PEACE,' WHEN THERE IS NO PEACE.

Jeremiah 6:13-14

Phillip Keller's formative years were lived out in East Africa. His neighbors were wooly creatures and sheep herders whose rearing practices were akin to shepherds in the Middle East. Eight years of his adult life were spent as a sheep owner and rancher in British Columbia. These experiences primed and prepared him to compose impressions about the twenty-third Psalm from the vantage point of a bona fide shepherd who lovingly cared for his sheep.[12]

About the four-legged critters he watched for endless hours he noted,

> Sheep do not 'just take care of themselves' as some might suppose. They required, more than any other class of live-stock, endless attention and meticulous care.[13]

It is unremarkable that God refers to those of us who love Him as sheep and the spiritual leaders of His flock He calls shepherds. Based on Keller's bird's eye view of scads of shepherds, he penned these words:

...the lot in life of any particular sheep depended on the type of man who owned it. Some men were gentle, kind, intelligent, brave, and selfless in their devotion to their stock. Under one man sheep would struggle, starve, and suffer endless hardship. In another's care they would flourish and thrive contentedly.[14]

Similarly, it is a sizable tragedy when shepherds of people fail to protect their flock and instead prey on those entrusted to their care. The consequences of these vile actions are fierce. Through the prophet Ezekiel[15] we are given a sneak peek into God's huge heart for His sheep and His fierce reaction when earthly shepherds fail to represent Him well.

Woe, shepherds of Israel...
...you slaughter the fat sheep without feeding the flock.[16]

Here God lists five specific ways that Israel's leaders have neglected their followers:

They have not strengthened the sickly,
They have not healed the diseased,
They have not bound up the broken,
They have not brought back the scattered,
They have not searched for the lost.[17]

They were guilty of not caring for the flock, and as a result, the flock was "scattered" for lack of a shepherd. Of course, there were shepherds around by title, but they were not fulfilling their role, and so it was as if they were non-existent.[18]

God's response to these failed shepherds is severe:

Surely because My flock has become food for all the beasts of the field for lack of a shepherd, and My shepherds did not search for My flock, but rather the shepherds fed themselves and did not feed My flock... Behold, I am against the shepherds, and I will demand my sheep from them and make them cease from feeding sheep. So the shepherds will not feed themselves anymore, but I will deliver

My flock from their mouth, so that they will not be food for them. [emphasis added][19]

The severity of God's statement here not only highlights the direct damage of Israel's leaders, but also their failure to respond when the flock was in desperate need. God was dealing with these shepherds for their neglect. He was letting them know that to do nothing for the flock was to do something very damaging indeed. It breaks God's heart when our spiritual leaders find out that abuse is happening under their watch and when they refuse to respond.

Doing Nothing Is Doing Something

WE WILL HAVE TO REPENT... NOT MERELY FOR THE
HATEFUL WORDS AND ACTIONS OF THE BAD PEOPLE BUT FOR
THE APPALLING SILENCE OF THE GOOD PEOPLE.
Martin Luther King, Jr.

"Oh, my God, he stabbed me! Please help me! Please help me!" she shrieked.[20]

"I didn't want to get involved" was the explanation from one of the 38 neighbors who heard but did nothing.[21]

"I don't know" was another reason given for not helping this woman.

"I was tired...I went back to bed," said a third neighbor.[22]

On March 13, 1964, at about 3:15 a.m., Catherine (Kitty) Genovese was savagely stabbed twice in the back as she walked 100 feet to her apartment building door. When Kitty screamed the first time, a neighbor yelled, "Let that girl alone," prompting her assailant to flee. She struggled to make her way to the side of the building to get to her apartment but during a 35-minute period, her attacker returned twice. He stabbed her a total of 17 times, and during his third return, while she lay crumpled and dying, he raped her.

Not one of her neighbors, from the safety of their homes, called the police during the vicious stabbing and rape. After Kitty was assaulted for the third time, the first call came to the police and within two minutes the police arrived. They explained that if they had been called sooner, Kitty's life could have been saved.

In recent years, considerable attention in writing and speaking has concentrated on the role of bystanders in the accounts of genocide, ethnic cleansing, and other forms of mass violence. Bleak are the accounts of unfolding evil when bystanders do nothing. Global observations have led many to conclude that indifference and passivity enables evil to scatter like gossip in a small town. When it comes to these vile acts of humanity, the case has been made that appreciable responsibility resides with knowledgeable third-party observers. It is unacceptable to say, "We did not hurt these people" when we knew what was occurring, we had the resources to prevent it, and yet **We Did Nothing.**

Contemptible & Culpable Ignorance

No snowflake in an avalanche ever feels responsible.

Voltaire

Of course, parents, leaders of nations, organizations, and churches, do not always know about the deeds of perpetrators. Individuals who abuse are better at weaving deceit and snipping off loose ends than others are at unraveling their ball of lies. However, far too often there is a systemic similarity in the response to mass or individual abuse. **See no evil, hear no evil, speak no evil.**

Sometimes families and organizations do not want to know about the abuse because knowing means entering into the victim's morass of torment. The pain is wide and deep. So turning away and driving on from the scene of the accident is easier, at least in the short run.

"Keep it a secret. Don't tell anyone. Don't make us look bad." Admonishing congregations to stop talking about the fact that one of the teachers from the Christian school molested a bunch of high schoolers = DENIAL. Abuse exerts influence on victims and everyone who comes across its path. All parties need room to respectfully voice the impact of the blow.

Alternatively, when abuse is acknowledged, a seismic blame-shift lurks in many pews. For example, within one congregation that Tammy worked with, even *after* the pastor admitted to sexually violating several adolescents while he "counseled" them, several church members still blamed the youth or maintained that the pastor couldn't have done it!

Time to heal is an important gift that congregations are wise to lavish upon members that have been abused by pastoral staff. Hastened healing may work in the short run but rarely in the marathons of life.[21]

Too often, the gruel of "forgive and forget" meals are served after abuse has been perpetrated by one of the church leaders. Without a doubt, forgiveness is paramount in the process of healing from abuse and we will further explore this topic in a later chapter. But when a Christian leader or counselor bulldozes this agenda onto a person who has yet to even recognize the extent of the damage arising from her pastor molesting her instead of counseling her, the resulting pressure serves to only deepen the damage. Indeed, God wants us to forgive so we might follow in His footsteps and so that we might be free, *not* so that we can sweep the abuse under the proverbial carpet. One author emphatically stated that "a pastor should not undertake to counsel victim(s) unless he or she has special training in counseling sexual abuse victims and is comfortable talking about sexuality."[24]

When a Christian leader has been found guilty of abusing one of the sheep, the desire for a repentant heart is a worthy aspiration and, not to mention, biblical. One of the optimum ways to help a shepherd repent is to avoid shielding him from the consequences of his actions. Cooperating with criminal justice agencies is not only required by law, but it also helps the perpetrator to see and taste the gravity of his actions.

When instead of fanning the flame of denial, a Christian organization supports the victims, conveys an attitude of concern, places the responsibility of the abuse on the perpetrator, and protects the victim from further abuse,[25] these actions serve as a healing balm to infected wounds.

When churches and other religious institutions hire people who violate individuals under their care, the leadership of these institutions is wise to authentically voice two simple words: "I'm sorry." However, an attorney who spends his time suing religious institutions when child sexual abuse has occurred has never heard this kind of apology.

> Believe it or not, I have never gotten an unequivocal apology for any of my clients from the Archdiocese of Portland (or from any Archdiocese for that matter), from the Latter-Day Saints Church, from the Seventh Day Adventist Church, or from the Boy Scouts of America.
>
> Oh, they will agree to letters of regret, they will agree to letters acknowledging the victim's pain and suffering, or the wrongness of the abuse. But I have not yet been able to get an institutional official to say: 'As a representative of this institution, I apologize profoundly to you for what our man did to you. It was wrong, he betrayed you and betrayed your trust. And, because he represented us, we betrayed you and violated your trust. I apologize and am so sorry.' Why is that so difficult? Governments get it—governments are issuing apologies all the time, to individuals or peoples wronged throughout history. Why can't spiritual and moral leaders get it?[26]

Another act that conveys care and understanding on the part of Christian leadership is offering a symbolic gesture. Similar to war memorials, specific actions or concrete memorials can serve as a visual reminder of what happened and provide promptings not to forget. Leadership paying for the counseling of survivors, pursuing changes in policies that require criminal background checks and other measures to protect individuals, and engaging in face-to-face conversations with survivors helps survivors know that leadership is along for the journey of healing. These measures also reveal that the leadership realizes that healing from Christian leadership violations takes time, understanding, financial and collective support, and the humble and praying posture of shepherds.[27]

And He Failed to Restrain Them

The concern of protecting and loving victims of clergy abuse instead of enabling the abuser to go on is not new. God required this of the priest Eli when it came to his two sons. And Eli did confront his sons.

> Now Eli, who was very old, heard about everything his sons were doing to all Israel and how they slept with the women who served at the entrance to the Tent of Meeting. So he said to them, 'Why do you do such things? I hear from all the people about these wicked deeds of yours. No, my sons; it is not a good report that I hear spreading among the Lord's people. If a man sins against another man, God may mediate for him; but if a man sins against the Lord, who will intercede for him?' His sons, however, did not listen to their father's rebuke...[28]

Eli made a satisfactory first step. He rebuked his boys. However, when they didn't take notice, Eli failed to remove them from office. And there were harsh consequences for Eli. The Lord told Samuel:

> See, I am about to do something in Israel that will make the ears of everyone who hears of it tingle. At that time I will carry out against Eli everything I spoke against his family—from beginning to end. For I told him that I would judge his family forever because of *the sin he knew about*; his sons made themselves contemptible, and *he failed to restrain them*. Therefore, I swore to the house of Eli, 'The guilt of Eli's house will never be atoned for by sacrifice or offering.' [emphasis added][29]

Yikes. As a Christian leader, each time I (Tammy) read this passage, I feel an enormous amount of responsibility. God demanded much of Eli. It was not enough for him to simply chide his sinister sons. The required response of Eli as God's chief shepherd (with hefty implications to Christian leaders [i.e., cardinals, pastors, elders, boards of trustees, parents]) was to oust these men from their ministry position so others would be protected and God's name honored. When Eli was remiss in his responsibility to hand out harsh penalties to his priestly sons, cruel consequences were meted out to Eli and his sons.

Failure to face evil and failure to restrain and punish shepherds who fleece their flock is unacceptable in God's eyes and it breeds massive betrayal among victims.

When I (Hannah) read the Eli passage, I can't help but think back to Tamar and wonder *where was David's rebuke?* Tamar was drowning in the pools of betrayal all around her. Her own brother violated her. Another brother silenced her. Her dad was "angry" but did nothing.

Where were David's five stones now?

This leads to one further form of betrayal found carved in the lives of most survivors somewhere along the journey. The question **"Why didn't you stop the abuse, God?"** stands like a towering billboard on a desert highway, unable to be ignored.

Guiled by God

Pastor and teacher A.W. Tozer once said, "What comes into our minds when we think about God is the most important thing about us."[30] If Tozer's statement is true, then it is important to explore the impact of abuse on one's view of God. When I (Hannah) was in a survivors' group, our leader passed around a sheet of paper that listed (front and back) all the different names/titles of God and asked us to respond to the question, *How would you describe, from this list, who God was at the time of your abuse?*

It felt like a trick question.

You see, all this list had on it were names from the Bible – positive names. Nowhere on this list were names like "The God Who Abandons," "The God Who Is Not There," or "The Passive God." And the sad reality is that many people who are abused struggle to have a positive image of God, especially when their abuser claimed to be a representative of Him.

Several studies have highlighted that abuse correlates with loss of spirituality,[31] loss of faith in God,[32] and the development of more negative images of God.[33] While many in various denominations look up to leaders in the church as surrogate parents, the Catholic church demonstrates this to a significant extent, in its use of familial terms, referencing leaders as "father," "mother," "sister," and "brother." And because a "father" is not merely that, but also a representative of *the* Father, the implications are severe.[34] One clergy abuse victim stated, "I don't think I'll ever step foot in a church again… I lost my religion, faith, and the ability to trust adults and 'institutions.'"[35] Another man stated, "I felt it was God's representative on earth that opened my eyes to God's failing. I don't believe in God today at all anymore."[36]

Abuse by someone who represents the living God not only produces massive revulsion toward the clergy but often toward God as well.

> The fact that it was a priest [who abused me] was cataclysmic. It taught me that there is a lie in the world. I developed a slowly evolving cynicism. As I got older and gave up on my piety, I grew to hate the smells, sounds, feelings of Church— the incense, the collars, the robes. My spirituality and ability to believe in a higher power were destroyed.[37]

When sexual abuse is also spiritual abuse, as in the story of Renee Altson, the journey to healing is lengthy, and the seeds of confusion, doubt, and anger are buried deep. Her abuse story begins with this

chilling fact: "My father raped me while reciting the Lord's Prayer
... my father molested me while singing Christian hymns..."[38] As
one would only imagine, Renee struggled with frequent references
to God as "Father":

> My father sometimes forced my eyes open, made me look at
> him as he raped me. I live with the visions of his face still.
> Sometimes from the depths of the middle of the night I
> wake up screaming. Sometimes I pray, and my father's face
> is the face of God I see in my mind. His face comes to me
> in the middle of church, as I'm driving down the road, I see
> him in the soap bubbles in the sink. Out of nowhere I see
> his eyes behind the eyes of a friend... I want this God, but I
> don't want this God. God has my father's face. God has my
> father's hands... I feel an ongoing fury at the comparison
> of God with father. I swallow tears every time, every single
> time, someone prays to our "heavenly Father," "Father in
> heaven," or any variation thereof... How can you dare to
> compare yourself to a father, God? Who are you to think
> that I can ever trust you with that perception? Who are you
> to give me that image that went so badly? Why did you in-
> sist on a relationship that was so wrong?[39]

The Bible uses a variety of metaphors to describe our relationship
with Him,[40] which is so wise of God because here on earth, many
experience a lot of these human relationships in evil ways. In other
words, if you or your client, or someone else close to you has a hard
time relating to God as a father because your earthly example was
neglectful, absent, emotionally-distant, addicted, demeaning, or
sexually abusive, that doesn't mean that you can't relate to God.[41]
He gives us many pictures: father, king, shepherd, mother hen... It
is quite possible that each of these images of God may be trouble-
some, difficult to relate to, fear-provoking. But He is in no rush. An
imposter has lied, cheated, and violated. He realizes that identity
theft takes time to resolve. He will wait. He lingers with anticipation
that we will, some day, realize that He is not at all like our abuser. He
couldn't be more different. And in the meantime, He longs for the

day we might realize that He adores, esteems, values, and cradles His kids. He always did and always will have our best interests in mind, even when it doesn't seem like it.

Where Was Jesus?

In the movie *Our Fathers*, a survivor of Catholic priest abuse attends a men's support group and stands to share a segment of his story. He deliberates over the question that burned brightly in his heart as a 12-year-old boy—a boy who gazed out the window and stared at a cross while the priest's hand moved up the boy's thigh to his genitals. He was hoping Jesus would have been like a strong fireman who rescued him before he was burned. Instead, third degree burns in the form of a question was branded on his soul. It is the question that continues to smolder among many survivors too: *Where was Jesus who didn't let death have him? Death is having me now....*[42]

The question over God's presence crackles as the flames of suffering sear and scorch. In the thick of Job's agony, he was desperate for a sense of God's nearness. "If only I knew where to find Him; if only I could go to His dwelling...But if I go to the east, He is not there; if I go to the west, I do not find Him."[43]

I (Tammy) recall a time when I was acutely desperate for a tangible sense of closeness with my Father: Following the funeral of my mom. As family members flew home and my departure to go back home to Indiana was imminent, I ached at the thought of leaving Winnipeg. Returning to Indiana meant leaving the people who knew my mom, loved her, and loved us both. The awareness that no one I met from that day forward would ever know her plagued my soul.

The morning I was to depart, I cried in anguish to my Father, "I cannot get on that plane unless you go with me." At that moment in time, I didn't doubt He loved me. What I wanted was a palpable sense of His nearness. Years later, I realize I was really saying to my Father, **please don't die on me too.**

At the airport, the customs official asked me the reason for my loads of luggage. I burst out crying as I told him my mom died. On the bus ride from Chicago a passenger attempted conversation as he noted the amount of all my luggage. I looked at him and told him, "My mom died." Talk about a conversation stopper.

In the days, weeks, and months to come, I spent hours with the Lord in the morning before I began my day. Never have I felt so close to my God. He walked with me, carried me, and comforted me. His presence was palpable. In the midst of my greatest grief, the answer to the age-old query of **Where was Jesus?** was revealed in the sweetness of His companionship with me and etched in the words of Isaiah 43:2: "When you pass through the waters, I will be with you; and when you pass through the rivers, they will not sweep over you. When you walk through the fire, you will not be burned; the flames will not set you ablaze. For I am the Lord, your God, the Holy One of Israel, your Savior."

The flooding waters compelled me to gasp for air. The blazing fire's heat was severe. But my Savior was there and He was enough.

What Now?!?: Ten Easy Steps?

WE MUST CHOOSE BETWEEN THE DELIGHTS &
PLEASURES OF SAFETY OR GROWTH.
Abraham Maslow

We would like to think at the rock-bottom moments in our lives that we would all find ourselves willing and able to stumble into a church with open doors and discover within those walls some sort of hopeful message. But when it is in these buildings that we have been hurt or when hurt has come by way of people who represent God, the limp we walk with only seems to get worse the closer we draw to *that place.*

Solution #1: There are no simple solutions.

When a sheep has not merely wandered into the woods on its own, but was essentially maimed and kicked out of the flock, it becomes difficult to trust other sheep. It becomes even more difficult to trust a shepherd. Restoration in one's own heart and into healthy relationships with others and with God is a long process that starts in different ways for each person. For some, it involves going to the Shepherd and lodging a complaint before even considering rejoining the flock. Others may be decidedly angry at the Shepherd, and need to be pursued by the flock before they can consider trusting the Good Shepherd (John 10).

Despite our soldier-like resolve to NEVER TRUST AGAIN, God's response to His sheep is one full of compassion. God steps into our fields and seeks out all of us who are scattered. God stepped into the dark field of Renee Altson's life and found her in her most lost place.

> I chose to believe that I was better off alone, protected from the ninety-nine, isolated and untouchable. I chose to sit in the wilderness, believing it was my home, struggling to make it comfortable, trying to convince myself that I belonged there. And I did belong there. I belonged in my desperate aloneness. I belonged in my lack of belonging. My hurt was raw, the damage done to me was real and tangible; a trail of blood showed the woundedness was not just in my imagination… I heard the shepherd coming a long way off. He was whistling. 'Hey,' he said to me. 'I have missed you. I am so glad I have found you.' He extended a hand to wipe my tear-stained, dusty cheeks. 'Come back with me,' he said. 'Come back to the others.' I shook my head and pulled away. 'No,' I said. He looked surprised, but it did not change the immense compassion on his face. 'No,' I said again. 'I can't go back. I don't want to. I don't trust the other ninety-nine. I don't want to be hurt again.' The shepherd sat down on the ground next to me. 'Okay,' he said quietly, 'I'll just stay here with you then.' [44]

The Good Shepherd's promise is that He will find us, rescue us, and stay with us as long as it takes. God Himself highlights these promises through the prophet Ezekiel[45]:

I will deliver my flock (v.10)
I will search for my sheep (v.11)
I will care for my sheep (v.12)
> I will bring them out (v.13)
> I will gather them (v.13)
> I will bring them back to their land (v.13)
>> I will feed them (v.14)
>> They will have rest (v.14)
>> I will bind up the broken (v.16)
>>> I will strengthen the sick (v.16)

May you become increasingly aware of the presence of the Good Shepherd in your life, and lean into the One who will never steal, kill, or destroy… so that you might become increasingly more in tune and equipped to protect the flock and seek after the ones who are dying in their desperate aloneness.

…HE WILL CARRY THE LAMBS IN HIS ARMS,

HOLDING THEM CLOSE TO HIS HEART…

Isaiah 40:11

Never

trust again

DISCUSSION STARTERS

1. As with Renee Alston, is there a name or title of God that you struggle with? If so, what is it? Is there a name of God that touches you deeply?

2. What is your reaction to Eli's failure to restrain his sons? OR what about David's failure to protect his daughter?

3. How would you like churches to respond when a minister is found guilty of abusing one of the flock?

4. Is there a "Where was Jesus?" time in your life? Can you put words to this? Draw it?

5. When is the last time you have been aware of being carried in His arms and being held close to His heart (Isaiah 40:11)?

THERE ARE TWO KINDS OF SECRETS: THOSE WE KEEP FROM
OTHERS AND [THOSE] WE HIDE FROM OURSELVES...
SOMETIMES WHEN WE BELIEVE WE ARE KEEPING A SECRET,
THAT SECRET IS ACTUALLY KEEPING US.
Frank Warren

NOTHING MAKES US SO LONELY AS OUR SECRETS.
Paul Tournier

THE MAN WHO CAN ARTICULATE THE MOVEMENTS OF HIS INNER
LIFE, WHO CAN GIVE NAMES TO HIS VARIED EXPERIENCES, NEED
NO LONGER BE A VICTIM OF HIMSELF, BUT IS ABLE SLOWLY AND
CONSISTENTLY TO REMOVE THE OBSTACLES THAT PREVENT THE
SPIRIT FROM ENTERING. HE IS ABLE TO CREATE SPACE FOR HIM
WHOSE HEART IS GREATER THAN HIS, WHOSE EYES SEE MORE THAN
HIS, AND WHOSE HANDS CAN HEAL MORE THAN HIS.
Henri Nouwen

MUSIC IS THE SHORTHAND OF EMOTION.
Leo Tolstoy

THIS IS A PRIVATE MATTER AND I BEG OF YOU TO LET IT SLEEP.
Mr. Hyde, Robert Louis Stevenson's Dr. Jekyll and Mr. Hyde

NONE OF US CAN EVER EXPRESS THE EXACT MEASURE OF
HIS NEEDS OR HIS THOUGHTS OR HIS SORROWS;
& HUMAN SPEECH IS LIKE A CRACKED KETTLE
ON WHICH WE TAP CRUDE RHYTHMS...
WHILE WE LONG TO MAKE MUSIC THAT WILL MELT THE STARS.
Gustave Flaubert, 1856

Anguish
u n v o i c e d

Wherever sexual abuse resides, secrets flourish. Scads of people who have been molested haul around narratives that are seemingly impossible to voice. Individuals who sexually violate others bank on these stories being kept under wraps. A pedophile who molested more than a thousand boys explains:

> For me, secrecy was the glue that held my fantasies together. Secrecy was the element that added a feeling of excitement, heightening the overall thrill I got from offending. It represented a twisted sense of personal power and personal worth, and ultimately it was my critical weapon both to entice and ensnare my young victims.[1]

Psychiatrist Rolland Summit explains that survivors are close-mouthed about abuse for a host of other reasons:

> "Nobody will believe you," "Don't tell your mother; (a) she will hate you, (b) she will hate me, (c) she will kill you, (d) she will kill me, (e) it will kill her, (f) she will send you away, (g) she will send me away, or (h) it will break up the family and you'll all end up in an orphanage." ... "If you tell anyone (a) I won't love you anymore, (b) I'll spank you, (c) I'll kill your dog, or (d) I'll kill you."[2]

When survivors gather the courage to speak about the trauma, they may tell tentatively, as though a bomb were strapped to their words. The weight of the hurt seems to seep over the sides, yet the descriptions of the hurt are lean and spare, as language can be limited and inadequate as a way to convey the complexities and the weight of trauma. Some experiences are *ineffable*—i.e., the trauma defies expression or description. For example, a client shared with Tammy that as a young girl she would spend the summers at the home of her aunt and uncle. A ritual began where her uncle would haul her to the back shed, lock the door, and then proceed to molest her. On one occasion, her whimpering was extinguished when her uncle told her,

"God wanted me to do this."

God wanted her uncle to do this? How could words ever adequately depict her confusion, her helplessness, her savage experience, her narrative?

For some, telling is not part of the plan. It's not safe to speak.

Makin' Mud Pies

WHAT CANNOT BE SAID WILL GET WEPT.

Sappho

The sexual abuse that Antwone Fisher endured began at about the age of three and lasted for many years. Willenda, a neighbor who "helped out" by babysitting, would lug Antwone to the basement like an overstuffed bag of unwanted belongings *en route* to the garbage dump. What went on downstairs should never happen to a little boy.

> Then she's finished. Her voice lays empty as she says,
> 'Where your clothes at? Put some clothes on.'
> She sounds like it's my fault I don't have clothes on.
> She dresses, tosses my clothes at me, and says,
> 'Go on outside in the shade and play.
> I think they makin' mud pies out there.'
> For a second Willenda smiles. But then her face flashes a warning.
> She doesn't even need to tell me in words. I know what it says—

> ncver, never, never tell, or something more horrible than
> you can ever imagine will happen to you.

And it wasn't really the fear of her punishing me that kept
me from telling anyone all those years. It was the unspeakable shame I felt about what went on with her in the basement, and *my unspeakable shame* that maybe it was my fault.
[emphasis added][3]

There are certain types of stories that you don't want to jab with a
stick. We let them go on sleeping because we fear that if they are
roused they might growl and reveal their pointed teeth.

Unable to Face It

IF YOU DO NOT TELL THE TRUTH ABOUT YOURSELF YOU CANNOT
TELL IT ABOUT OTHER PEOPLE.

Virginia Woolf

Muteness about abuse is crystallized for other reasons. Talking about
the abuse means admitting at a deeper level, it really did happen. To
speak of it "give(s) it shape and substance and permanence."[4]

Telling sometimes jeopardizes the loss of the one we love. The one
who ravaged may also be the one who taught us to let the clutch out
slowly when we put our foot on the gas; she may be the one who
inspired us to dream, who fed us our food, who taught us at Sunday
school. Voicing the abuse risks erasing all the memories on the chalk-
board, the bad and the good.

Sue William Silverman's father was the United States Chief Counsel
to the Secretary of the Interior from 1933 to 1953, and he went on to
be the president of several prominent companies. Sue had pictures of
her father with President Harry Truman and other influential political
figures. An unrecorded point on his vitae however, is that he molested
his daughter throughout her childhood and adolescence. Sue buried
this secret for years. Decades later, when her father was living in a

retirement complex and his friends exclaimed to Sue how wonderful her father was, a torrent of emotions and thoughts surged through her:

> Even if I told these people in the restaurant the truth about my parents, they would not hear me. The truth would be too difficult to consider. After all, each table is set with linen and flowers. The arrangement is too pretty. Who would want to disturb it? Who would want his or her equilibrium interrupted? No one wants to hear; so no one will know. But of course *I* am the one who says nothing, who can't tell these people, who can't confront my parents. So maybe I—not these people, not my parents—really, *I am the one unable to face it.*[5]

In my (Tammy's) family there were a lot of secrets. My mom developed a bipolar illness after giving birth to me. Her sad times were punctuated by times of elevated energy: singing hymns at the wee hours of the morning, shopping for peculiar gifts for people with money we did not have. Her illness began in the 1960s when mental illness was not understood or common dialogue. When my mom was depressed, I told people at church she was "sick." When she was manic, well, she was "sick" again. The thought of anybody knowing our family secret was frightening for a little girl who was trying to protect her dad's job and her mom's dignity and trying to stave off her own feelings of helplessness. So by the time I was sexually abused at nine years of age, I was already a seasoned veteran at stashing secrets in our family vault.

In contrast, another survivor determined to speak the unspeakable may freeze when it comes to the prospect of telling. The fervent passion to get it out is simultaneously fused with feeling incapable of doing so.[6] The prospect of releasing the secret feels like death.

Some survivors come to the point where they can bear the silence no more, and the stories rush out like a midnight-black Labrador retriever yanking on the leash, waiting to run. With a friend, or in the office of a caregiver, the tale of trauma is disclosed at break-neck speed following a hasty "Hello." No longer is the secret tolerable. He has resolved that the story must be told. Sometimes there comes a point when it is more painful *not* to speak.

All in all, the reasons people don't tell are just about as numerous as there are survivors.[7]

On the Other End of the Continuum

We realize that for some victims of abuse, blurting out stories of trauma is a more run-of-the-mill occurrence. There are those who prattle on about their trauma with no-holds-barred, almost as if they are discussing report cards or basketball statistics with buddies. "Look at me! Listen to this!" Abuse stories are paraded and one-upping becomes the norm. Just ask your local adolescent-group-home therapist who spends a lot of time with kids who are hungry for attention and bereft of boundaries.

The task of caregivers when journeying with a person whose abuse is worn like a leopard skin coat and knee-high, blood-red leather boots will inevitably be quite a different path. Somewhere the survivor may have learned that the way to secure involvement with others is to flaunt a more grisly war story than the next girl. Boundaries may have been non-existent in her family-of-origin and telling all to anyone is par for the course. Caring involves modeling appropriate self-disclosure. It is helpful when caregivers endeavor in non-judgmental ways to plumb motivations for "flashing" abuse stories. Dialoguing with survivors about the fact that the price of admission to real relationship does not require bunches of battle scars can shed new light and open the door to authentic living.

Setting the Narrative Free

A GREAT DEAL OF HEALING AND INTIMACY BEGINS
WITH THE WORDS, "LET'S TALK ABOUT IT."
Barry Allen Farber

Disclosure is a relational venture. The outcome of the unveiling of the abuse narrative is impacted by both the teller and the tellee.

This is why disclosure is defined as a shared process: "The telling of the abuse and the response to the report."[8] The therapeutic connection in the revealing and receiving of the secrets is a mainstay in the healing process.[9] Professionals' and family members' responses to the stories of abuse hold the capacity to aid in both healing and harming.

When the abuse secret and the survivor are received with disbelief, shame, blame, or distancing, many learn to put the story under wraps, never to be told again. Or at least not for a long, long time.

When Tess, the title character in Thomas Hardy's *Tess of the D'Urbervilles*, finally garners the courage to tell her new husband about the time she had *been with* another man (she was raped when she was 16), the response she receives is like pouring acid in a freshly opened wound.

"I repeat, the woman I have been loving is not you," he says.[10] In a surprising moment of clarity and vulnerability in the midst of a dreadful moment, Tess defends herself.

> 'Angel!—Angel! I was a child—a child when it happened!
> I knew nothing of men.'
> 'You were more sinned against than sinning, that I admit.'
> 'Then will you not forgive me?'
> 'I do forgive you, but forgiveness is not all.'
> 'And love me?'
> To this question he did not answer.[11]

In the 1998 film adaptation of this classic, Angel looks to his wife and asks if she could *swear* that the man was entirely to blame for what happened.[12] She responds in the only way shame knows how: she buries her head into her chest, weeps, and shakes her head no. He blamed her. She blamed her.

Conversely, when a survivor unveils her narrative and it is greeted with comfort, belief, and support, frequently there is a yearning to reveal more chapters, more stories, and more of one's soul. Fisher's daring disclosure with his military appointed psychiatrist engendered freedom and a desire to speak further:

> Before that meeting with Commander Williams, I had never told anyone my story. I had never been given the chance to connect the dots of my existence, to see the shape and the course of my life, to observe for myself how everything that had happened had its reason, its lesson. To talk was liberation from the prison of silence, from the burden of my own secrets. But by the end of the hour, I had only begun.[13]

Scores of abuse survivors have revealed to Hannah and me words something like, "I've never told anyone this before." What caregivers do with these first, second, third-time revealed horror stories is important. But often, even more important during the sharing of secrets is the connection between the caregiver and the survivor.

This is why *relationship* is so vital in counseling.

As the therapeutic alliance is developed and deepened, a survivor may learn that a godly therapist, while imperfect, can be a tried and true recipient for his or her stories. Over time, a survivor learns that the caregiver will wait until he or she is ready to convey what happened.

Because so many who have been abused have a sort of autobiographical laryngitis, the caregiver's task is to help the victim of abuse reclaim his voice. Sometimes we have to make the first move as counselors—not pushing our clients in any way, but simply by being willing to hear and enter into their stories *in whatever language they are speaking.*

Being a counselor at times feels like being a linguist of the emotional languages of people. It seems that each person, each client who has been abused, whether speaking words or not, is communicating his or her story in some way. Some become violent; some mark on or shrink their bodies. It is important that we listen with our ears and our eyes.

Tamar told her story both in words *and* in action. Scripture tells us that after the rape, "Tamar put ashes on her head and tore her long-sleeved garment which was on her; and she put her hand on her head and went away, crying aloud as she wept."[14] There are a lot of verbs in that one verse, a handful of actions that Tamar recruited to aid in communicating her anguish. Who was her counselor? Who was the first to *hear*—the first to partake in the process of healing or continued damaging? Her brother Absalom. Absalom, who apparently failed his counseling courses miserably; Tamar was forced to contend with an insensitive platitude doled out by her brother:

"Don't take it to heart."

Absalom responded in a way that distanced and silenced Tamar, and his response had weighty consequences. We can be quick to judge and react to behaviors that we don't understand. Unlike Absalom, we need to savor each word as monumental; stand in awe that a person has chosen life and chosen to speak; be curious about what has kept that person alive; listen to people's earthly stories and help them to see the bigger story: the eternal story; ferret out the portraits of hope and underscore God's fingerprints in the midst of the pain.

Baring One's Soul

I FOUND I COULD SAY THINGS WITH COLOR AND SHAPES THAT I COULDN'T SAY ANY OTHER WAY... THINGS I HAD NO WORDS FOR.
Georgia O'Keeffe

Survivors may take umpteen approaches in revealing long-kept secrets. Paintings, sketches, images in clay, play, sand trays and collages are venues that help some utter their angst.[15] Invitations to image experiences may be a means to self expression and communication. For some survivors, words are not their first language. Thus, it is important to familiarize oneself with the dialect of the particular survivor. This may be particularly true for survivors in cultures where telling the secret of abuse would result in death for the survivor for bringing dishonor to the family name.[16] Telling may need to be done in different ways.

Music can embody the mood of one's soul while lyrics furnish words to experiences, impressions, and feelings. The secretiveness girding abuse engenders isolation, feelings of difference, and feeling poles apart from others. Lines from a poignant song can link the lyricist and the listener, signaling their relatedness.[17] The Psalms are teeming with songs of anguish. In fact, approximately one-half of the psalms are laments.[18] The Lord kindly designed music as a way to express the innermost self. Thus, a useful therapeutic endeavor involves inviting the survivor to select and share a song that most expresses his present experience, mood, and secrets not yet ready to be directly disclosed.

Painting, sketches, or clay can also provide a helping hand in the telling of the story. Jenny Murphy explains, "Art therapy can be seen to offer a transitional space which is experienced as a safer and less intense than a verbal therapy relationship... These art materials or images provide a means of expressing, holding, and recognizing the feelings."[19]

Like a prisoner set free after a 20-year-sentence, long-kept secrets can be unshackled through writing.

Poetry, short stories, a memoir—the writing possibilities are profuse. For example, Virginia Woolf, hailed as one of the twentieth century's most innovative writers, applied the literary approaches of stream of consciousness, indirect narration, and poetic impressionism.[20] Embedded in her writing was a chronicle of incest. Woolf declared she was abused as a child and adolescent, and she made these previously kept secrets known in a passel of ways. As a child, she endeavored to tell her parents about the abuse. She compiled stories in the family newspaper to "tell" indirectly; however, no one seemed to get the drift of her plight.[21] As an adult, with her trusted friends, she unpacked her epic tragedy in black and white details. Her childhood horror was also divulged through her fictional characters, who wore sundry symptoms that Woolf personally exhibited throughout her life. Lenore Terr explains:

> ...her fictional characters ... were, like Virginia, very, very much afraid. And what did Virginia's characters fear? They

feared sex and losing control, the very same thing that Virginia herself feared.[22]

Woolf penned an autobiographical essay four months before her suicide. *A Sketch of the Past* details a sexual violation by her 16 or 17-year-old half brother, Gerald Duckworth, when Woolf was only five or six years old.[23]

> There was a slab outside the dining room door for standing dishes upon. Once when I was very small Gerald Duckworth lifted me onto this, and as I sat there he began to explore my body. I can remember the feel of his hand going under my clothes; going firmly and steadily, going lower and lower. I remember how I hoped he would stop; how I stiffened and wiggled as his hand approached my private parts. But it did not stop. His hand explored my private parts too. I remember resenting it, disliking it—what is the word for so dumb and mixed of feeling? It must have been strong, since I still recall it.[24]

Woolf also disclosed that her second half-brother, George Duckworth, sexually abused her and her sister for several years during their teenage years.

It was not until after I (Tammy) graduated from a counseling program, began counseling, and subsequently sat in an abuse seminar that I talked about the specifics of my abuse. I had always remembered my abuse but it took a decade and a half for me to realize that God wanted to work *in* me so that He could work *through* me and that I was a limited vessel for His plans until I allowed Him license to the secrets of my soul. During this process, I thought about abuse when I woke up in the morning and before I went to sleep. Memories hounded me through the day. Over time, I realized my Father wanted to release me from the poison of my fear, hate, and unforgiveness and that the Great Physician's intent was always to heal, not hurt, His girl.

Over the past few years, as I travel to various countries and share my story of sexual abuse, I have individuals who tell me, sometimes through translators, sometimes on a sheet of paper, and sometimes in their own words for the very first time, "It happened to me, too." And another one of God's kids begins his or her journey of speaking the truth so that he or she might be set free and He might be loved.

Culture, Concealment, & Candid Accounts

The knottiness of disclosing trauma is exacerbated by cultural differences.[25] Western cultures tend to attach high value to articulating thoughts and feelings. However, for some steeped in collectivist cultures, the practice of breaking secrets may not be highly regarded. Because telling secrets might cast aspersions upon family members or someone highly respected in the community, this practice is often discouraged in Asian and Latino families. In contrast, shrouding certain information may be perceived as exhibiting greater respect.

A missionary working with Muslim women emailed Tammy awhile back. She had gained the trust of the women in her community. Over time, my missionary friend received scores of invitations for tea which segued into disclosures of abuse. There were countless tales about an uncle, father, brother, or cousin robbing young girls' bodies. Prying open this can of *words* could merely serve to brand the woman as **ADULTERER**, and having lost her virginity, she would be considered fair game for other men to seduce or assault because she was trash anyway.[26] Confronting is a complex consideration only intensified in contexts where "izzat (honour/respect), haya (modesty) and sharam (shame/embarrassment)" require protection of the family or community.[27] An attempt to ignore izzat can result in being disowned, banished, or shunned. In some societies, life-threatening danger may be lurking for those considering telling.

Danger must always be assessed. It is not prudent to confront perpetrators in every circumstance or culture. At times, as long as the adult victim of the abuse remains in dangerous settings or cultures, secret telling is done with trusted individuals in the absence of confronting the perpetrator.[28]

Giving voice to secrets looks different around the world. There are countless survivors waiting for godly caregivers to listen to tales that no one else wants to hear. Generalized assumptions about culture are as unhelpful as being blind to culture.[29] Closing our eyes to the other ingredients that make up a person besides culture is equally unhelpful.[30] Getting to know unique individuals and learning to recognize the consequences of disclosure that stem from cultures and faith traditions can help survivors overcome the barriers to speak the unspeakable.

Revealing Secrets to God

LET ME HEAR YOUR VOICE.
Song of Solomon 2:14

Healing involves divulging our secrets to God as well. For some, contending with God is the starting point on the healing journey. We clung to Jesus and blurted the events of the abuse in His ear. For other survivors, wrestling with God comes much later. We may not have known Him when the abuse happened or even if we did, it was hard admitting what happened to ourselves, so talking to God about it, well, seemed unimaginable.

Catherine Foot wrote *Survivor Prayers,* a wise and vulnerable book of poems and prayers to God about abuse:

> As wounded children we learned to conceal the levels of pain and loss from family and friends because we were told to, or because we feared the truth would not be believed, or because it seemed too overwhelming. Many of us have learned also to "hide" from God. Talking to God about our childhood sexual abuse means placing before God all the fears, the rage, and the confusion of the hurting child. Breaking silence with God may mean standing before God and asking why. It may mean ending a pattern of 'taking care' of God, trying to put a nice face on the raw pain, or ending every

prayer with a 'happily ever after' in an attempt to keep God happy. We may have had a tendency to say, 'Well, yes, it was hard, but everything's OK now, so please don't leave me.' Breaking silence with God means telling God the truth.[31]

There is so much more to say about this whole talking-to-God business, and we will look more in depth at this important topic in our chapter on abuse and prayer. But for now we understand that sometimes it feels like the greatest risk is (ironic as this is) telling our story (His story) to the Author Himself. And yet, He already knows.

If you are graced with the gift of journeying with others as they voice the truth of their past and the impact of this history on the present, we pray that His kindness, patience, and wisdom flow through you. If the mountain before you is telling one person in the world that you were abused, we pray for courage for you. If facing your greatest fear involves voicing to a friend or counselor, the details, the specifics, the where, when, and what happened during the abuse, we ask for boldness, His wisdom and His timing. And if you sense He is calling you to tell Him the truth about what happened, how you felt, how you feel, we want you to know that even while you fear uttering these words to Him and your chin is down and you are unable to look Him in the eye, He is there waiting to gently cup your face in His hands and whisper *Let me hear your voice ...*

DO NOT BE AFRAID; KEEP ON SPEAKING; DO NOT BE SILENT.

Acts 18:9

Anguish
unvoiced
DISCUSSION STARTERS

1. Without using words, how could you give voice to a secret that is weighing you down?

2. Psalm 33:3 says, "He will give us a new song." What does your new song sound like? What are some of the lyrics?

3. Caregivers: What are ways you may have given the message "Don't take it to heart?"

4. Caregivers: How can you create an atmosphere to help survivors express their story?

I AM DYING OF THIRST BY THE SIDE OF THE FOUNTAIN.

Charles D'Orleans

IT IS THE NATURE OF DESIRE NOT TO BE SATISFIED
& MOST HUMAN BEINGS LIVE ONLY
FOR THE GRATIFICATION OF IT.

Aristotle

OUR HEART WILL CARRY US EITHER TO GOD
OR TO ADDICTION.

Brent Curtis & John Eldredge

HUMAN BEINGS ARE IDOL-MAKING FACTORIES.

John Calvin

DO NOT WORSHIP ANY OTHER GODS BESIDES ME.

Deuteronomy 5:7

DIAGNOSIS WITHOUT PRESCRIPTION IS A CRUEL THING.

Mark Buchanan

MAN IS A HUNGRY BEING.
BUT HE IS HUNGRY FOR GOD.
BEHIND ALL THE HUNGER OF OUR LIFE IS GOD.
ALL DESIRE IS FINALLY A DESIRE FOR HIM.
Alexander Schmemann

Unrequited Love

addicted to turkish delights

Enchanted Turkish Delights

Narnia, the land beyond the wardrobe, a place where beavers talk and children dream, is also a region where enticing food was dangled before the eyes of a young boy. Edmund and his siblings had been sent away from their parents in London due to the air raids of World War II. Added to this, Edmund was out of sorts with his brother and sisters and quarreling had characterized their interactions. Life was not care-free.

The Queen of Narnia asks Edmund what he would like to eat, and he requests Turkish Delights. Quickly, Edmund began eating – it was the most delicious thing he had ever eaten, and he started to feel warm and comfortable when he was previously shivering with cold. Edmund ate and ate and ate until the Turkish Delights and his disappointments were all gone. Secretly Edmund hoped that the Queen would offer more. She knew that he wanted more – that if given the chance, he would never stop eating because the Turkish Delights were in fact, enchanted. So much so, that anyone who took just one Turkish Delight would never stop.[1]

Just like Edmund, most of us are inclined towards escaping our disappointments. We all have our "Turkish Delight," something that offers a temporary relief from pain. Whatever the disappointment, we are prone to search for a soothing balm, even if it is temporary, and even when it is ultimately more damaging to oneself, others, and God. In this chapter, we want to look at a few of the common Turkish Delights that dangle before survivors. Specifically, we will address the addictive allure of substances, disordered eating patterns, self-mutilation, and false forms of sexual intimacy.

Ad·dic·tion [uh-dik-shuhn]

I NEVER MET A FEELING THAT WOULDN'T BE A GOD IF YOU LET IT.

Andree Seu

Psychiatrist Gerald May explains that addictions are all about attachments. The French word *attaché* means "nailed to." Picture a pair of 2 x 4s being nailed together. Addictive behaviors enter the scene of our lives as we nail gun our desires to behaviors, things, or people because we believe that they will bring stability and life to the empty places in our souls.[2] Picture what happens when you hurl a piece of Velcro into the dryer along with a pair of tights. Say goodbye to those stockings after they become entangled and ultimately destroyed by the Velcro because of this thing called attachment.

The book of Isaiah has a lot to say about attachment. People are described as "forming an alliance," "relying on," and "depending on" something other than God.[3] Enslavement to substances or things emerge in an array of shapes and colors. Whether we can't live without

more trophies on the mantle,
the bottle of Dewar's in the cupboard,
the romance novel on the nightstand,
late-night internet porn,
the Snickers bar hiding in the glove compartment,
her phone number in your address book,
his seductive glance from across the room,
admiring faces from the people staring up at you in the pulpit…

ADDICTIONS WORK FOR A SEASON.

Perhaps it is hard to believe that a hunger for applause could possibly be in the same genre as a hunger for ecstasy. However, John Eldredge sheds light on the fact that our slavery comes in contrasting configurations.

> Don't be fooled by the apparent innocence of the object you've chosen. Most of our idols also have a perfectly legitimate place in our lives. That's their cover. That's how we get away with our infidelity... Addiction may seem too strong a term to some of you. The woman who is serving so faithfully at church—surely, there's nothing wrong with that. And who can blame the man who stays long at the office to provide for his family? Sure, you may look forward to the next meal more than most people do, and your hobbies can be a nuisance sometimes, but to call any of this an addiction seems to stretch the word a bit too far... If you don't think [they are], then prove it by letting go of the things that provide you with a sense of security, or comfort, or excitement, or relief. You will soon discover the tentacles of *attachment* deep in your soul.[4]

Sometimes it is hard to see past the behavior of a teenage daughter who gets in trouble at school for carrying a flask of vodka and who spends most of her Saturday bent over a toilet bowl recovering from the night prior. Compassion may be difficult to dredge up for the man who seduces a different woman each weekend and who trades these encounters for badges of so-called manhood. And yet so many who have been abused find themselves leaning over toilet bowls or slicing up their arms or engaging in some other behavior that we often don't understand.

What we must understand is that these people are running *from* the personal **HELL** they've experienced through the trauma of sexual abuse or another type of pain—and that the desire underneath all of this poisonous behavior is, in fact, *Heaven.*
Perhaps Freud said it best in his "pleasure principle": that we are people who continuously seek pleasure and avoid pain.[5] In other words, we seek Heaven and want to avoid Hell.[6]

Not having been made for an imperfect home, our hearts grow weary from existing in this endless world of imperfections. Having been made for Heaven, we continually grapple with dissatisfaction and groan for a place that is too magnificent for our imaginations to handle.

Edmund was weary from his pain, and he wanted something better. He wanted to be a prince. And in his intensely passionate search for Heaven, he was called out by an enchanted rival. His rival promised to deliver exactly what he desired. Initially, it even seemed like those promises would be delivered. But like a rose, its attractiveness hid prickly thorns.[7]

Still Taking Shots

One kind of alluring rival is chemical addictions. Many have studied the impact of drugs and alcohol and we now understand that there are "reward circuits" in the brain that are activated by a variety of things, including chemicals. This is what heightens the desire or craving for more. Addicted folks know this as "**chasing the dragon**," that glorious first high and the never-ending pursuit to experience it again. What begins as a pursuit of the next rush can eventually resemble a relationship with a mistress. Carolyn Knapp describes the path of obsession with her lover:

> It's not at all unusual in AA to hear people refer to alcohol as a best friend, and to mean that on the most visceral level: when you're drinking, liquor occupies the role of a lover or constant companion. It sits there on its refrigerator shelves or on the counter or in the cabinet like a real person, as present and reliable as a best friend. At the end, when I started hiding bottles of Scotch around the house, and tucking nips of brandy into my bathrobe pockets, I did so in the manner of a child who's afraid to be without a favorite blanket or a teddy bear. Protect me. Shield me from being alone in my own head.[8]

It might be difficult to imagine how a substance could take the place of relationships, but one need only watch an episode of *Cheers* - or even listen to the famous intro song – to get a better idea of how this works. We want to be known. We want to enter a room filled with people who are happy to see us.

Doesn't that sound enticing? A place to belong. Relationships, especially the ones at home, can take a lot of work. When there is chaos or rage or a deafening silence, home can feel pretty lonely. So a seat at a local bar can be pretty irresistible. The bartender knows your drink without even asking. No one is judging you or telling you what to do. There is finally a routine, a habit, a "home" where you are known. And these people understand because they're not going home either. So they become the new "family." Thus, when someone having a love affair with alcohol decides to give up drinking, he's not only giving up a substance, but a family. He is daring to feel unknown for a time. It is a huge risk to take.

A few years ago, I (Tammy) returned from taking a group of graduate students to Ukraine, a sizable country once part of the former Soviet Union. We visited dirty-clothed, unwashed, and unwanted children, packed like sardines in orphanages they called home. The stench made us gag. The inability to make it all better for the children made our hearts ache. Does it surprise you that Ukraine has a high rate of chemical dependencies? During this overseas trip, I observed that chemical abuse is often an attempt to balance the fulcrum of a staggering economy and massive pain, and alcoholism, as an attempt to cover torment, is as much of a problem in small towns as in metropolitan America. Savage drinking serves to shield us from our hurt.

Abuse & the Chemical Connection

Recovery is...about dealing with that hole in the soul.
William C. Moyers

Does it surprise you that sexual abuse and later-in-life drug and alcohol abuse are commonly linked?[9] A few years ago, a group of folks did a sizable study of over 17,000 adult insurance members in California about childhood abuse and health related issues.[10] They found that both men and women who reported CSA were more likely to marry an alcoholic, have alcohol problems, or engage in illicit drug use. We know that approximately one-half of sexual assaults are committed by men who have been drinking and when you add to this that about one-half of all sexual assault victims report they were drinking alcohol at the time of the assault, alcohol is bad news when it comes to assault.[11]

Of course chemical addiction makes sense for survivors of any kind of trauma. If you have ever sat near family or friends following a complicated surgery, many receive sizable doses of morphine with **open arms**. In fact, if Uncle Joe was able, he would probably dance a JIG in his hospital room when the morphine arrives. Similarly, when a survivor comes face to face with the option of feeling the pain of the memories of abuse, or one more bottle of Pabst Blue Ribbon, well, what's behind door number two becomes rather attractive, even downright appealing.

Using can also hinder a survivor from recognizing in the first place that the sexual violations were, in fact, abuse. However, because chemicals merely *cover* rather than *cure* the angst,[12] the problem mushrooms. It becomes a **vicious cycle**.[13]

The added irony for the survivor entering recovery for chemicals is that he or she must come face-to-face with the pain—that "hole in the soul"—that he or she was trying to avoid with drugs.

Stuffed: Broken Forms of Eating

THE SORROWS OF THOSE WILL INCREASE
WHO RUN AFTER OTHER GODS.
Psalm 16:4

Calorie-counting journals. Mirrors. Scales. Cheetos under the bed. Laxatives. Fitness magazines. Running shoes. The list could go on, but these are just some of the idols we bow before as men and women who struggle to eat in the way He intended.

Childhood sexual abuse commonly has a direct impact on the development of an eating disorder, at least in part because a child's self-image grows distorted when his or her body has received unwanted sexual attention.[14] For some, disordered eating is employed as a way to stuff feelings of helplessness. Because the person could not keep the abuse from happening, he or she becomes determined to simplify life to the lowest common denominator: eat or don't eat. It's a simple choice and an easily controlled one, when everything else feels out of control. For some, binging and purging becomes almost an obsessive compulsive behavior; like someone who showers repeatedly after being raped, purging is a way to try to "rid" the evil that has been done. In some cases, a survivor feels betrayed by his or her own body for responding to the abuser's touch, so restricting and/or binging and purging become ways to punish one's body. The reasons why sexual abuse frequently marshals one into various patterns of disordered eating are profuse.

One woman writes her story of controlling and eating this way:

No, I wasn't going to allow anyone to 'feel me up' anymore. I didn't want that. But I was also going to dress very carefully, fold my collar just so, and walk with my heel touching first, my knees very rigid, and my posture erect. I was going to run between the two piers on the beach every day and do my series of floor exercises. I could only eat once a day, and only after postponing it (mainly with exercise) as long as I could. In fact, eating was not allowed unless I had completed my exercise rituals and organized certain of my belongings in special ways. I carefully selected and measured portions of the same ('healthy') food day after day, chewing each bite a certain number of times and putting my fork and knife down between bites. I changed my writing style by printing very neatly and extremely small.

I also changed my tempo of speech and I chose when and to whom I spoke. I started withdrawing from people and feelings because I felt that I could maintain my path better without these interferences. I became extremely controlled in all areas of my life, especially those related to eating and exercising. With this new lifestyle, I started losing weight and defying puberty …Indeed, these obsessions were my *salvation* [emphasis added].[15]

Her *salvation*. When we think our lovers will save us, that is addiction. This piece of cake will save me from feeling this pain. If I run eight miles, it will save me from taking up too much space. If I purge, it will save me from being noticed, from being ugly. If I starve, I will save myself from my own desires.

While research on men with eating disorders is substantially eclipsed by the expanse of research presented in regards to women, this is a very real and growing problem for men, with current statistics at 5-10 percent of all reported eating disordered cases.[16] With females making up the majority of those struggling with eating disorders, and the inference of this as a "female problem" even in the very diagnosis of anorexia (i.e., an absence of menstrual period as a DSM diagnostic criteria amenorrhea as criteria), it can feel especially vulnerable for men to acknowledge this as a struggle. While body dissatisfaction is not the only factor involved with the development of an eating disorder, it is a very common and a growing issue for men. One author points out that while articles and advertisements concerning weight loss present with higher frequency in women's magazines, they are becoming more common in the most popular men's magazines at a ratio of 10.5:1 (coincidentally about the same ratio of eating disorders between women and men).[17] Body dissatisfaction for a man is as likely to lead him to want to gain weight as it is to lose weight, a body image and disordered eating problem described today as *reverse anorexia* or *muscle dysmorphia*.[18]

A friend told me (Hannah) on one occasion, in the midst of struggling with an eating disorder, she found her dusty Bible buried, as she described it, underneath her calorie-counting, weight-recording journals and magazines. What a powerful visual image of what we do… bury the truth and cover it up with the dust of our own addiction. We put God on the back burner. And we believe that we are always one step away from being enough, from being lovable. If I just lose two more pounds, then no one will ever leave me again. If I just gain a bit more weight, no one will notice me again.

The mirror is a terrible lover, because it almost never tells us that we're ok. It almost always shouts at us that we are not enough, that we are a problem, that we could never be loved looking like *that*. But even as a culture, we have sort of a Stockholm syndrome[19] attachment to the mirror, don't we? It beats us up, but we always go back for more, because we don't know who we are without it.

Are you getting that this is a lover which will not satisfy?

When was the last time you looked into a mirror and worshiped Him more because of that simple glance?

> As our culture screams at you to change your appearance, listen closely for the still, small voice of Jesus. He is inviting you to live life unashamed of how He created you, like a child who isn't caught up in the latest trends but happily worships using his entire body.[20]

The New Anorexia

Eating disorders and self-injury appear to be next of kin. Cutting, like starving or binging, is a means of expressing emotional pain through battering the body. In the 1970s, when anorexia came on the scene fast and furious in the lives of young girls, the idea of starving oneself seemed perplexing, bizarre, and incomprehensible.[21] However, over time, as therapists and researchers became more familiar with the dynamics behind the incessant restriction of food, they began to see that these girls were *starving* for control and most importantly, relationship. Since then, self-injury has been tagged as the "new anorexia of our time."[22] It has become the current mode by which scores of individuals give voice to their angst. And common in the lives of many cutters is sexual abuse.[23]

Reading between the Scars: Self-Injury

Cutting is like a secret inside, burning to be told, to be heard, to be understood. For some, self-injury is like slipping into a bulky sweater on a crisp fall day. It feels comfortable, familiar. It fits. Cutting for others is like a best friend that comes in the form of a razor, exacto knife, or lighter. This companion *gets* the pain and will take all the drama pent up inside and will bleed or burn it out.

What is the purpose or *raison d'etre* behind self-injurious behavior? The reasons are abundant.[24] Emotions that have not yet found their way into words are heard loudly in these seemingly silent symbols on the body.

Folks who self-injure sometimes speak of an analgesic experience: Cutting delivers a soothing sensation for the soul. Shame, panic, rage, and grief intensify, but with a slice of a blade, the rushing river of emotions is whooshed away. A strange sense of calm washes over. In the same way, mutilating activities can be an attempt to become unsullied and washed clean. The sense of dirtiness stemming from abuse frequently engenders a desire to scrub the floors of the soul dirt-free, using hair pulling, burning, or other types of self-mutilation as a type of bleach.

Like early morning ocean waves that obliterate the previous day's marks in the sand, the self-harming behavior rids traces of our emotional rot. Some people who self-injure use harming themselves as a way of communication.[25] "Scars are stories, history written on her body."[26] The scars tell a story, sort of.

> Self-mutilation speaks of distress, torment, and pain. The act of wounding onself *embodies*—literally—an implicit

connotation of something unbearable, unutterable, that is communicated in this act… One of the most distressing features of abuse is its demand for secrecy and silence; victims who wish and long to be heard are forbidden from speaking by various means… [S]elf-inflicted injuries, while telling an 'unspeakable secret,' can also be used to deflect from it. Thus self-mutilation can be used to speak and not to speak.[27]

Cutting can also be a way of reminding oneself, *I am still alive.* Self-injurers have learned to disconnect, dissociate, and become like strangers to their own bodies and emotions. Numb is the sensation she feels as she slices her skin; thus, ironically, cutting is a way of associating, signalling a return to life.

Self-injury can serve as an attempt to quell the helpless feelings, to get back control. Sexual abuse is an experience bruised with helpless feelings, so the control over the splitting of skin becomes one arena where control can be seemingly captured. A young girl or boy may not have easy access to drugs, alcohol, or even binging… so they turn to the one thing they do have: their bodies.

A need to grab people's attention may also inspire self-injurious behavior. Blood, scars, and sharp instruments have a way, like ambulances, police cars, and crashed vehicles on the side of the road, of causing folks to look. A few crumbs of negative attention are better than no attention at all.[28]

One young woman described her relationship with self-harm in this way: "It's like what people describe as being in love… that 'weak in the knees' feeling… compared to anything else, it was just heaven." [29]

As stated, the reasons for self-injury are profuse. However, the common theme among all the whys and wherefores behind mutilating activities is pain. Instead of running into the arms of the Great Lover whose blood was spilled out for us, we spill our own to control our pain the best we can—we try to cut out our need for His help.

Sex & Sensibility

When a child is prematurely sexually stimulated, a fusion may form between sex and abuse. When this happens, one's sexuality may come to be experienced as a commodity that can be used to gain money or favors.[30] When the synthesis between attention, privileges, rewards, and abuse occurs, this can be a corrosive combination. A pimp explains his philosophy of business principles:

> And how do you get obedience? You get obedience if you get women who have had sex with their fathers, their uncles, their brothers—you know, someone they love and fear to lose so that they do not dare to defy. Then you are nicer to the woman than they ever were, and more dangerous as well. They will do anything to keep you happy. That is how... Both those girls were had by their fathers. Now they make me rich and they are *happy*.[31]

Happy? Quite a convenient and profitable conclusion.

Among men and women, various forms of sexual activity can become addictive replacements for the kind of intimacy God had in mind. Every second, about 28,000 internet users are viewing pornography.[32] Billions of dollars are spent each year on this global industry. In the past, porn has been primarily the domain of men, but recently the statistics for women involved with pornography are snowballing.

Why risk being rejected by a real-live person when a "yes" can be nabbed from someone I don't even have to bother getting to know or romance? An apology for leaving the toilet seat up will never be required. She will never ask that the trash be taken to the curb. He will never reject me... never turn me down... never make me feel undesirable. The person on the screen *always* wants me. Oh yeah, and she's physically flawless.

Sounds pretty enticing.

And to the soul that has been violated, made to feel so small, dirty, rejected at the core... it's not only enticing. Paradoxically, it feels like *LIFE*.

Same-Sex Attraction

For some who have been sexually violated, femininity is worn like a lime-green, home-made, polyester outfit to a high school dance. It feels awkward and shameful. For some, avoiding that place that causes us to cringe and even feel nauseated is found in the comfort of a relationship with someone of the same sex. Sexual abuse is not the "cause" of same-sex attraction (SSA) or the only predictor, because there are a variety of influences (i.e. biology, personal experiences, thoughts, emotions, relationships, self-concept) in each person's story. Considering all these factors, it is crucial to remember that there is more to hungering for someone of the same sex than meets the eye, and, as one author points out, "same-sex relationships are, at their core, a reflection of our God-given need as human beings for identity and attachment, albeit often confusedly sexualized or misappropriately directed."[33]

This soul craving is seen in the life of Christopher Yuan. His discovery of porn when he was a boy and his sense of never quite fitting in with others, left a large hole in his soul. The gay community became a place of belonging.

> …When I stepped into the gay community, I was introduced to a world of outcasts who had come together and become family. They stood up for one another, supported one another. They laughed with me, cried with me, and accepted me for who I was—gay.[34]

This universal hunger for love takes center stage in this story by Niki, who journaled her story specifically for this book:

> As early as four years old, I remember pleading with my mother, "I want to be a boy!" This desire came from deep inside, and I felt estranged from my own body and the label "girl." I could not escape the expectations of who I was supposed to be, a charming little girl twirling in satin dresses with her beloved Barbie. This stood in stark contrast to the

competitive little tomboy who loved to get dirty and begged to tag along with my older brothers playing G.I. Joe.

The weight of these expectations only grew heavier throughout my childhood. I didn't know why I felt as I did; only that it felt horrible being caught between two genders. I was only sure that I felt very different from the other girls and yet I knew I was not a boy.

My father did not mind my "tomboy" mindset. He was far more comfortable raising his two boys, seeming to be at a loss on how to relate to his little girl. The apparent distance between he and I [sic] was reinforced by his avoidance of my emotional needs. He did not verbalize his love for me. He overindulged in my competitive athletic performance, the one area where he could relate to me.

I felt like a disappointment to my mother. She longed for a little girl that she could dress up and have pretend tea parties with, which of course did not happen. This letdown coupled with difficult circumstances in her life left her appearing fragile, weak, and unstable in my eyes. Since she was the only female model I had, I began viewing femininity in light of these negative attributes. "If women are fragile, weak and emotionally unstable, I want nothing to do with it." I was determined to be "one of the boys," rejecting girlish outward appearances and shutting down my emotions.

Unfortunately, my confusion was compounded by a childhood that quickly became unsafe. Starting around the age of 7, I began experiencing sexual abuse from a male in my life that I should have been able to trust. This experience stole my innocence and awoke a part of my sexuality that was not yet meant to be awoken [sic]. The abuse took on many forms, including exposure to female pornography. The combined effect of the abuse and gender confusion influenced me to identify with the pornographic images I saw. I felt these women represented who I was, while also being sexually attracted to them. This dichotomy caused me great shame. By the time I was a teenager I was addicted to pornography. For me, it became a way to escape from reality, to feel *something*, to try to regain control. It was a secret that would enslave me for years to come.

As I transitioned into high school, I was confused about my gender, broken by abuse, sexually addicted, and socially awkward. It was a deeply painful, dark, and lonely time in my life. Playing sports was the only thing that brought a semblance of meaning to my life. I had also become convinced that I was a lesbian. I was addicted to same-sex pornography, had difficulty forming female friendships, and continued to fail in my efforts to date guys. My attempts at socially acceptable dating gave me intense physical nausea, which only reinforced that something was surely wrong with me.

Try as I may, I could not escape my attraction to women. They were a mystery to me. I longed to be connected with and loved by a woman. Because of the painful social pressure to conform, I sought out professional counseling. The counselor told me that I was a lesbian, and the sooner I accepted that the better. I left feeling relieved to finally have an answer, and yet apprehensive on how to live it out.

Like a painful elementary school memory, sexual abuse pokes, jabs, and spits on our sense of femininity or masculinity.[35] The excruciating journey into this place of feeling uncomfortable in your own gender may only be matched with the sobering and awkward journey toward becoming more at ease in your God-given masculinity or femininity. More will be said about this topic as we continue reading Niki's story in the next chapter.

Other Lovers

During a YouTube live concert, Bono holds up the mic in the direction of the throngs of fans, waving cell phones and lighters, who chant repeatedly, that they cannot find what they are searching for.[36] The lyrics resonate in the souls of U2 followers and the rest of the planet. Despite all the mountains we've climbed, bottles we've drunk, Oreo bags we've devoured, scars we've carved, and one-night stands we've chosen, our addictive behaviors reveal that our desperate attempts have not satisfied us. The addictions we have discussed may seem pretty "modern," but this is no contemporary-born issue. Since the beginning of time, we've been declaring to God that He is not enough despite the fact that "He carried the cross and loosed our chains."[37] Our addictive behaviours declare He hasn't satisfied our needs or our aches so we go looking for other lovers.

Let us make one thing crystal clear if it hasn't been so far. Abuse is a loathsome experience and it is unmistakable in Scripture that God hates what is evil. Abuse was not part of His original plan for His kids and it grieves Him when they are hurt. BUT when we stand before Him, *our response* to the abuse is what matters.

A couple of years ago, Hannah and I attended a national abuse conference and appreciated wisdom gleaned from the speakers. At one point, a renowned and learned trauma researcher and writer stated that when it comes to addictive behaviors, caregivers and clients are all in the same proverbial boat. The only difference between you, me, and others is "luck." Thus, if carving stories on our genitals is *not* working, then we need to get a different coping mechanism to make life work.

Now, I agree that we are all sinking in the same boat. Whether my addiction is buying one more gotta-have book to lift my spirits and your addiction of choice is a carton of Moose Tracks ice cream at the end of a hard day, or you're addicted to your kid's addiction,[38] they all drive us to the same dead end. And the goal of tracking down and embracing a different coping mechanism? Well, there are plenty to choose from. However, the problem with the "luck" premise is that it obliterates repentance and it stomps out our need for a Savior. Choosing a different coping mechanism is not the answer. Choosing Him in the midst of facing the angst of abuse and any other sorrow, loneliness, or boredom *is what we are searching for.*

Since the beginning of time, He has been warning that if we continue to pursue these ends, "[we] will surely die" (Gen. 2:17). For Adam and Eve, it wasn't about the food. It wasn't the fruit that was the problem; it was their dissatisfaction with both the world God placed them in and their God.[39] One book later in Scripture, the Israelites found themselves rescued by God out of bondage, and repeatedly, they wanted to go back to Egypt. In Jeremiah, these addictions are referred to as "broken cisterns" (2:13). In Ecclesiastes, they are our "devices" (7:29). In the book of Hosea, God calls these things our *other lovers* (2:13). Throughout Scripture, these addictions are referred to as our idols (Ex. 20:4, Lev. 19:4, Ps. 96:5, Acts 15:20, 1 Jn. 5:21).

Caregivers can support survivors by understanding how sexual trauma may be affecting their lives, and by helping survivors relinquish dysfunctional coping mechanisms with skills that will truly serve them. However, beyond replacing coping skills, there seems to be *something more* needed in order to weather the storm of addictions stemming from abuse. We need something far more powerful to enable us to "get up and walk." Because the power of the addiction is tenacious, we need something or someone that can break through the magnetic force of addictive substances. Turkish Delights will always be there, and the Queen will always be nodding with a "come hither" look offering a silver platter full of these delectables.

We need to find something that satisfies our souls, someone whom we can rely on, depend upon, become attached to. We need to find a love that will not be left unrequited.

Unrequited Love

addicted to turkish delight
DISCUSSION STARTERS

1. Have you ever felt the angst of an unrequited love—the feeling of loving someone or something that didn't love you back? What was that like?

2. What is your Turkish Delight, and who or what is the Queen of Narnia in your life? What "hole in the soul" is your Turkish Delight attempting to assuage?

3. How would you describe your relationship with your body?

4. Paul David "Bono" Hewson captured a universal truth in the lyrics to his song, "I still haven't found what I'm looking for." What are you still searching for?

I MAY LIKE TO THINK I AM AUTONOMOUSLY CHARTING MY OWN
COURSE, BUT I KEEP DISCOVERING THAT MY LITTLE SHIP HAS
BEEN ANSWERING TO DEEPER, HIDDEN CURRENTS ALL ALONG.
Gerald May

AND HERE AT LAST WE FIND STRICT DIAGNOSIS OF OUR MALADY,
WHICH IS, IN SHORT, THAT MAN IS HEAVEN-STARVED—
MEN ARE BORN THIRSTING FOR INFINITY.
E. Stanley Jones

O GOD, YOU ARE MY GOD, EARNESTLY I SEEK YOU;
MY SOUL THIRSTS FOR YOU, MY BODY LONGS FOR YOU IN A DRY
AND WEARY LAND WHERE THERE IS NO WATER.
Psalm 63:1

THE CENTRAL PARADOX OF OUR CONDITION [IS] THAT
WHAT WE HUNGER FOR ... IS TO BE KNOWN
IN OUR FULL HUMANNESS, AND YET THAT IS OFTEN JUST
WHAT WE ALSO FEAR MORE THAN ANYTHING ELSE.
Frederick Buechner

COMMUNITY [IS] WHERE NO ONE REMAINS UNKNOWN,
UNEXPLORED, UNDISCOVERED, OR UNTOUCHED;
WHERE WE DISCOVER OUR TRUE SELVES; WHERE WE REALIZE
THAT WE REALLY ARE PASSIONATE FOLLOWERS OF JESUS;
WHERE PEOPLE BECOME SPIRITUAL FRIENDS.
Larry Crabb

IT IS FOR FREEDOM THAT CHRIST HAS SET US FREE.
STAND FIRM, THEN, AND DO NOT LET YOURSELVES BE
BURDENED AGAIN BY A YOKE OF SLAVERY.
Galatians 5:1

Requited Love

thirsty in the desert

The Ultimate Unrequited Love

It began with "I do," and God pronounced them husband and wife. But this was no run-of-the-mill marriage. It was the divine call of a man to wed a wife unfaithful. From day one, this marriage was saddled with sorrow and unrequited love.

God uses a feast of metaphors in Scripture to describe our relationship with Him, but in the Old Testament book of Hosea, He uses the metaphor of a marriage covenant. As Hosea is the husband and Gomer is the wife, God is the husband and the church is His bride. Better than any Lifetime TV love story, Hosea's story is about carrying an unfading commitment to Gomer despite her sustained whoring around.

Why would Yahweh give a godly prophet such an outrageous directive?

In part, because all of us seek other lovers. By marrying an unfaithful wife, Hosea was called to feel a piece of the pain that our Holy God bears daily as His kids attach to alcohol, a no-sugar-vanilla-skim-extra-hot chai, bragging rights over seeing the most clients in a day, keeping a vise grip on their kids so they look good…whatever it is that they do to make life work. Our Groom takes our other lovers seriously. They hurt Him. And yes, He understands that pain often precedes our other-lover-seeking behavior.

And to that pain He offers *Himself.*

After all our sleeping around, God doesn't kick us out or even make us sleep on the couch. He does whatever it takes to draw us away from our drug of choice. Because He knows our lover will eventually cheat on *us*. It will fail us. So He leads us to a solitary place so He can speak tenderly,[1] a type of holy-motivational-interviewing, and helps us become aware of how thirsty we really are. "*I will make her like a desert, turn her into a parched land and slay her with thirst.*"[2] As author and speaker Larry Crabb says, "We will not win the battle against addiction without discovering our desire for God."[3]

Then, after all our tramping around, He whispers words a lover would express to his bride in private, away from the crowd.[4] No matter how low our bottom gets, no matter how sharp our segue into self-loathing becomes, His gaze on us is love.

And if we will tell Him we are sorry and we relinquish our compulsion, obsession, or preoccupation that enslaves us,[5] if we will return home to our Spouse, a new beginning, a "door-opening of hope" awaits.[6] "*There I will give her back her vineyards, and will make the Valley of Achor a door of hope.*"[7]

Frequently, we fear that life without cutting, porn, control, will be like an engine without oil. It will seize and cease running. However, *despite all the*
  morning afters,
    regrets,
      blackouts,
        job losses,
          lost ministries and reputations…

He releases us, like dawn to a new day. Prostitutes, addicts, liars, cheats—all of us can begin again.

A Modern-Day Hosea

Remember Niki from the previous chapter who struggled with sex addiction and same-sex attraction? Take notice of God's relentless pursuit of her:

> My public high school chemistry teacher shared that God loved me. Up until this point, I did not have a belief in God and was closed to the idea of His existence. The difference now was that my pain and confusion were so great that I *needed* there to be a God. After months of discussion and seeking truth, I realized that it came down to faith, and Jesus entered my life. Due to the encouragement of this teacher and my desire to know more about God, I attended a Christian college a year later.
>
> My experience at this college provided a safe environment, which I desperately needed in order to learn more about God and His purpose for my life. However, I still did not know how to deal with the pain and confusion I held inside. Just because I believed in God did not mean that my struggles disappeared. I basically detached myself from my gender identity struggles and tried to shut off my sexual desires. This avoidance continued until circumstances forced me to confront these issues.
>
> My sophomore year, I attended a chapel service about sexual abuse. I was overwhelmed by childhood sexual abuse memories. They came suddenly and with startling clarity. I sought out help immediately and began four years of intensive counseling. It was a journey through the deepest, darkest pain of my life into the healing and restoration of my Lord Jesus.
>
> In addition to my cherished and enduring counselor, the Lord brought me my own modern-day Hosea. He was a man of faith and integrity who looked past my walls of self-protection and fear of intimacy. He saw past the shame of

my false identities, respected my boundaries, and took the time to build trust. He believed in the woman God created me to be and trusted that I would one day walk in that design with confidence. He took a risk, aware that other routes were easier, and chose to pursue what the Lord had for our relationship.

Out of that constant pursuit of love and acceptance, the Lord asked him to take me as his bride. Marriage was something I never thought would be possible for me. For so long I had believed the lie that I was incapable of being loved, especially if [men] knew my secrets. Also, I strongly doubted that I could authentically love a man. Our love did not come quickly or easily. It was slowly built in a safe environment through trust, prayer, and perseverance.

Out of that place the Lord brought deeper intimacy, a miracle undeserved. Out of desperation over what I had done and what had been done to me, I reached out to my Savior. Pleading with the Healer through tears of faith, I longed to hear that I was forgiven and that my life could be filled with love. He took hold of me and lifted me up to stand with dignity, knowing that I have been forgiven. My Redeemer rescued me from the lies and false beliefs that had enslaved me and replaced them with truth.

"I am a beautiful daughter of the most high King, created to live out of my design as a woman."

There are days when the old lies creep back in to my mind and I struggle with same-sex attractions. However, instead of being controlled by fear, I ask for forgiveness and invite the Lord to reveal the longing beneath the struggle. He graciously brings me back to my need for His love, my desire for my husband, and my yearning for emotional connection with women.

The road is not without obstacles or without struggle for Niki, and her journey continues *in His grace.*

In His Grace

THOSE WHO CLING TO WORTHLESS IDOLS FORFEIT
THE GRACE THAT COULD BE THEIRS.
Jonah 2:8

Indeed, there are lots of ingredients to "addiction recovery," if we want to call it that. The starting point is a familiar word: grace.

We need the grace to acknowledge the simple truth that *I have a problem, and I need help.* Some have said that "church" should be run more like an AA meeting. This may be a curious thought, but the essence of why some folks say this is wrapped up in one thing:

Honesty.

Recovering alcoholics, drug addicts, sex addicts, food addicts, and so forth have one thing that many of us sitting in pews don't realize about ourselves: They *know* they need help. Certainly, recovery does not involve simple steps, but this seems to be an important start for anyone who has found their "lover" to become unsatisfying—to anyone who has finally hit rock bottom.

But it's not easy. When we get used to a chemical, a pattern of behavior, or a way of life for an appreciable period of time, our body and our soul begin to rely on that object being there. We become dependent upon that to which we have become attached. Giving it up will likely entail agony. Considerable agony. Because even after you quit slamming dope, your husband may still leave. The journey to learning how to endure our internal angst without the aid of our painkillers is *not easy.* Merely stopping the addictive behavior doesn't delete the desire that led us to our watering hole in the first place. We must enter our disappointments and the messes we have made so that we may "[come] to [ourselves] in a dark forest," as Dante, the fourteenth-century Florentine poet, wrote in *The Inferno.*[8]

```
We admitted we were powerless over our addictions
    - that our lives had become unmanageable.[9]
```

Wander into any Celebrate Recovery or 12-step group and within seconds you are likely to hear folks divulging their darkest secrets. "My name is Charity and I'm a food addict." "My name is Dave, and I'm addicted to porn." Imagine if the forced fellowship time in church went something like that. "My name is Pastor Steve and I'm addicted to having people affirm my sermons." "My name is Nancy and I'm addicted to church committees." Every addict learns to pass out lies to themselves and others like a Las Vegas casino dealer. Thus, the power of addiction recovery is in the exposure of secrets: bringing into the light what was in darkness. Light prompts denial to flee like Florida roaches. We can see what we need to deal with in the glow of day.

Honesty is of utmost importance and not a mere step to be checked off a list. The pool of honesty needs to be dived into daily. Many come to admit at some point that they are powerless over their addiction and that their lives are unmanageable. But the struggle to be honest doesn't stop there. The decision to live truthfully requires a return performance. "Today I refuse to dress up my disappointment so others won't worry that I will go back to carving on my body." "I admit that this afternoon I craved a hearty porn binge to remedy my mood." "Late last evening, every fiber of my being screamed for something to fill me, so I scoured the cupboards and ate until a Raisin Bran box, barbeque chip bag, and two Snickers wrappers lined my garbage pail." Each day requires another batch of truth, including our triumphs and our trials.

Brennan Manning, author, speaker, and recovering alcoholic, writes about an AA meeting that he attended where a man named Phil had just recently been drunk for a five-day period after seven years of sobriety. Admitting this to the group was especially painful for him. He was broken. The group responded:

> "The same thing happened to me, Phil,
> but I stayed drunk for a year."
> "Thank God you're back."
> "Boy, that took a lot of guts."

"Relapse spells relief, Phil," said a substance abuse counselor.
"Let's get together tomorrow and figure out
what you needed relief from and why."
"I'm so proud of you."
"I never made even close to seven years."
"You old ragamuffin," said Denise, "Let's go.
I'm treating you to a banana split at Tastee Freeze."[10]

Do you know what that sounds like? The pouring raindrops of *grace*.[11]

After trying many faulty cures, the cofounder of Alcoholics Anonymous, Bill Wilson, finally

> ...reached the unshakable conviction, now a canon of twelve-step groups, that an alcoholic must "hit bottom" in order to climb upward. Wilson wrote his fellow strugglers, "How privileged we are to understand so well the divine paradox that strength rises from weakness, that humiliation goes before resurrection: that pain is not only the price but the very touchstone of rebirth." The irony continues throughout recovery. Although an alcoholic may pray desperately for the condition to go away, very few alcoholics or other addicts report sudden, miraculous healing. Most battle temptation every day of their lives. They experience grace not as a magic potion, rather as a balm whose strength is activated daily by conscious dependence on God.[12]

Does this sound familiar? This is the life-changing concept that Paul speaks of in his second letter to the Corinthians, when he is explaining his own "thorn in the flesh" after having pleaded with God to just take it away: "And He said to me, 'My grace is sufficient for you, for power is perfected in weakness.' Most gladly, therefore I will rather boast about my weaknesses, so that the power of Christ may dwell in me."[13]

It is this grace that allows us to "boast in weakness." It is grace that makes it possible to say, "My name is Hannah, and I'm addicted to being wanted." It is grace that permits me to say, "My name is

Tammy and I'm addicted to getting my own way." It is grace that is honored and experienced every day we manage to flee from our "lover." It is grace that makes this kind of raw, vulnerable honesty *possible*, and even exciting, when we realize we're boasting in Jesus.

> The Good News means we can stop lying to ourselves. The sweet sound of amazing grace saves us from the necessity of self-deception. It keeps us from denying that though Christ was victorious, the battle with lust, greed, and pride still rages within us. As a sinner who has been redeemed, I can acknowledge that I am often unloving, irritable, angry, and resentful with those closest to me. When I go to church I can leave my white hat at home and admit I have failed. God not only loves me as I am, but also knows me as I am. Because of this I don't need to apply spiritual cosmetics to make myself presentable to Him. I can accept ownership of my poverty and powerlessness and neediness.[14]

This journey of recovery may indeed be lengthy; however, it is comforting to know that as the bumps and turns along the trek escalate, so does His grace. Just as the manna was in proportion to the Israelites' hunger during their desert travels, His grace is in proportion to our need.[15]

Another travel tip we'd like to mention: we need fellow passengers. As Henri Nouwen said, "the way to 'God alone' is seldom travelled alone."[16]

Community

YOU HAVE NOT FULLY TAKEN YOUR FIRST STEP UNLESS YOU HAVE SHARED IT WITH OTHERS.

Patrick Carnes

Come in close, so we can whisper this in your ear:

You can't do this on your own.

That's right. This includes those of us whose "Turkish Delight," our addiction, is helping people. We realize, however, that community can be a place of pain. It may have been in our church community that the abuse happened. Or in our earliest community, we may have learned from our chemically dependent, mentally ill, or incessantly fighting parents that it was our job to temper the conflict. Consequently, we spend our adult careers managing other peoples' pain. We *help* people. We don't *need* people. Thus, the idea of sharing our secrets, being "weak" in another's presence, is daunting. We teach other people to take off their masks, to come out of hiding, to share secrets, but we don't do this very well. We were hurt in relationships and re-entering and unpacking our emotional suitcases is risky. Yet when people face their junk together, something beautiful can happen. "The healing path always leads us back into the human fray to be betrayed *and* to savor both human and divine love."[17]

Allowing yourself to need a support system comes in a variety of shapes and sizes. It may involve daily accountability with some trusted friends. It may mean checking in with a pastor or mentor. It may mean taking classes, participating in group therapy, or going to a Celebrate Recovery, AA, or OA (and every other letter under the sun) meeting. For Niki it meant turning to a trusted counselor.

Scripture makes it clear that we are created in the image of God and created for relationship. God has been communicating this essentially since the beginning of time.[18] No one hates loneliness more than God.[19] The phrase "one another" shows up (depending on what version you're using) up to 150 times in Scripture, indicating that this is pretty important to God. We are who He wants us to be in the context of relationship. We cannot love on our own, be gentle on our own, or bear our burdens alone. In the book of Galatians, Paul says it pretty directly: "Bear one another's burdens, and thereby fulfill the law of Christ."[20] Paul wisely reminds us a little later, though, that this does not make other people responsible for our decisions: "For each one will bear his own load."[21] Each one of us will have to give an account for the decisions we have made. Please understand this tension: we are meant for relationship, and it is good and biblical to ask others for help, but this will never make those around you responsible for your decisions.

While developing a community of trustworthy people to journey with is essential, it is also important to apologize for the ways we hurt others along the way.

I'm Sorry

REPENTANCE IS NOT JUST GETTING GOD TO LOOK AT OUR SIN;
IT'S OUR WILLINGNESS TO STAND TOGETHER WITH GOD
WHILE WE BOTH LOOK AT OUR SINS.
Calvin Miller

I'm sorry. Vital words in the healing process. Twelve step groups include them, spouses rollick when they hear them, Jesus requires them in order to have a real saving relationship with Him, yet they can be agonizing to say.

In the Dr. Seuss story, *Bartholomew and the Oobleck*, the King made a mess of his kingdom. But his king-sized pride nipped any apologies in the bud. That is until a little boy named Bartholomew Cubbins couldn't stand it anymore, so he turned to the king and tells him that he ought to say he *is* sorry. Incredulous, the King tells this pint-sized kid that kings don't say they are sorry because…they are kings! Undeterred, Bartholomew tells the king that he is no king at all if he can't say that he is sorry.

Suddenly, the king cried and cried and cried. He was sorry. He was very, very, very sorry.

> And so the story goes that the very second the king expressed his sorrow over what he had done, magic happened. All the oobleck that covered the people melted away.[22]

God melts too when one of His kids says the words, "I'm sorry."

"I'm sorry for hating you, God, for making me a man."

"Mom, I'm sorry for all the nights you left the porch-light burning, waiting for me to come home when I was high."

"I'm sorry, Dad, for the rage I've nursed and brick wall I built around myself."

"I'm sorry for trying to starve myself."

"I'm sorry for pushing you away after letting you in."

"I'm sorry for trying to change you to be what I wanted you to be so I wouldn't be so afraid."

"I'm sorry."

Not a smidgen sorry for the abuse—that is the perpetrator's responsibility lock, stock, and barrel. Sorry for the hurtful ways I have responded to the abuse.

I (Tammy) remember when my junior high Sunday school teacher, Mrs. Henshell, had our class memorize a verse. We went over it week after week. At the time, it seemed a little overdone. Decades later, I realize the gift she gave us.

> If we confess our sins, He is faithful and just and will
> forgive us our sins and cleanse us from all unrighteousness.
> *1 John 1:9*

Confessing connects us with our forgiving Father.

I'm sorry…Two little words strong on courage and mighty on freedom.

Saying Goodbye

> It is a wonder what God can do with a broken heart,
> if He gets all the pieces.
> *Samuel Chadwick*

If you thought asking for help was difficult, try saying goodbye.

Saying goodbye, letting go, unrequited love—all are themes in lyrics of popular songs. Everything from *It's so hard to say goodbye* to *Yesterday* to *I will survive*. Letting go of an addiction is in some ways like breaking up with a lover or grieving the loss of a loved one. It involves saying goodbye to what is familiar, predictable, and known.

It may be obvious that you have to say goodbye to your favorite beer or Friday night bar, but it may not be obvious that you'll have to let go of your drinking buddies, favorite shot glasses, dance music, or the high of the nightlife. It might make sense to finally let go of that guy you've been holding onto, but you may not realize you also need to say goodbye to the stack of pictures and letters, and delete his emails along with the determination to get him back. Logic may tell you that throwing away your calorie-counting journals and diet pills are important, but what about the jeans you keep in the back of your closet, hoping you'll fit into them again someday?

Saying goodbye is more than just throwing pipes, bongs, syringes or any other drug paraphernalia into a dumpster or deleting his/her information from your contacts list. It is a mental shift. A surrendering of what *you want* to what *He wills*. Letting go is another part of this journey that is both a moment in time and an ongoing process. Today I choose sobriety, and one day at a time I'll continue to make that choice of surrender—no matter how much it hurts to let go.

In the process of letting go, there may be some type of "replacement" behavior that offers a less damaging way of coping. As an example, it is dangerous for a person addicted to heroin to "say goodbye" to the drug cold turkey, as there can be serious medical complications. Instead, a medically supervised withdrawal period that usually involves increasingly smaller dosages of a painkiller will help this person "detox" safely and develop better ways of coping in the process.

There is truth to be mined for other addictions as well. For the person who struggles with cutting, holding ice cubes tightly is considered a less-severe form of self-mutilation, but the challenge for this person ultimately is to sit in the pain without having to "purge" it. Holding ice cubes, although maybe not dangerous, is still a way of toughening up. Ultimate healing for this person is to release the grip and with open hands welcome the pain and the comfort that is to follow. This is the same idea for a person in drug or alcohol recovery who takes up smoking or the intake of high doses of sugar to deal with cravings— perhaps less destructive, but still a means of coping rather than going to God. This is also the idea that baby steps count. Spending less on books each month *is* progress for the professor addicted to Amazon. com, eating more calories *is* progress for the girl struggling with anorexia. Thus, letting go can be a lengthy process.

As we are learning to surrender these behaviors more and more, may we also have the courage to ask the following question…

WHY DO I DO THIS?

UNDERSTANDING THINGS WILL NOT CHANGE AN ADDICT'S LIFE.
DOING THINGS DIFFERENTLY WILL.

Dr. Walter Ling

Jesus *is* the answer, but it's not as simple as just saying, "Jesus is the Answer." For those of us who acknowledged Jesus as the Lord of our life and said that we are sorry, Jesus has set us free, but because we are not yet satisfied, we tend to live as slaves. And there will continue to be a little slave in all of us *until that Day.*

> Often I have been asked, "Brennan, how is it possible that you became an alcoholic after you got saved?" It is possible because I got battered and bruised by loneliness and failure; because I got discouraged, uncertain, guilt-ridden, and took my eyes off Jesus. Because the Christ-encounter did not transfigure me into an angel. Because justification by grace through faith means I have been set in right relationship with God, not made the equivalent of a patient etherized on a table.[23]

An honest examination of our yoke of slavery involves asking ourselves *Why do I do this?* This is not a "next step," but something that will more likely take place throughout your journey. In the beginning, we may ask ourselves why or how our relationship with _____ even began. This may mean looking at memories of sexual abuse or other victimizing experiences. It might involve exploring family dynamics and/or generational sin.

What this looks like is this: when you are driving home from work on a Tuesday afternoon thinking, *Man, I really want to stop by the liquor store* or *What I wouldn't give to go purchase one more pair of black pants*, it is important to stop and ask yourself, *What is this about? What happened today that I feel so vulnerable to this? What has been bothering me lately? What would it be like to just go home and be quiet?* And as already suggested, asking these questions with the help of friends or a trusted counselor can be especially helpful in the process of self and most importantly, God-discovery.

Hype but Lacking Substance

LET ME NOT EAT OF THEIR DELICACIES.
Psalm 141:4

Satisfaction is only one purchase away. In Augusten Burroughs' memoir about his raging addiction to chemicals, he pushes back the advertising industry curtain to reveal that many ads are merely smoke and mirrors designed to speak to our soul cravings.

> Sometimes when you work in advertising you'll get a product that's really garbage and you have to make it seem fantastic, something that is essential to the quality of life. Like once I had to do an ad for a hair conditioner. The strategy was: *Adds softness you can feel, body you can see.* But the thing is, this was a lousy product. It made your hair sticky and in focus groups, women hated it. Also, it reeked. It made your hair smell like a combination of bubble gum and Lysol. But somehow I had to make people feel that it was the best hair conditioner ever created. I had to give it an image that was both beautiful and sexy. Approachable and yet inspirational.

> Advertising makes everything better than it actually is…It's
> an industry based on false expectations.[24]

The packaging and catchy sales pitches flirt with us and whisper, "You want me. You need me." But we soon find out that what we think we gotta have doesn't deliver. Addictions work a lot that way too. The gut ache after the binge, losing our home after shooting a pile of meth, credit card bills piling up, getting caught embracing another woman… For a brief moment, we realize that our lover didn't satisfy. We may ditch this unsettling notion with another high, one more affair, our next shopping binge, or another drama, or we may pause and allow ourselves to want something more.

We were made to be attached. And to this God-formed need our Father speaks. In Acts 3:19, words of *something more* march in.

"Repent, then,
   and turn to God,
      so that your sins may be wiped out,
         that times of refreshing may come
            from the Lord."

The word "repent" involves a turning from our alcohol, our controlling ways, our porn.[25] But that's not all. Our wise Father who molded us knows that we must go somewhere with our need to be attached so we don't swap one idol for another. Luke explains, "Repent, then, AND *turn to God*…" Like the father of the prodigal son, He waits with open arms for us to make an about-face in His direction. "Attach to Me," He whispers. "Tell me about your aches, your disappointments. Tell me '*so that your sins may be wiped out.*'" Regarding the bulky bag carrying all the stories about people we have hurt through our addictions, He invites us to place this at His feet. For this is why His Son died. And after we have turned from our addiction, crawled up into His loving arms, and told Him we are sorry, there's something more. *That times of refreshing may come from the Lord*. He's planned a party. The invitations have been mailed and you are the guest of honor.

The Quintessential Party

BECAUSE YOUR LOVE IS BETTER THAN LIFE,
MY LIPS WILL GLORIFY YOU...
MY SOUL WILL BE SATISFIED AS WITH THE RICHEST OF FOODS...
MY SOUL CLINGS TO YOU; YOUR RIGHT HAND UPHOLDS ME.
Psalm 63:3-8

No matter how long you go without your substance of choice, there may be a lingering dissatisfaction and loneliness that follows. As thoroughly as you may have processed the pain and worked through the false beliefs attached to your addiction, the pleasure that you long for is simply *not enough* and the pain is still *too great*. As we mentioned in the previous chapter, you are not meant for this world, and this world will never provide full satisfaction. And while the cliché answer is to tell you "God will satisfy," the truth is that even this relationship is not experienced yet in the fullest sense— loneliness and dissatisfaction in the soul of one who walks with God is completely normal, because we are not yet face to face with Him.

Last February, I (Hannah) was throwing a surprise birthday party for a good friend of mine named Bethany. Bethany was one whom I specifically spent Friday nights with, week after week. It was "our time." Her birthday this year landed on a Wednesday, but I decided to plan her party for the Friday two days after her birthday. If you've ever done anything like this, you know that you also have to celebrate on the *actual* birthday so that there are no hints of a surprise party around the corner. So we celebrated on Wednesday. And then Friday came. Our time. I sat in a coffee shop for hours that afternoon with another friend of mine, while my "party committee" was busy decorating the house and making finishing touches to the surprise. So this whole time I'm sitting there drinking coffee, I'm getting periodic text messages from Bethany, who was getting increasingly more desperate:

"Hi friend. What are you up to?"
"Hey, do you still want to hang out tonight?"

"Are we going to get a chance to connect?"
"Is there anything special you'd like to do?"
"Was Wednesday supposed to count as our time?"
"Do you even want to hang out?"

The whole time I'm not even paying attention to my phone, so when I finally left the coffee shop, I noticed I had all these messages from her. Bethany was beginning to doubt my desire to be with her. Slowly but surely, she was questioning her value in my eyes—Where did she stand with me? She was questioning my very love for her. And all the while, a surprise party was being planned for her—something bigger than what she ever expected or imagined from me.

Isn't that something of a picture of the love of God? When things are not happening as I had hoped or expected, I am quick to "text" God, desperately seeking out His love that I feel has waned. Has He forgotten me? What good am I to Him? Does He even care? What I fail to realize is that He has the biggest surprise party that He is planning in a place where I won't ever have to question His love again.[26]

As we move farther and farther away from the second-rate parties we settle for in this world, may we hunger increasingly for the God of the quintessential party.

Requited Love

thirsty in the desert

DISCUSSION STARTERS

1. What is it like for you to ask for help?

2. Who are the people in your life to whom you can talk about your struggles? Do you have a sense of authentic community?

3. Since we are all Gomer, what words do you long to hear from your Hosea?

4. Do you remember when your relationship with your "Turkish Delight" began?

5. Imagine for a moment what you think "the quintessential party" might be like. In your wildest imagination, what would Heaven be like? Is that something worth waiting for?

WHAT WE CALL OUR DESPAIR IS OFTEN ONLY
THE PAINFUL EAGERNESS OF UNFED HOPE.
George Eliot

IN THE MIDST OF THE SORROWS IS CONSOLATION,
IN THE MIDST OF THE DARKNESS IS LIGHT,
IN THE MIDST OF THE DESPAIR IS HOPE,
IN THE MIDST OF BABYLON IS A GLIMPSE OF JERUSALEM,
AND IN THE MIDST OF THE ARMY OF DEMONS
IS THE CONSOLING ANGEL.
Henri Nouwen

NEVER, NEVER, NEVER, NEVER GIVE UP.
Winston Churchill

A FRIEND HEARS THE SONG IN MY HEART
AND SINGS IT TO ME WHEN MY MEMORY FAILS.
Anonymous

TO LIVE WITHOUT HOPE IS TO CEASE TO LIVE.
Fyodor Dostoevsky

WE HAVE THIS HOPE AS AN ANCHOR FOR THE SOUL,
FIRM AND SECURE.
Hebrews 6:19

HOPE IS SYMBOLIZED IN CHRISTIAN ICONOGRAPHY BY AN ANCHOR.
AND WHAT DOES AN ANCHOR DO? IT KEEPS THE SHIP ON COURSE
WHEN WIND AND WAVES RAGE AGAINST IT.
BUT THE ANCHOR OF HOPE IS SUNK IN HEAVEN, NOT ON EARTH.
Gregory Floyd, A Grief Unveiled

...AND HOPE DOES NOT DISAPPOINT US...
Romans 5:5

Indomitable Hope

In·dom·i·ta·ble (n-dm-t-bl) adj.
Incapable of being overcome, subdued,
or vanquished; unconquerable.

Hope is a Dangerous Thing

Andy Dufresne was sentenced to life in prison for a crime he didn't commit. Talk about a hopeless situation![1] Yet there was something different about Andy. From day one he involved himself in personal hobbies and made a few friends along the way. As time went on, Andy, who had been a banker on the outside, became even more involved by assisting inmates and staff with their taxes and helping inmates achieve their high school equivalency. He made the most out of a sad situation. Andy also wrote letters to request books for the new library at Shawshank Prison. After years of writing letters, he received scads of books and a few records along the way. Andy loved music. So in a moment of pure rebellion, he played an Italian opera on the speaker system for the entire prison to hear, after locking one of the guards in the bathroom. Andy's fellow inmate and close friend, Red, described hearing that beautiful music in prison. His heart soared because for a brief moment as he listened to the music, he was free.

After Andy was forced to spend two weeks in solitary confinement, he sauntered into the cafeteria with an unusual glow, and the boys began to ask him how he did it—How was he this untroubled after two weeks of solitary confinement? He took the music with him, was his reply. Confusion sprawled all over their faces since the warden wouldn't have permitted a record player in solitary confinement. Andy explained that he carried the music in his heart, that the music awakened his *hope*. Red became unglued. Hope only makes a man go insane, he shot back. Hope has no use in prison …it is a dangerous thing.

Hope is not a game many survivors play anymore, as **hope is a dangerous thing.**[2] When daddy lifted me onto his lap, I hoped this time he would just hold me, spend time with me, love me. Yet when incest trails the hope and desire for love, these longings become despised enemies. Hope feels like foreplay to violation. Consequently, a survivor may train himself not to hope, not to expect, not to allow himself to yearn for something more as a protection from betrayal and one more grand let-down. Eventually, he learns not to hope from others, himself, and from God. And yet God fashioned a place in the souls of His kids to hope.[3] Victor Frankl, a Jewish psychiatrist, discovered what permeates the pages of Scripture—hope is critical for life. He stumbled on this truth in what seems the most unlikely of places: a dark and dehumanizing WWII concentration camp, a place where his wife, father, and mother died. Frankl witnessed that while he and fellow inmates couldn't make sense of their abject suffering, those who had nothing to live for quickly died. Yet those who did not lose hope, survived. For many survivors, to inch toward hoping again is a mammoth step because as John Eldredge says, "Hope rouses the desire from its slumber and makes us even more vulnerable to disappointment."[4]

Survivors of evil need hope for today and they need hope so they can crawl, walk, and eventually run into tomorrow. In this chapter we want to see, taste, smell, and hold onto this thing called hope.

BUT

The American Heritage Dictionary says that hope is "to wish for something with expectation of its fulfillment."[5] We hope that it stops snowing or we hope that we get an A on the exam. Secular award-winning author Rebecca Solnit wrote in her book, *Hope in the Dark,*

"Hope is an ax you break down doors with in an emergency... Hope just means another world might be possible, not promised, not guaranteed."[6] This kind of earthly hope is bereft of assurances. This kind of hope is like a spider web. A quick wave with a broom can sweep it all down.[7]

In contrast, the variety of hope that Scripture talks about is different. Hebrews 11:1 says that "Faith is being **sure** of what we *hope* for and **certain** of what we do not see" (emphasis added). This brand of hope is not illusory or wishful thinking. Biblical hope is being confident that nothing passes through His hands that He has not permitted and that He will see us through. "Biblical hope is not hope for something, it is a type of hope in Someone."[8]

Paul spoke about this kind of hope in the fourth chapter of 2 Corinthians as he was walking in the damp and dreary tunnel of heart-breaking trials. As I (Tammy) began to study this passage, despair was knocking on my door. I was brooding over some circumstances that left a gaping wound and a well of confusion. I was trudging along a potholed path and I couldn't see past my situation. I wondered if I dared work on this chapter, knowing the state of my heart. Desperation surpassed my hesitation.

For God, who said,
'Let light shine out of darkness,'
made His light shine in our hearts
to give us the light of the knowledge
of the glory of God in
the face of Christ.

In a vast stadium of darkness, a light flickers. Paul directs our gaze to another light, far off in the distance. "Then God said, 'Let there be light;' and there was light" (Genesis 1:3). Steady and sure, Paul wrote that the same God who created light in the physical world has a torch burning for the dark and discouraged crevices of our souls. And His light cannot be extinguished.[9] Swimming against the tide, Paul's strength and hope came not from the change in his circumstances but by looking into the illuminated face of Jesus. Thomas Merton penned,

The soul of man left to its own natural level, is a potentially lucid crystal left in darkness. It is perfect in its own nature, but it lacks something it can only receive from the outside and above itself. But when the light shines in it, it becomes in a manner transformed into light and seems to lose its nature in the splendor of a higher nature, the nature of the light that is in it.[10]

BUT we have this treasure
in jars of clay
to show that this all-surpassing power
is from God and not from us.[11]

Packaging is EVERYTHING in sales. The glitz and glamour connected with presentation sells perfume, detergent, and even presidents. Still, in God's economy what is in the package is what counts. We are clay, fragile and easily broken, hardened in the kiln of life. Yet the God of the universe has chosen to dwell in the available chipped and cracked jars so that His power might be displayed and so that there is no mistaking where this power for living comes from.

We are
hard pressed
on every side,
BUT not crushed...

Not crushed. The god of this world loves to take abuse and squeeze the life out of survivors. He presses hard and leaves his mark. We may be backed into a corner, yet our God guarantees that His grace will be sufficient.[12] Guarantees.

Perplexed,
BUT not in despair...

The Greek word for perplexed means "not to know how to decide or what to do."[13] The evil of abuse is confusing. Despair, however, means to be utterly at a loss, utterly destitute of measures or resources—and it involves renouncing all hope.[14] Yet, even when we don't know how to proceed or why evil has happened, Paul encourages us not to give way to despair and abandon hope because hope was not designed to be based on our circumstances. Circumstances can change. As I studied this passage, the words "But not in despair" shot up like a flare. Paul knew despair. He had been there and done that. Earlier in 2 Corinthians 1:8, Paul describes a time when despair was heavy on his heart. Yet, now in chapter four, he tells us that we don't need to reside in the land of hopelessness. Confusion, yes. Heartache, yes. But not despair. So Paul passes on a lesson about hope that he has learned first-hand. No matter how dark the night, we can trust that God will provide a way.

Studying this passage did not begin as a lesson for you, the reader. It was personal. I was hungry. As I began to smell the aroma of the feast before me of which Paul had learned, I ate this passage up like manna from heaven. The words nourished and filled me. As I read these words, I grabbed Paul's hand and said with him, *Perplexed, but not in despair.* And I felt less alone. My chin was lifted so my gaze could return to my Jesus. Thank you, Father.

Persecuted,
BUT not abandoned

To be persecuted literally means to be hunted like an animal. This is the image with which some survivors are all too familiar—when a perpetrator undresses his victim with his eyes, words, or his hands or when he adamantly denies his violating actions. Yet Paul says that even at the most evil hour, God will never leave you.[15] On this our palace of hope is built. Wherever there is persecution, He is.

Struck down,
BUT not destroyed.

The Enemy has been behind the striking down of survivors world-wide. And his plan from day one has been to use the abuse to destroy—to put an end to, to ruin, to render useless.[16] But for those who love God, Paul says, this is impossible. The Enemy cannot ruin those whom God redeems. Without offering spiritual placebos, Paul closes the chapter with a call to lift our gaze.

Therefore we do not lose heart.
Though outwardly we are wasting away,
yet inwardly we are being renewed day by day.
For our light and momentary troubles
are achieving for us an eternal glory that
far outweighs them all.
So we fix our eyes not on what is seen,
BUT on what is unseen.
For what is seen is temporary,
BUT what is unseen is eternal.[17]

On these rock-solid promises which emanate from the trustworthy Promise Giver is the only place where indomitable hope stands tall.

The Day the Music Died

HOPE IS THE THING WITH FEATHERS
THAT PERCHES IN THE SOUL,
AND SINGS THE TUNE—WITHOUT THE WORDS
AND NEVER STOPS AT ALL...

Emily Dickinson

Emily Dickinson painted poetry with hues of depth and complexity.[18] In her poem called "Life" she portrayed hope as a bird who sings a sustained song even in the darkest of days. Hope has feathers that allows one to fly to new beginnings.

Bird lovers attest to the fact that a male nightingale sings loud songs with a stirring range of whistles and gurgles late in the evening when other birds are silent. Moreover, the male nightingale sings even more forcefully in urban spaces in an attempt to overcome the background noises.[19] Just like the nightingale, people were made for song. Dan Allender tells the story of a former student and an interaction this student had with a client in a nursing home. The elderly woman had sailed on the *Lusitania*, and Dan's former student proceeded to ask some basic questions:

146

> **Student:** How did you get on the boat,
> and what were you doing on that?

> **Elderly Woman:** I was 13, and I was coming to
> the United States. I was a musician and in that, I loved
> the opportunity to meet Americans and to play for the
> very first time in America. I don't play anymore. In
> fact, I didn't play after I came back from America.

> **Student:** You used to play, and now you don't? And
> then you said you didn't play soon after you returned?

All this person had done was restate what the elderly woman had said with a tone of compassion and concern, and the elderly woman began to look very uncomfortable. The woman explained that she had **NEVER** talked about what happened so many years before.

> **Student:** You've never talked about it
> ...about why you stopped playing?

> **Elderly Woman:** My parents and friends
> asked at the time, but I couldn't say.

> **Student:** What is it that brought you to a point
> where you made the decision [not to play]?

> **Elderly Woman:** My teacher went with me
> on the *Lusitania* and he did things to me
> that ought to never have been done to a 13-year-old.

The woman who uttered this sentence was a 92-year-old woman. From age 13 to 92, no one had asked the simple question as to why she stopped making music. Yet, when someone finally asked, she expressed with all sincerity, "That day, when he did those things, the music died."

For many survivors, to hope is like being asked to wade in deep, turbulent waters. Waters that have hidden below the surface, a dangerous undertow. Waters that will knock you down and lead you down current without something to grab onto. Thus, the invitation to hope must be given gently, carefully, without pressure. Hope must often be eased into. Singing again takes time. Singing again involves being given the chance to share about the day the music died, about the day a voice was lost, and the day we locked our instrument in a secured box, never to play again. It brings great comfort to know that the One who longs the most for us to sing again, is the One who gives us a new song and writes the lyrics. "He puts a new song in my mouth, a hymn of praise to our God" (Psalm 40:3). May we sing louder than the sounds of persecution, despair, and affliction. May we fly to new perches on the branches of the One who is hope.

Companions

CHRISTIAN DID NOT PRESS ON ALONE,
FOR ANOTHER PILGRIM NAMED HOPEFUL JOINED WITH HIM AND,
BY MEANS OF A BROTHERLY COVENANT,
AGREED TO BE HIS COMPANION.
The Pilgrim's Progress, John Bunyan

One of the most challenging times of my (Hannah's) life was walking through the failure of a romantic relationship—a relationship that had ended in betrayal and a great deal of pain. It was a dark time. Hope seemed hard to track down. My best friends Ashley and Laura joined me in this difficult chapter of my journey and agreed to be my companions. They reminded me a new day would come; they helped me to keep going forward and to refrain from turning back. They did this by frequently asking me what I needed, even weeks and months after the break-up. They let me be a total mess— sometimes wanting to go out and get my mind off things, other times wanting to stay in bed and weep. I was on a roller coaster, and they decided to ride with me (and Laura doesn't even like roller coasters!). When I struggled to believe that I had any value, they were quick and long-suffering in reminding me about the beauty they saw in me. In short, they brought powerful, sustaining words of hope to a despairing twenty-something-year-old.

Tamar needed words of hope from a faithful companion. Instead, her brother Absalom said to her after the rape, "Be quiet now, my sister; he is your brother. Don't take this thing to heart."[20] Tamar needed a Laura, Ashley and Hopeful at her darkest hour: friends who would hope for her on the day her hope tank was empty. Yet even if we are so fortunate to have hope helpers in our lives, if He is not trustworthy, if He is not good, then there is no reason for hope. As A.W. Tozer said,

> As long as we are in the hands of chance, as long as we look for hope to the law of averages, as long as we must trust for survival to our ability to outthink or outmaneuver the enemy, we have every good reason to be afraid.[21]

Hope and trust are cousins. Indomitable hope is only possible when in the midst of suffering, there is a trustworthy God who will never allow more suffering than we can bear. Indomitable hope is only possible in the midst of suffering when there is a God whose love for His kids never wavers.

> The love of God is one of the great realities of the universe, a pillar upon which the hope of the world rests. But it is a personal, intimate thing, too. God does not love populations, He loves people. He loves not masses, but men. He loves us all with a mighty love that has no beginning and can have no end.[22]

A World Beyond

GOD IS ALWAYS BEYOND.
Michael Card

On the days that our hope may be dim, we are told to fix our eyes on the face of Jesus and keep trusting the One who is our hope. He promises to give us the precise amount of hope we need in the desert of our lives, in the same way He provided manna for the Israelites every morning.[23] "Some gathered much, some little."[24] And on days when we can't see where the manna is, we need hope helpers to lead us to the meal awaiting.

But that's not all. When it comes to hope, He offers something more. He reminds us that this world is not all there is. There is a world beyond the wardrobe. A world beyond anguish. A world beyond abuse. A world beyond desolate. A world where hope will be fully satisfied. And one day in that world beyond,

HE WILL WIPE EVERY TEAR FROM THEIR EYES.
THERE WILL BE NO MORE DEATH OR MOURNING OR CRYING OR PAIN,
FOR THE OLD ORDER OF THINGS HAS PASSED AWAY.

Revelation 21:4[25]

Indomitable Hope

DISCUSSION STARTERS

1. Was there a day in your life when the music died?

2. When is a time that you have chosen to step into hope, to embrace hope, to choose to hope, even when your circumstances seemed bereft of hope?

3. What are some of the things you look forward to most in the world beyond the wardrobe?

REMEMBER THE DAYS OF OLD;
CONSIDER THE GENERATIONS LONG PAST.
Deuteronomy 32:7

THE ONE THING WE LEARN FROM HISTORY
IS THAT WE DO NOT LEARN FROM HISTORY.
Hegel

GOD DOES NOT TAKE AWAY OUR PAST; GOD GIVES IT BACK TO US—
FRAGMENTS GATHERED, STORIES RECONFIGURED,
SELVES TRULY REDEEMED, PEOPLE FOREVER RECONCILED.
Miroslav Volf

MY MEMORIES OF THE ABUSE WERE LIKE A SPOT ON THE HIGHWAY
BEHIND ME, WHICH I WATCHED RECEDE IN THE REARVIEW MIRROR;
IT BECAME SMALLER AND SMALLER UNTIL IT VANISHED.
Richard Berendzen

YOUR FUTURE DEPENDS ON HOW YOU DECIDE
TO REMEMBER YOUR PAST.
Henri Nouwen

THESE STONES ARE TO BE A MEMORIAL
TO THE PEOPLE OF ISRAEL FOREVER.
Joshua 4:7

Marching
down memory lane

Some years back, Sandra, Anna, Barb, and Debbie, best pals from high school, piled into one car and drove to my (Tammy) high rise apartment in downtown Winnipeg. They hauled our high school yearbook, '80s music, and bags of clothes to exchange among our group. For an evening, we were in high school again. We laughed till our stomachs hurt, and memories of teachers, friends, and high school, good-old-times, were rekindled. It was a night to remember.

Memories can also bring a mixed bag of sentiments. While we were writing this chapter, our community lost a beloved police officer after a long battle with cancer. At the police station, a memorial was built including Officer Polston's van and handfuls of markers for students and loved ones to sign. It was a poignant experience to see very little space left on that van. The van was covered with signatures and notes from people who would never forget the impact he had on their lives. In Officer Polston's lifetime, he touched a lot of lives. His loving impact is something that ought to be remembered. As I saw people of all ages with tears running down their cheeks, I (Hannah) thought *what a gift* it is to be able to remember and reflect on a man who gave and gave, a man who was grounded in God.

While reminiscing is the substance of conversation and delight for many seniors, family gatherings, and old friends congregating, for many survivors, remembering abuse spells **DANGER**. Some survivors wish their uninvited memories would vacate the premises. Yet, like unwanted salespersons, these traumatic memories keep re-dialing, in the form of nightmares and flashbacks. Desperate attempts to scrub these memories clean like Lady Macbeth and her spots of blood occur through abusing chemicals, multiple sexual partners, living life in the busy lane, and a panoply of other addictions. For others, memories of childhood seem to have been cut away like an appendix through a surgical procedure. Desperate attempts to obtain that which is missing become the focus of countless hours and enormous energy. For others, remembering is smothered in ambivalence— wanting to remember and yet not wanting to remember. Wrestling with memories and looking for direction from our omniscient and loving Father is the tenor of this chapter.

The Dialectic[1] of Remembering Abuse

THE CONFLICT BETWEEN KNOWING AND NOT KNOWING,
SPEECH AND SILENCE, REMEMBERING AND FORGETTING,
IS THE CENTRAL DIALECTIC OF PSYCHOLOGICAL TRAUMA.

Judith Herman

Over the years, I (Tammy) have journeyed with survivors who carried fragments of intense sensations and feelings, along with sparse or absent narratives related to their childhood trauma. I have also worked with survivors who have always remembered their abuse. Still others carry a hodgepodge of recollections: certain aspects are vivid while other specific memories are MIA. The subject of memories for abuse was the subject of my doctoral dissertation.[2] The topic of delayed recall for abuse has intrigued a lot of people including survivors, therapists, researchers, family members, and lawyers, triggering a thorny and polarizing controversy and acrimonious discourse over the last couple of decades.

While there are stacks of studies on abuse memories, let's look at the gist of the memory controversy. On one side of the delayed memories three strand, twisted tug-of-war rope are researchers and clinicians who maintain that individuals sexually abused as children can "forget" the abuse and then later remember.[3] Thus, individuals who have experienced complex trauma learn to block out past hurts through dissociation.[4] Way down on the other end of the tug-of-war rope, experts argue that delayed "memories" of abuse are a "myth". The bulk of these memories are false and these pseudo-memories have either been implanted by therapists who have used leading questions or clients have read or heard others talk about trauma and have falsely believe the trauma happened to them when it actually happened to someone else.[5]

There is compelling evidence that people who were sexually abused in childhood can experience a lack of recall for the abuse and then later remember.[6] Like unwanted clothes crammed into cardboard boxes in the attic, unwanted memories are stored away in the mind. Then, at some point along the journey, these unwanted memories strike like a hit-and-run driver leaving debris scattered all over the boulevard. On the other hand, we have also learned that people can sincerely believe they have recovered a memory of abuse but, in actual fact, they are mistaken.

What is often true in many contentious polemics[7] is that truth takes up a great deal of space and it is often hidden from those peering from one side of the spectrum. It is wise to learn from members on both ends of the contentious debate so that visual perception is more accurate for researchers, therapists, and survivors, and ways of responding to people sharing memories are marked by wisdom and compassion.

Je Me Souviens... Me Acuerdo... I Remember

For some survivors, traumatic memories simmer for years and finally come to a boil when the past is relived through flashbacks and nightmares. These flicks of traumatic memories come surging back as exposure to elements connected with the trauma occur[8] (e.g., the smell of gasoline; an old song on the radio; words or phrases seen or heard; sexual intimacy). Trauma research has shown that survivors may actually experience physical changes to the hippocampus, a part of the brain involved in learning and memory and the handling of stress.[9] It may well be that alterations of memories for abuse like flashbacks, dissociation[10], and intrusive memories may be related to the impairment of the hippocampus. There is still a lot to learn about exactly how a child or adolescent who has experienced complex trauma dissociates the traumatic memory.

Trauma experts have learned that survivors can become overwhelmed if they prematurely dive into the discussion of complex traumatic memories without the ability to adjust their extremes of emotions.[11] Talking about complex trauma memories too quickly is like jumping into the deep end of the pool when you don't know how to swim. Instead, it is wise to learn to wade in the shallow end of the pool, and with a trustworthy swimming coach, learn how to pace wading workouts before approaching deeper waters.

Trauma researcher Christine Courtois and her colleagues explain that there are three phases or stages involved in wrestling with complex traumatic memories:[12]

Phase One involves the development of safety and learning to manage their emotional thermostat. Many survivors of complex trauma have learned to live in relational and circumstantial chaos and violent relationships are familiar. Thus, it is vital for survivors to enter into relationships with a godly community where violence is not part of the décor. This phase of the healing journey also involves learning to identify and experience emotions versus seesawing between emotional extremes (e.g., numbness, rage, despair).

Phase Two: When personal and interpersonal safety has been established (e.g., sobriety, choosing not to engage in self-injurious behaviors) and the survivor has learned to embrace emotions without becoming overwhelmed, the second stage of the healing journey can be approached. This phase of the journey involves entering the deeper waters of traumatic memories. One of the important tasks during this stage is that survivors learn to grieve over the losses of loving relationships and the evil that has happened to them.

When traumatic memories are allowed to take center stage, certain memories may hit with fury. It is important to remember that survivors are reminded that He won't allow one memory to arrive on the scene before its rightful time. However, becoming overwhelmed can be a signal that we may need to tap on the brakes, slow down, and return to phase one and lay some more groundwork. When all of these steps have been down, and decisions are made to face the pain of the past, we discover that it takes a lot of energy to keep memories at bay. It also takes great courage to turn our face toward and not run from the pain of the past. Flashbacks, nightmares, and night terrors remind us that we are not yet finished and at peace with the traumatic events.

We wonder, did Tamar experience night terrors due to Amnon's caustic words—"Get this woman out of here and bolt the door after her"[13]? Did her body tremble every time she smelled baked bread? Did she want to bolt when men with Amnon's similar stature came near? These questions are unanswered on the pages of Scripture. We do know however, that for the Tamars of this world, when there is an atmosphere of safety and supportive help, and there is opportunity to devote attention to intrusive memories, the choice to face and contend well with these memories is more likely.

Bearing witness to the specific stories of the past is a significant portion of phase two but remembering alone is insufficient.[14] Since survivors of complex trauma are prone to believing lies about him or herself, others, and God, the survivor and caregiver together can examine the assumptions and beliefs related to the trauma in a new light. For example, consideration as to the power and size of the perpetrator, the options available at the time of the abuse, and the rationalizations of the perpetrator are important conversations. Briere and Lanktree call these discussions cognitive reconsiderations.[15] These topics are worthy dialogues as specific memories are examined, however, the usefulness is limited. In addition, it is important to learn to hold up the specific traumatic memory in front of the gaze of God so He can speak and bring truth in place of lies. Ultimately, we want God's perspective regarding the events of the past and help with what we have learned to believe as a result of the past. Miroslav Volf, Director of the Yale Center for Faith and Culture, explains that true healing comes when the painful memories of the past have been:

> (D)islodged from the center of our identity and assigned a proper place on its periphery, and that its hold over how we live in the present and how we project ourselves into the future has been broken.[16]

Thus, during phase two, emancipation from our painful past comes as we face the specific memories of abuse; moreover, we obtain a shift in perspective as lies are replaced with truth. No longer are we merely a victim of our past. Rather, we realize we are someone who has suffered but also we are someone who has been delivered by God and given a new life. Volf explains that we begin to see ourselves like the ancient Israelites, who walked out of Egypt with their heads held high seeing themselves, not first and foremost as victims of Pharaoh, but as individuals *delivered* by their God.[17] "I am the LORD your God, who brought you out of Egypt so that you would no longer be slaves to the Egyptians; I broke the bars of your yoke and enabled you to walk with heads held high" (Leviticus 26:13). The evil that has happened is not allowed to have the last word.

> If we remember a wrongdoing—no matter how horrendous—through the lens of remembering the Exodus, we will remember that wrongdoing as a moment in the history of those who are already on their way to deliverance.[18]

Throughout the emotionally laden memory work of phase two, balance is the key. Remembering is an important part of being freed from the Egypt of our past but the remembering during this phase of the journey was not designed to be the central focus. As Courtois and her colleagues explain, "At no point should therapy substitute for living life."[19] We may need to take some items off of our proverbial plate as we are prone to piling more of life on. However, choosing to love in relationships, carrying on with work, and living is vital as we deal with past issues. Similarly, as was true for the Israelites, breaking free from Egypt was so important, but the sole purpose was to worship God in the desert (Exodus 7:16). In the desert of our painful memories, worship is our destination.

Phase Three: The third phase in working with complex traumatic memories involves the continuation of a long walk toward intimacy in relationships. The focus becomes increasingly on the present and on taking risks because we believe He is strong enough to catch us if our risk-taking doesn't turn out the way we hoped. We continue to remember so we can forgive and be forgiven regarding the ways we have handled our painful past. We persist with grief work as we face the cumulative losses attached with abuse over our lifetime. During the vicissitudes of life, we learn to approach the fountain of joy and even kick off our shoes and splash around in it.

The phases of counseling for complex traumatic memories are not linear, unswerving, or nonstop. Instead, the periodic need to return to earlier phases and to pause is part of the journey.[20] Pacing is important.

Years ago, when I (Tammy), was a speed swimmer, we raised support for our swim team through swim-a-thons. We swam two hundred lengths of the pool as fast as we could. We needed to swim up and down the pool at such a pace that would allow us to keep going to finish the race. Younger swimmers, who were first-timers at the swim-a-thon event, frequently went too fast at the beginning and after a while, these red-faced kids had to hang on the side of the pool to cool down and catch their breath. Wise pacing when we face the past is important too.

When memories do come, a closer look at some of the specific challenges involved in facing memories, through the life of Peter can help along the memory journey.

Peter: Life beyond the Rooster

> Having arrested Him [Jesus], they led Him away and brought
> Him to the house of the high priest; but Peter was following

at a distance. After they had kindled a fire in the middle of the courtyard and had sat down together, Peter was sitting among them. And a servant-girl, seeing him as he sat in the firelight and looking intently at him, said, "This man was with Him too." But he denied [it,] saying, "Woman, I do not know Him." A little later, another saw him and said, "You are [one] of them too!" But Peter said, "Man, I am not!" After about an hour had passed, another man [began] to insist, saying, "Certainly this man also was with Him, for he is a Galilean too." But Peter said, "Man, I do not know what you are talking about." Immediately, while he was still speaking, a rooster crowed. The Lord turned and looked at Peter. And Peter remembered the word of the Lord, how He had told him, "Before a rooster crows today, you will deny Me three times."

And he went out and wept bitterly.[21]

...And Peter lived a desolate life. No, this wasn't the ending of Peter's story. His later chapters in Scripture are dissimilar from Tamar's story. While the reasons for their shame were very different—Tamar's as a result of something done *to* her and Peter's shame as a result of something done *by* him—both were swathed in shame. Imagine for a moment if Peter had never moved beyond the guilt and shame over his denial of our Lord.

After a night of bitter weeping, did Peter awaken once again to the sound of a rooster crowing, and re-experience his shameful betrayal? Did the memories replay over and over again in his mind? What was it like when he remembered the time he pledged his life to Jesus, even if it cost him everything?[22]

How did Peter cope with these memories, with this pain, with the lie in his head: *I said I would die for Him, but it must not be possible. I'm not faithful enough, not good enough. I don't love Him enough?* Was Peter able to sleep, dreading the sound in the morning that brings it all back? Did he wake up before dawn and run as fast as he could to avoid hearing the crow, but still it haunted him? Did he just learn to live with it, to bury it as deep as he could, to pick himself up by his sandal-straps and work hard to prove his love? We wonder …

Peter's guilt and shame is different from the my-fault-kind-of-shame we talk about in *Beyond Desolate*. His shame was about something Peter had done, and not something that was done to him, as is the case in abuse. However, they both experienced much anguish over what occurred and their futures may have been similar. Did something happen in between that caused this man to live so courageously, so *beyond?*

Jesus called him
to
remember.

Sort of. He didn't sit down with Peter and say, "Let's review what you said to me that one time and what you told those who asked if you knew Me. Tell me as many details as you can recall." The point in shedding His light was not to review the details and get the facts straight, but to *slay the lies* that were believed by Peter with His truth.

> Jesus came and took the bread and gave it to them, and the fish likewise. This is now the third time that Jesus was manifested to the disciples, after He was raised from the dead. So when they had finished breakfast, Jesus said to Simon Peter, "Simon, son of John, do you love Me more than these?" He said to Him, "Yes, Lord; You know that I love You." He said to him, "Tend My lambs." He said to him again a second time, "Simon, son of John, do you love Me?" He said to Him, "Yes, Lord; You know that I love You." He said to him, "Shepherd My sheep." He said to him the third time, "Simon, son of John, do you love Me?" Peter was grieved because He said to him the third time, "Do you love Me?" And he said to Him, "Lord, You know all things; You know that I love You." Jesus said to him, "Tend My sheep. Truly, truly, I say to you, when you were younger, you used to gird yourself and walk wherever you wished; but when you grow old, you will stretch out your hands and someone else will gird you, and bring you where you do not wish to

go." Now this He said, signifying by what kind of death he would glorify God. And when He had spoken this, He said to him, "Follow Me!"[23]

It may seem here that Jesus is offending Peter, but in fact, His words are healing. Three times Peter denied the Lord, and three times Jesus asked Peter, "Do you love Me?" Ed Smith said this about Jesus' three-times-posed-question:

> Jesus deliberately asked Peter three times if he loved Him, which we are told hurt Peter. In the setting of the charcoal fire, it appears that Jesus was intentionally triggering Peter's memory-based pain by way of association. Jesus' kind but unrelenting confrontation positioned Peter to hear the truth he so desperately needed to hear. The truth was immediately forthcoming. Jesus told Peter that when Peter grew old, he *would* die for Him; his death would be difficult, but his courage in enduring it would bring glory to God.[24]

So, if in fact Peter had believed he was not faithful enough, not good enough, he didn't love Jesus enough, then Jesus put an end to these ways of thinking. He spoke the truth, and the truth set Peter free. Jesus wanted Peter to be delivered from his past so he would enter unencumbered into the mission God had for him.

And Peter did.

In true Jesus-inviting-us-to-live-beyond-desolate fashion, Peter later wrote to "always [be] ready to make a defense to everyone who asks you to give an account for the hope that is in you, yet with gentleness and reverence."[25]

Peter, whose terror ushered him to betrayal, whose silence spoke a denial, tells *us* to always be ready to give an account. God thought that was something worthy enough to be published.

Missing Pieces

In contrast to those who were abused and wish they could forget knowing memories, there are some who long desperately to remember what feels blurry, fuzzy, unknown. There is a sense of something terrible that has happened, but only enough pieces of the puzzle remain to know that the picture is incomplete, only enough to be enveloped by desperation that begs, *why can't I remember?* The hunger to remember may be fueled by the desire to know one's history, to have a sense of one's self as a child, and to make meaning out of all this pain. Yet, some memories may remain inaccessible and the loss of not-knowing waits to be grieved.

For those who wish they could remember, the question becomes: How do you manage what you have been given? Do you remember the story about the rich land owner who, before leaving on a journey, entrusted different amounts of money to his three servants while he went away?[26] A major point of the story is that each of the servants were responsible for the portion of money they were given. We can apply this principle to dealing with memories as well. Some remember much, while some remember very little. What we do with the memories we have been given is what is important.

Added to the principle of being faithful with what we have been given, there is research which suggests that remembering every detail is not as important as confronting the lies that were established in those experiences.[27] In fact, a ceaseless search to remember may end up hurting more than helping.[28] There are certain memories that need to be spoken out loud, in detail, in the presence of a wise person, so the lies of the enemy can be demolished and the truth of our omniscient God can be spoken and embraced. Still, even if a person does not remember all the details of the abuse, but she learns to live with integrity and her faith in our great God is deepend, this is what is most important.[29]

The legitimate hunger to remember and the acceptance of not remembering is truly a high calling to hold in balance. Along the courageous walk down memory lane, it is helpful to remember that memory retrieval is not the goal. Knowing and loving Him is what we were made for.

HIS Words

You're sitting in a counseling office, buried into the comfy couch and playing with a loose thread on the pillow you're gripping. The lighting is dim, almost as if turning lights brighter would hurl you into panic. Self-help books surround you. The clock on the wall ticks.

Maybe you're the person re-telling your story (as much as you can recall) one more time, hoping that this time something magical will happen and that you'll leave the memory and all its anxiety in the counselor's wastebasket.

Maybe you're the counselor, hoping that as he tells the story, you'll speak the right words that will make the difference; this time, he will know it wasn't his fault, he will get that he is the son of the King. But in the back of your mind, you sense that it won't work now because it hasn't worked before. Shame is inevitable, and you start to wonder if you're doing more harm than good.

Ed Smith describes his early counseling experiences this way:

> I can remember having them revisit their traumatic memories over and over, but nothing significant happened. I watched them abreact in deep emotional and physical pain as they experienced their memories, only to have the pain remain. During this abreaction I tried to give them the truth, but they could not embrace it. I would have them tell me the truth (It wasn't their fault; they were safe now; they were not dirty, shamed, defiled) and acknowledge it themselves out loud, yet they could not make it their own.[30]

It is these kinds of experiences that prompt victims and helpers alike to long for something more.

For quite some time, we haven't known how to put this into words. We've felt the frustration, and we've experienced the "something more." It happened the day we were hiking and I (Hannah) was *stuck* at a particular memory as I was sharing my story with Tammy. Processing this day later, Tammy recalled that it felt like she was being almost too obvious as she was speaking truth to me, as if she were being asked to convince me of something that she could not do. My memory of that day was that she *wasn't clear enough,* not that I blamed her for that. Not only could I not believe what she was saying, but I also felt like I couldn't understand it, couldn't grasp what was true. But something changed when she began to pray and when she asked the Lord to show me a picture of His face during the incident in which I felt so stuck.

She knew that I needed the truth that only He could give because, "No person, including ourselves, is capable of talking us out of the lies we believe. We will be free only when we receive the truth from the One who is Truth (John 16:12)."[31]

Ed Smith, in his book on Theophostic Prayer Ministry, describes a woman who was experiencing depression and anxiety who went to see her pastor:

> The pastor prayed, asking for guidance and discernment, and then used the principles he had learned to help her follow her fear to its origin in her memory. Within a few minutes an enormous amount of pain began to surface and she began to describe a very disturbing memory of childhood pain and emotional wounding ...

Shari began to experience intense depression and anxiety in this session, stating that she believed she was going to die.

> While tempted to reassure her that she was only in a memory and was completely safe, the pastor refrained ...Instead, he had her embrace the fears and encouraged her to feel them completely. Little by little Shari came to understand and identify the true source of her pain, which she discovered

was not the memory itself but the false beliefs in the memory …In the midst of her immense emotional and physical pain, the pastor invited the Holy Spirit to reveal truth to her in the midst of her fear and panic. Suddenly, everything changed. The pastor watched as a calming wave of peace washed over her. Shari immediately stopped expressing pain; her breathing relaxed, and her countenance changed from one of panic and anguish to one of complete peace and calm.[32]

So how do we describe *these* kinds of moments? The kind that Jesus had with Peter? To be honest, even if Tammy or I knew how to describe it, I don't know if we would. Our fear would be that as soon as we put words to this, some would take it as a formula, a guaranteed three-step process to healing and would apply it to every client with memories. Pray these words, do these three steps and Shazaam, he's healed!

What we can say is that these are moments in which a helper realizes his limitations and refers his client to the One who can bring the healing. It is a moment in which a counselor helps someone, "to position themselves at the feet of Jesus so He might do all He has promised."[33]

And then we help them to listen. Listen to the Shepherd who calls, who heals, and who seeks each one who is lost, alone, abused, withdrawing, distant, who longs for us to hear how He feels about us…

So how do you describe this encounter?

Perhaps that's like providing a linear explanation to other life-changing experiences: Jesus interacting with the woman who poured perfume on His feet or the woman who had been bleeding for years, Peter's post-rooster exchange, or Jesus' dinner at Zaccheus' home. Our words can't quite capture the moment. Yet, HIS words make all the difference.

Establishing Ebenezers

SAMUEL TOOK A SINGLE ROCK AND SET IT UPRIGHT
BETWEEN MIZPAH AND SHEN.
HE NAMED IT "EBENEZER" (ROCK OF HELP), SAYING,
'THIS MARKS THE PLACE WHERE GOD HELPED US.'
The Message- 1 Samuel 7:12

A couple of years ago, Hannah and I traveled to Stuttgart, Germany, together. One morning Giselu took us to Zeichen der Erinnerung, translated as Sign of Remembrance, where the remains of four railway tracks were standing. These tracks marked the spot during WWII where Jews purchased tickets and boarded trains under the pretense of traveling to safety. Instead, these trains escorted their Jewish passengers to concentration camps and, for many, to their eventual demise. Beside the tracks stood a large wall with engraved names of each Jewish child and adult who boarded these death cars. Giselu quietly translated the plaques on this monument that were designed to help visitors remember and to keep historical events "alive." This was a somber morning as we allowed the significance of this historic site to permeate us.

Building monuments out of stones was a frequent practice of the Hebrew nation in the Old Testament as well.[34] Jacob used a stone to commemorate that God met him at Bethel in an "awesome"[35] way. Joshua placed twelve stones to remember where God led the Israelites across the parted Jordan River.[36] Then we see Samuel continue this monument-building tradition. Following a time of fasting and real repentance, the Israelites defeated the Philistines. "Then Samuel took a stone and set it up between Mizpah and Shen. He named it Ebenezer, saying, 'Thus far has the Lord helped us.'"[37]

Stone upon stone was placed as a permanent reminder that God had been faithful and acted on behalf of His people. These monuments served as a visual remembrance that their victory was not due to their power or their brilliance, but because of their great God. These stone monuments stood as reminders to future generations that God helps His people. Building Ebenezers was an act of worship.

When I (Hannah) was a senior at a Christian college, I had the privilege of serving as a resident advisor, and I lived on a hall with mostly juniors and seniors. My responsibilities with upperclassmen were few, but one task was to come up with a "theme" for my hall: I chose *Ebenezer*. The idea was to decorate the hall with pictures, words, verses, and lyrics of experiences that reminded the women of something God had done in their lives. For example, I chose to put up two pictures – one was a photograph of my car, and the other of the roof of a house. Let me explain.

My 1997 maroon Chevy Lumina had become a place where I had many meaningful conversations with the Lord. I can remember sitting in my parked car in random lots and staring at the raindrops as they drizzled down my windshield and just *weeping* before the Lord. I remember driving around and talking to Him, screaming the lyrics of "Everything" by Lifehouse to Him, one of my favorite pastimes and a personal spiritual discipline. Because He had been so faithful to provide a vehicle and to meet me there, I wanted to remember Him every time I stepped foot in my Lumina.

The picture of a roof was one that I cut out of a magazine. It may seem silly to think of a roof as an "Ebenezer," but it was on the roof of my parents' house one summer evening that I surrendered my life to Jesus. I was thirteen and recovering from bulimia, not knowing how to really get out of that kind of bondage and feeling alone – the kind of alone that is also accompanied by guilt because I acknowledged that it was I who had pushed everyone else away. I had heard about Jesus and had His love modeled a great deal, but this was *it* – this was the moment when I really *needed* Him. I guess it wasn't a "typical" conversion – instead of the classic Romans Road, I was praying out of Psalm 13: *How long, O Lord, will you forget me forever?* I viewed Him in a lot of ways as my "last resort," my Lifeguard who might be able to save me from drowning. But I did give Him my life that night, and now, when I get an opportunity to be on a roof, I want always to remember how the Lord saved my life from bondage that one hot summer.

So, that senior year in college, it was a beautiful thing to see new pictures and items posted on the wall as we got to walk by every day and *remember* what He has done because indeed, *He has done great things for us, and we are filled with joy.*[38]

So here's an idea we would like to present to you, our reader. Imagine if survivors commemorated the ways God has helped, times when God has led to freedom from our sins, turning point experiences He has brought us to, and ways God has remembered us. Some may not remember all the abuse experiences but what we can remember is even more important. We can remember God's grace that is placed stone upon stone in our lives.

Your Ebenezer may be your dad's tattered old Bible as a symbol of the way he prayed for you. It may be a picture of someone who told you about Jesus. It may be an object that reminds you of the time when someone offered you a safe harbor in a raging storm. Perhaps it's the words written on a slip of paper that Jesus whispered when you asked Him how He feels about you.

As we gaze upon our hall of pictures, stack of stones, or prayer journal, we can echo the words of Samuel, "Thus far has the Lord helped us." And may we sing from deep inside of us, the lyrics of the classic hymn, *Come, Thou Fount of Ev'ry Blessing.*

> Here I raise mine Ebenezer;
> hither by thy help I'm come;
> and I hope, by thy good pleasure,
> safely to arrive at home.
> Jesus sought me when a stranger,
> wandering from the fold of God;
> he, to rescue me from danger,
> interposed his precious blood.[39]

Marching

down memory ~~Lane~~ ne
DISCUSSION STARTERS

1. Write the next stanza of Come, Thou Fount of Ev'ry Blessing. Thus far how has the Lord helped you?

2. What is forgetting/remembering like for you?

3. What do you think He wants you to remember most about Himself?

4. What's your Ebenezer?

You, God, who live next door—If at times,
through the long night, I trouble you
With my urgent knocking—this is why:
I hear you breathe so seldom.
Raineier Marie Rile, Book of Hours

Biblical prayer is impertinent,
persistent, shameless, indecorous.
It is more like haggling in an outdoor bazaar than
the polite monologues of the church.
Walter Wink

The best prayers often have more groans than words.
John Bunyan

How long, O Lord? Will you forget me forever?
How long will you hide your face from me?
David, Psalm 13:1

God does His most stunning work where
things seem hopeless & wherever there is pain,
suffering, and desperation, Jesus is.
Jim Cymbala

Prayer Mosaic
the language of lament

Iridescent glass,
Ceramic scraps,
Discarded trinkets,
Porcelain tiles,
Stubby stones,
Flat backed marbles,
Shards of china,
Colored chunks of marble...

Forms of art birthed from a kaleidoscope of mediums converge into a *mosaic*.[1] Thousands of pocket-sized objects become transformed into colorful works of art. The language of God with His kids resembles a mosaic of sorts. God is multidimensional and He speaks to His people in a staggering selection of styles. Chris Tiegreen, author of *Creative Prayer*, explains,

> He speaks to us from the love of his heart with pictures, symbols, music, scenery, tastes, sounds of nature, smells of plants and incense and rain, and the soft, gentle caresses of the wind, of the waves, and of other human beings...God gave a rainbow to Noah, a ladder to Jacob, a burning bush to Moses, an ark and a tabernacle to Israel, a giant to David, a marriage to Solomon and his beloved, a family to Isaiah,

figs to Jeremiah, dry bones to Ezekiel, a wife to Hosea, a vine to Jonah, and horsemen to Zechariah and John—to name a few. His voice has come in the sound of thunder, a waterfall, singing, a fire, a wind, a gentle whisper, and more. God expresses himself in terms of fragrance, sound, touch, taste, and anything else our senses can take in.[2]

When it comes to God's people conversing with Him, this bears resemblance to a mosaic as well. We speak to God in many forms, such as the iridescent glass of heartfelt thank-yous, porcelain-tiled love notes about His character, ceramic-scrap apologies, and the shabby stones of please-help-me requests. Each of these expressions to God is vital and part of the magnificent mosaic of prayer.

But intimacy with God includes sharing other expressions and emotions that at first glance may appear less attractive, less neat and tidy, less Christian-like. This type of prayer is called a lament and is defined as a complaint[3] or an expression of sorrow that is often composed as a song, hymn, or prayer.[4] Contained in these cries are two central questions, including, "God, where are you?" and "God, if you love me, then why?"[5] The Old Testament is packed to the brim with laments or prayers that are "violent and visceral, exuberant and exhilarating, passionate and pointed... and God responds to them without rebuke. And it seems that He does not just tolerate our feelings; he *desires* them."[6] Pastor and author Eugene Peterson explains,

> It's an odd thing. Jesus wept. Job wept. David wept. Jeremiah wept. They did it openly. Their weeping became a matter of public record. Their weeping, sanctioned by inclusion in our Holy Scriptures, a continuing and reliable witness that weeping has an honored place in the life of faith.

> But just try it yourself. Even, maybe especially, in church where these tear-soaked Scriptures are provided to shape our souls and form our behavior. Before you know it, a half-dozen men and women surround you with handkerchiefs, murmuring reassurances, telling you that it is going to be alright, intent on helping you to 'get over it.'

Why are Christians, of all people, embarrassed by tears, uneasy in the presence of sorrow, unpracticed in the language of lament? It certainly is not a biblical heritage, for virtually all our ancestors in the faith were thoroughly 'acquainted with grief.' And our Savior was, as everyone knows, 'a Man of Sorrows.'"[7]

Just as mosaic art is frequently formed from broken pieces, prayer often emanates from a broken heart. As wise Norwegian seminary professor Ole Hallesby said, "prayer and helplessness are inseparable."[8] Consequently, healing involves getting up-close-and-personal with the tattered piece of the prayer mosaic that is frequently cut out of the canvas and swept up in a pile on the art gallery floor. This broken-heart type of prayer, as a medium toward deep and intimate conversations between Yahweh and His people, is the central focus in this chapter. It is on this lamenting segment of the prayer mosaic that we want to linger, specifically as it relates to intimacy with God among survivors.

Abba Father

To many, the word "Father" conjures up colorful images of

warm embraces,

belly laughs,

protective arms,

walking in the woods,

helpful advice,

wrestling & more wrestling,

early morning on his knees,

loving conversations.

175

In stark contrast, for others, "Father" implies graphic depictions of

Shouting Arguments,
Cold & Angry Stares,
Drunken Slurs,
Sexual Violation.

Our earthly fathers were designed to give us a greater glimpse of how a loving father interacts with his kids. And on an eternal landscape, our father-daughter/father-son relationships were intended to help us catch sight of a heavenly Father who adores His children. Abusive dads teach opposite lessons. These experiences can impact the way we relate and speak with our Heavenly Father. This is problematic because prayer is all about intimacy.

So if the essence of prayer is intimacy, how does a caregiver help someone crawl up on the lap of God the Father in prayer when crawling on the lap of a trusted someone resulted in violation?[9] How do you lead a hurting soul in the direction of a face-to-face with Jesus when the windows to their soul were smashed and left lying in broken pieces on the ground? Their eyes were trusting, then fearful, then ignored, then cynical, cold, and empty over time. How do you help someone lift their chin and gaze into His eyes when they have learned that it is easier to look away?

Falling in Love

The process of the journey of healing and becoming intimate with Jesus can perhaps be better understood by recalling the process of falling in love, when your favorite place to be is gazing into each other's eyes.

You are noticed, or you notice someone.
   There is eye contact,
      Perhaps an awkward introduction.

Some flirting, shameless attempts to impress,
    Increasing vulnerability,
        Dates, dates, & more dates.
           Finding commonalities & differences.
      Thinking about him or her all the time.
    Knowing.
    Being known.
  A conversation that you realize you never want to end.
You want the rest of your life to be a conversation with this person.
I love yous.
  A proposal.
    Vows exchanged.
    Consummation.
  Sacrifice.
Till death do us part.

The journey of newfound love is sweet and good. Often, however, this trek toward relationships with loved ones is re-routed for survivors.

Ambivalence: You want to—but don't want to—be noticed, seen.
  You're suspicious of their motives—*What do you want from me?*
    Attempts to prove he or she cares for you, but can't convince you.
    It's so difficult to be real, to show the real you.
      Mute your longings,
        Dance around topics in conversations.
    Imbalanced giving: like a tennis match—
  they serve & the ball drops before you,
Or you do all the serving,
Push him away before he leaves you.
  Sexuality offered. No soul attached.
    Or, *My sexuality is the enemy. Don't touch me.*
    Push her away or make her so miserable she pushes you away.

The pushing away, fear of intimacy, deep distrust, and offering of body instead of soul are lived out in the life of the main character in *Redeeming Love*. Angel had been viciously and repeatedly raped and sold to men for their pleasure since she was a wee little girl. Life was one crushing blow after another, so she muzzled what was left of her desire to be loved. Paradoxically, the act of sex became her life and career.[10] Because she was practiced in the art of surrendering her body but not an ounce of her soul, prostitution became her gig. Customer after customer took possession of the only part of her that seemed to matter--she was an expert at accommodating, even though in her head she might be staring at some detail in the ceiling or thinking about her chores. Angel spent years prostituting herself and avoiding intimacy with the one man who loved her and wouldn't violate her. *Redeeming Love* is a story of relentless love by a man, but even more so about the loyal love of God.[11]

It is our belief that the colors and contours in the journey of falling in love with a person resemble the journey of becoming intimate with God in prayer—in a sense, falling in love with Jesus. And for the survivor of abuse, the process may involve a lot of kicking and screaming in the wild ride of becoming intimate with Jesus. Letting Him come close feels like opening ourselves up to violation all over again. But becoming intimate with Jesus is precisely the remedy for a broken and troubled heart.

Thankfully, the Word of God is teeming with stories of men and women who kicked and screamed, wrestled and wept, argued and pleaded, and eventually, waited and worshiped. People who held fast to the belief that a dance with the Savior would one day follow the dirge.

Deus Absconditus-The God Who is Hidden

HE IS NOT THERE.
Job 23:9

In the movie *Forrest Gump,* Jenny takes Forrest by the hand and runs as fast as their little legs will carry them away from her drunken, molesting father. They come to a hidden place in the cornfields. As dad searches for her and spews her name in the distance, Jenny kneels with Forrest on the ground. She prays repeatedly that God will make her a bird so she can fly away.[12]

Yet in this fictional film, God did not make Jenny a bird. And she did not fly away. So too, in the non-fictional lives of many survivors who prayed and pleaded in faith that God would stop the abuse: He did not stop it. This leads us to ponder: "God is omnipotent, yet he did not rescue. God is love, but he allowed an innocent child to suffer torment. God hates evil, but he did nothing to prevent it."[13]

Do we dare ask God why He allowed such events to take place in our lives? Can we bring Him our battered bag of grief, betrayal, despair, and sense of injustice? These emotions are messy, bereft of neat and tidy. Will He silence us and turn away?

Grief was meant to run behind the cart of loss. Grief is natural when God does not stop Satan's vicious blows. Moreover, when emotional abrasions are kept hidden, or left unattended, infection spreads. This is because unprocessed grief does not remain locked away in the past. It storms into the present, with arms folded and stomping foot, demanding attention.

> Perhaps grief and loss issues related to childhood abuse are best described as a type of disenfranchised grief... as 'grief that persons experience when they incur a loss that is not or cannot be openly acknowledged, publicly mourned, or socially supported.'[14]

In contrast to keeping the anguish of abuse locked up tight, C.S. Lewis encouraged us to "lay before Him what is in us, not what ought to be in us."[15] However, this suggestion flies in the face of a Christian world that commonly prizes perpetual victory with Sunday morning smiles and upbeat answers to personal inquiries. And when it comes to the lengthy process of grieving over the evil of abuse and rape, many survivors receive slogans that drip with sentiments like advertisements tucked under the windshield wipers of our cars.

In stark contrast, the pages of Scripture are filled with characters who are real, raw, *and* reverent.

For example, Jeremiah, caged in a dungeon well, laments the dissonance between the way things are and they way things were meant to be. Habakkuk faces violence and law-breaking throughout Judah and God tells him that the wicked Babylonians who raped their way through villages would teach Judah a lesson. In his prayer journal of sorts, Habakkuk pens the words, "How long, O Lord, must I call for help, but you do not listen?"[16] The Psalms are teeming with individuals who enter into authentic engagement with God. In fact, somewhere between "one-third to one-half of the psalms are laments."[17] Michael Card explains in his brilliant book, *A Sacred Sorrow*, fifteen stories in Scripture come from David's time in the wilderness as he flees from his enemies. And in the wilderness he "[wept] aloud until he had no strength left to weep."[18] The words of anguish expressed by these godly people were fast and furious, uncensored and loud to a heaven that seemed cold and silent.

And if all these examples were not enough, we are given a picture of Jesus during the hours before He was crucified. Jerry Sittser, seminary professor and author of *When God Doesn't Answer Your Prayer*, explains that as Christ hung in agony, mocked by many, "the Gospels record only seven sentences that Jesus spoke during those six or so agonizing hours. One was a direct quote from Psalm 22." Echoing the words of David, these words poured out to God the Father were on Jesus' lips as He was dying: "My God, my God, why have you forsaken me?"[19]

After Tamar was raped, she "put ashes on her head" and "tore the ornamented robe she was wearing. She put her hand on her head and went away, weeping aloud as she went."[20] Her agonizing, up-front-and-center lament began. When her brother Absalom heard about the violation of his sister, he shushed her: "Be quiet now, my sister; he is your brother. Don't take this thing to heart!"[21] We've all been "shushed" at one point or another. In childhood, this seems to be the work of well-meaning parents, seeking to care for their lamenting infants:

> As we began to try to understand the shape of the world into which we were born, we would all soon experience the 'shushing' of parents whenever we would inevitably erupt into the wailing of our first laments. Contained somewhere in the

heart of these demands to 'be quiet,' beneath the sincere attempts at comforting, lay a level of shame and the inescapable
message that we should not cry out, we should not behave in
such ways; that wanting the comfort of presence and the as-
surance of [God's love] were really somehow selfish. At that
frustrating moment we entered into the very human, fallen
aspect of denial, which is the polar opposite of lament.[22]

Absalom was essentially asking his sister to be in denial. *Don't take
this to heart.* Too often this message lives on for survivors today who
lament the evil that took place. This legacy of denial has continued
too long. Hearts are desperate to have a lament over the rape of the
body, mind, and soul that is understood, heard, and felt. The longer we take up residence, eat, sleep, breathe in denying the evil that
occurred, the closer we are to a story that ends like Tamar's. *Tamar
remained and was desolate in her brother Absalom's house.*[23]

If we don't wrestle through the anguish over the evil that happened,
we will spew our torment out on others nearby and ultimately never
move beyond in our relationship with God.

Because the struggle of faith is a battle of the heart, as well,
perhaps, as a struggle to regain meaning, it is important that
the abuse survivor is encouraged to allow his or her feelings of anger against God to be given expression. The greater
danger for the survivor of abuse is that those emotions will
remain repressed. If they remain hidden because the survivor
does not have a supportive environment in which the emotions can surface, they will continue to affect the believer's
life and faith in subconscious ways, and the process of healing will be hindered... Expressing rage at God is actually an
expression of great trust and faith. The young child who is
secure in his parents' love can say that he hates them... it
affirms in its own way the goodness of God.[24]

Remember Renee Altson, who was raped by her father and mistreat-
ed by the church? This is what she wrote about what really mattered
in her recovery:

There have been people in my life who have heard parts of my story and given me advice. They have tried to make me feel better… My initial response when I hear these things is always guilt: maybe I haven't really done enough… But I have spent my entire life trying to move on. I have been in therapy for a very long time. I've been on medications, been admitted to mental hospitals, and prayed for hours with pastors and exorcists. I have talked myself down from ledges. I have made hundreds of promises to myself and to others and to God. I have read my Bible over and over again, fasted and prayed, believed and disbelieved and believed again. I have deliberately made conscious efforts to move forward. I have written up manifestos and memorized scripture. I have tried to let go, I have begged with tears to be cleansed, I have fallen on my face in the bedroom and howled for change. My healing has only begun to happen when I have been honest with the pain that I have lived. Rather than simply putting it behind me, I am finding that I have to befriend it. Rather than choosing to forget what happened, I am finding that I must choose to remember.[25]

While it is important that the rage boiling inside is poured out, we are simultaneously afraid of being burnt and scalding others. As Dan Allender explains,

If she feels anger she may fear that vicious rage will pour forth and destroy the object of her ire. Both the fear of danger and of being dangerous to others coexist in the heart of the person who has been sexually abused.[26]

Yet despite our fear of what lies within and what might come spewing forth, we are called to engage, like 97-year-old Jacob, who haggled with God with his whole being, all night long.[27] "I will not let you go unless you bless me," he said.[28] In terms of physical strength, a 97-year-old man could hardly be a physical challenge to God. This was a spiritual struggle. Lamenting called Jacob, and calls the rest of us strugglers, not to let go of God. It requires that we stay engaged.

Through Jacob's persistence, it seems he crossed an invisible line where his character was transformed as he submitted to God's ways.

Moving Beyond the Invisible Line

The hope-filled purpose of lamenting prayer is not intended for us to stay stuck in the sludge and muck of wrestling, weeping, crying, and blaming God. Its purpose is that we go beyond. Beyond desolate.

I (Tammy) have told Hannah and others that when I die, they *can't* read my prayer journals. Maybe someday I might change my mind, but it's not likely (since most of them are shredded and living in a landfill!). You see, on many a day, a close reading of my prayer journals would reveal a cantankerous old goat. The thought of others seeing the depth of my crabbiness after I die is kind of an embarrassing thought. (Still, why should I care? I will be in heaven dancing before my Lord!) Despite my proclivity to grumpiness on certain days, repeatedly scrawled on *some* of the pages of my letters to God, is a transformation of sorts. From crab to confession, I learn to open my hands to a Father who knows me best and knows what is best. And sometimes I get beyond me and onto Him and those are treasured times. Perhaps in some minute way, this is what happens in the journey of lament throughout scripture.

Michael Card explains that in every one of the lamenting psalms, except Psalm 88, a transition occurs whereby the psalmist moves from "despair to hope, from complaint to praise."[29] This shift is most commonly marked by the Hebrew word "vav adversative." The term stands for the English words "but" or "then" and they signal a radical change. When you see the vav adversative, it is as if you were driving down the highway in one direction and then all of a sudden you make a U-turn and begin driving in the opposite direction. It is in this about-face that we move from our self being the focus of the conversation, to God being the focus. We stop pounding on His chest and instead, allow Him to pull us close and embrace us. In the desert of our brokenness, we offer our ache to God and we worship.[30]

The language of lament spoken to God the Father by survivors is crucial because it is the part of the prayer mosaic that is a passageway leading *through* suffering to the waters of sweet worship.

Double-Decker Buses

The Washington Monument, Lincoln Memorial, and the Capitol Building stood tall from my front row seat on the tip-top of a crowded double-decker bus in Washington, D.C. A woman sat gently beside me (Tammy) while her family found seats across the aisle. We introduced ourselves and agreed that we were kindred spirits—she from India and me from Indiana! It was Ruby's first time to the United States so I asked her what stood out—the highs and the lows. She mentioned that comfort seemed to be important to Americans and I nodded as I sipped my Starbucks venti chai. Our conversation quickly entered deep waters. She grew up in a Christian family smack-dab in a country where Hinduism is the centerpiece of living.[31] Prayer became our topic, and without missing a beat, she said, "It is my breath. I talk with Him all day long." She spoke of prayer not casually, but desperately. A heavy heartache pressed down on Ruby, so with hands held and eyes closed, we spoke with someone more powerful than the tenant of the White House as our tour of deeper places intensified. Two sisters from diverse worlds were ushered before the King of Kings. These remarkable buildings suddenly didn't seem as important.

What happened next was not what I expected. On a crowded tour bus, this woman heavily-weighted by a bulky burden started singing *How Great is Our God*. Ruby didn't seem to notice the other passengers at that moment. She was too busy worshiping the King of India and the King of the rest of the world. Sadly, my first thought as she started to sing were the piles of people all around us. Second thought—*I am not ashamed of the Gospel*.[32] So I started to sing and we worshiped.

Pain was Ruby's intimate companion, which paradoxically had made her love affair with God all the sweeter. I may not meet this sister again until heaven, but that brief half-hour encounter on a double-decker bus was the high-water mark of my trip. She slathered God with unbridled affection, like a little girl who can't stop hugging her daddy. Her shameless sentiment made me thirsty. Moments with Ruby reminded me of the purpose of lament in the raging waters of suffering—so that we might grab hold of God and worship Him.

Michael Card concludes that the "goal of deliverance is always worship."[33] Beyond breaking free from the addictions that bind us is a kind of grateful and lavish love from one who recognizes who set him free. When the Hebrew nation was liberated after 430 years of slavery in Egypt, they worshiped God in a strange place: "Let my people go so that they may worship me in the desert" (Exodus 7:16). The desert. A pretty strange place to set up a praise concert.

Strange it seems, but if we allow it, the desert can be our learned instructor. Some of the harshest, scorching rays in the barren lands of my life have led me to lie prostrate before my God on my bedroom floor with tears streaming down my face. Repeatedly, He waits to show us that pain can be redeemed. I wouldn't trade those moments for all the venti chais at Starbucks.

Grumping at God Without Being Irreverent

Being honest. That's what He wants from us. Some survivors are able to start being honest with God before anyone else. Other survivors, however, step into trust and vulnerability in human relationships first before allowing themselves to fall backward into the arms of God. One study of 26 men who had experienced Catholic priest abuse explained that telling their story was an important part of their spiritual journey.

> A small group of men in their 40s and 50s spoke about their current search to reconnect with their spiritual lives. For these men, the process of telling and speaking out about abuse was part of this development. Several had gone back

to speak with priests other than their abusers with whom they had maintained connections. The abused men reported that these conversations with nonabusing priests—many who admitted culpability because they had known or felt that was something was happening but hadn't spoken out— were healing.[34]

Even when the many lamenting characters in Scripture held skewed perspectives on their situations, they were open with God about it. Prayers of complaint can still be prayers of faith. They represent a refusal to let go of the God who may seem to be absent, or worse, uncaring. If this is true, then lament expresses one of the most intimate moments of faith, not a denial of it. However, Howard Macy, author of *Rhythms of the Inner Life*, cautions, "We must not, however, confuse being honest with merely being crabby."[35] Crabby comes with a mind made up: *This is the way it is.* Instead, candid accounts with God come with awareness that we hold a limited view. As Philip Yancey explains in his classic book, *Disappointment with God,*

> From Job, we can learn that much more is going on out there than we may suspect… In the natural world, human beings only receive about 30 percent of the light spectrum. (Honeybees and homing pigeons, can, for example, detect ultraviolet light waves invisible to us.) In the supernatural realm, our vision is even more limited, and we get only occasional glimpses of that unseen world.[36]

The process of moving toward trusting God is the mortar that secures us when the storms of life rain down. Candid accounts advance us to a point of remembrance. "We must not seek to whip up feelings so much as to recall the character of God."[37] Instead, we recollect, "God, You did help me in the past. You showed me you loved me before." Expressions of honesty that make room for trust, lead to patience. Not a "Take your time, God" kind of patience. Rather, it is a growing patience that is built on knowing that His timing is best. These honest reflections of discontent *and* admiration, confidence in God's character *and* exasperation[38] that ultimately results in a deeper kind of faith that is revealed in a rape survivor's conversation with God during a church service prayer time:

> 'God, I hated you after the rape! How could you let this happen to me?' The congregation abruptly fell silent. No more rustling of papers or shifting in the seats. 'And I hated the people in this church who tried to comfort me. I didn't want comfort. I wanted revenge. I wanted to hurt back. I thank you, God, that you didn't give up on me, and neither did some of these people. You kept after me, and I come back to you now and ask that you heal the scars in my soul.'[39]

The lamenting pieces in the prayer mosaic are not designed to remain lodged in anguish. Honesty before God was intended to lead us to a grateful praise of Him who sees all and knows all. Kicking and screaming before Him is meant to convince our hearts that we can love Him, because He first loved us. This is different than the plastic-smile kind of praise that too often permeates our Sunday morning services.[40] "This is the kind of praise that only pours forth from lament. To be sure, it's a bruised and bloody praise... But it's a praise that can now hope all things, having been forced to let go of everything."[41] It's the kind of applause that is well aware of the throbbing hurt and in the midst of this ache, on some days shouts and some days whispers, "Great is Your faithfulness."

I REMEMBER MY AFFLICTION AND MY WANDERING,

THE BITTERNESS AND THE GALL.

I WELL REMEMBER THEM, AND MY SOUL IS DOWNCAST WITHIN ME.

YET THIS I CALL TO MIND AND THEREFORE I HAVE HOPE:

BECAUSE OF THE LORD'S GREAT LOVE WE ARE NOT CONSUMED,

FOR HIS COMPASSIONS NEVER FAIL.

THEY ARE NEW EVERY MORNING; GREAT IS YOUR FAITHFULNESS.

Lamentations 3:19-23

Prayer Mosaic

the language of lament

DISCUSSION STARTERS

1. When is the last time you sang a lamenting song or read a lamenting psalm in church? What do you think would happen if we engaged in laments in our Christian community?

2. Why do you think God is such a gifted interpreter for lamenting languages?

3. When was the last time you had a battle with God? What was it like?

4. Lamentations 3:23: "Yet this I call to mind and therefore I have hope: because of the Lord's great love we are not consumed, for His compassions never fail. They are new every morning; great is your faithfulness." What frees you to hope again and see His compassions every morning (even in the midst of difficult times)?

EVEN STRONGER THAN THE MESSAGE OF SUFFERING
IS THE MESSAGE OF FORGIVENESS.
Lewis B. Smedes

FORGIVENESS IS THE FRAGRANCE THE VIOLET SHEDS
ON THE HEEL THAT HAS CRUSHED IT.
Mark Twain

WE TALK GLIBLY ABOUT FORGIVING WHEN WE HAVE NEVER
BEEN INJURED; WHEN WE ARE INJURED WE KNOW THAT
IT IS NOT POSSIBLE, APART FROM GOD'S GRACE,
FOR ONE HUMAN BEING TO FORGIVE ANOTHER.
Oswald Chambers

NOT FORGIVING IS LIKE DRINKING RAT POISON
& THEN WAITING FOR THE RAT TO DIE.
Anne Lamott

I PARDON HIM AS GOD SHALL PARDON ME.
William Shakespeare, The Tragedy of King Richard the Second

FORGIVENESS CREATES THE POSSIBILITY
FOR JUSTICE, MERCY, AND GRACE TO MEET.
IT IS THE MYSTERIOUS WEDDING OF HOPE AND
LOVE THAT GIVES BIRTH TOTHE POSSIBILITY
THAT SOMETHING BEAUTIFUL WILL ARISE.
Myrla Seibold

Flying

above the fray

forgiving incalculable suffering

Letting Grudges Go

Many critics scoff at the idea of letting go of grudges for wrongdoings endured. The reasons for their onslaught of slurs concerning forgiveness are compelling.

One such rationale is found in the book and film *A Time to Kill,* set in sweltering Mississippi with racism as the backdrop of the story. Two white Southern men decided to rape ten-year old African American Tonya Hailey, but were not successful in disposing of her body. The men were drunk and didn't cover their tracks—in fact, they spent the day after the rape at the local bar, getting a notch above wasted. The courtroom thriller escalates after African-American Carl Lee Hailey, father of Tonya Hailey, decides to murder the two white men who raped his daughter. He shoots them in the courthouse on the way to their sentencing for Tonya's rape.

When the question of Carl Hailey's level of sanity is no longer a legitimate one in the courtroom proceedings due to his declaration that the men deserved to die and he hoped they'd burn in hell, the only debate that remained was: Did Carl Lee Hailey deserve to be punished for murdering the two men who raped his daughter? In a final statement made by the defense, Carl Lee's white lawyer asks the jury to close their eyes and listen. He tells a sad story which is Tonya's story – a girl who was walking to the grocery store only to be picked up by two men in a truck. The men take her to a field where they tie her up, strip her clothes, and take turns raping her and then throwing full beer cans at her, tearing up her skin all the way to her bones. Finally, after a failed attempt to hang her, they throw her body over a bridge down to a creek. Her body just laid there, raped, beaten, soaked in urine, semen, and blood. The defense rests with the lawyer's final line of this story: He asks the jury to imagine that the girl in the story is white.[1]

Jake Brigance appeals to the *hearts* of the jury—that place in them and all of us that longs for *justice*. Considering forgiveness in light of a little girl's rape is scandalous. The unseemly prospect of forgiveness for evil acts makes an appearance in all sorts of venues like music, literature, philosophy, and trauma literature. Let's take a look...

Goodbye Earl

When a woman lands in intensive care after restraining orders fail to halt her hot-tempered husband, forgiveness can seem a hard pill to swallow. The Dixie Chicks made this crystal clear in their popular country song, *Goodbye Earl*.[2] The lyrics tell us the story of the repeated beating of Mary Ann by her unsavory husband, which led this abused woman to the conclusion that Earl deserves death. A meal containing a few fatal black-eyed peas got the job done. The notion that some things are unforgiveable appeared to ring true with many in the United States as the song hit #13 on the Billboard Hot Country Songs chart.

Forgiveness wasn't on the Top Ten charts for Friedrich Nietzsche or Sigmund Freud, either. Victims forgiving evil people was interpreted as a mask for weakness or as a defensive illusion resulting from a fear of condemnation.[3]

Ellen Bass and Laura Davis, authors of the renowned *Courage to Heal* workbook had this to say about forgiveness:

Never say or imply that the client should forgive the abuser. Forgiveness is not essential for healing. This fact is disturbing to many counselors, ministers, and the public at large. But it is absolutely true. If you hold the belief survivors must forgive the abuse in order to heal, you should not be working with survivors.[4]

The seminal book *Trauma and Recovery* suggests that letting go of torture is the "fantasy of forgiveness."

…Some survivors attempt to bypass their outrage altogether through a fantasy of forgiveness… The survivor imagines that she can transcend her rage and erase the impact of the trauma through a willed, defiant act of love… the fantasy of forgiveness often becomes a cruel torture, because it remains out of reach for most ordinary human beings."[5]

My Solitary and Lonely Accomplishment

The theme of the unforgivable nature of sexual abuse unfolds in popular literature. In the Pulitzer Prize winning *A Thousand Acres*, Jane Smiley pens the story of a family living on a large plot of Iowa land. When the aging patriarch decides to hand over his farm to his three daughters, Ginny, Rose, and Caroline, the lavish gift whips up old memories of incest. Eventually, the family scatters and Daddy never admits the abuse. The farm falls apart. As the pages of the saga near the end, the oldest daughter, Rose, lies paper-thin, color-less, dying of cancer in a lonely hospital room. She lost her husband, lover, reputation, and farm profits. She weighs her life accomplishments. Rose, speaking to Ginny, lists her failures, and then angrily describes her solitary accomplishment: that she saw her father for what he really was, and that she didn't forgive the unforgiveable.[6]

Have Rose, the Dixie Chicks, Sigmund Freud, Jake Brigance, Judith Herman and so many others concluded correctly that some offenses are *unforgivable*?

Perhaps a reason why many survivors have such a hard time with the notion of forgiveness is because some of us in Christendom haven't done a very good job explaining *or* living it. In fact, too often, we have pummeled forgiveness down into denial-based smithereens. For many, forgiving becomes a detour from entering the gated-off section of our souls where anger breeds.

When I (Tammy) was a little girl, the tangled weeds on the side of our house were as high as an elephant's eye. I was embarrassed over our unkempt yard. The unwanted groundcover simply mirrored my mom's internal angst during the sinking times in her bipolar cycle. She didn't leave her bed much on those days. Her sad soul kept her from engaging in relationships and activities.

One summer day, I decided to rid these blemishes from our yard and our lives. After scouring the basement I located my artillery.

GIANT hedge clippers.

With all the moxie an eight-year-old could muster, I brought those handles together, whacking the enemy with each cut. On that warm summer day, like the walls of Jericho, those weeds came tumbling down.

All that shame, all that disappointment, all those secrets were chopped away. Or so it seemed.

But quick fixes are just that: temporary. Hacking off the top of those weeds only led to a short-term solution as those unwanted greens came back with greater vigor and brought their friends. Unbeknownst to little Tammy, all those thistles and tares needed to be pulled out cleanly and entirely by the roots.

So do painful memories.

Quick forgiveness merely chops the tops off traumatic events, leaving the hurt, the anger, the deep disappointment that is buried beneath the surface ready to rise again.

Forgiveness was never intended to be the denial of hurt.

Burying the Hatchet

You can learn more about what is NOT forgiveness by checking out well-worn idioms.

For example, there's the phrase **"burying the hatchet."** The Cambridge International Dictionary of Idioms says this means "to forget about arguments and disagreements with someone and to become friends with them again."[7]

But can you really "forget" about your trusted youth leader's wife who befriended you when you were an awkward, lonely teenager, prompted you to feel like one of the family, and then eventually had coerced sex with you? Does forgiveness mean that we bury those hurts by forgetting? Didn't we learn this through Scripture, which says we are to forgive and forget?

Actually, the phrase "forgive and forget" wasn't coined or inspired by God at all. It comes from Shakespeare's *King Lear*. Toward the end of this classic tale, the old king messed up and lost everything. He is then reunited with his devoted daughter, Cordelia, whom the king had callously disowned. He sees his sin and begs his daughter,

"Pray you now, forget and forgive."

"Forgive and forget" is one of those expressions that we need to return to King Lear, the rightful owner, because it's not doing Christ-followers any good. Even in Jeremiah when God says that He "will remember their sins no more," recall that God is omniscient.[8] He *can't* forget. Rather, His words carry the meaning of the mighty river of grace. He washes our sins away. He will not hold our wrongdoing against us. Forgiving is not forgetting.

Then there is the expression **"bury your head in the sand,"** which means "to refuse to think about an unpleasant situation, hoping that it will improve so that you will not have to deal with it."[9] However, this brand of forgiveness doesn't work for minor or major abrasions. When we shove survivors to the front of the forgiveness line without providing a spacious place to look at the loss, hurt, and rage connected with the "deep wounding"[10], we assist in the avoidance of authentic forgiveness. Perhaps our propensity toward quick forgiveness is hitched to our proneness to polarities. Either victims avenge their wrongs, or they absolve the offender... People invoke a form of forgiveness such as overlooking, excusing or condoning that seems to short circuit the process but really does not resolve it.[11]

So if forgiveness is not chopping off, burying, or forgetting that the painful events in our life ever happened, what is it?

The Heart of the Matter

Steven Tracy has penned a deep and wide study on the topic of forgiveness and sexual abuse.[12] He wisely explains that forgiveness is no uncomplicated matter. Unfortunately, a lack of biblical understanding about the complexity of forgiveness has provided a one-size-fits-all model of forgiveness across all situations. This can lead to re-victimization. A careful reading of Scripture reveals there are three forms of forgiveness: Judicial Forgiveness, Psychological Forgiveness, and Relational Forgiveness. Let's examine the brands of forgiveness.

Judicial Forgivenesss
Our sin + Repentance = God's pardon (judicial forgiveness)

"Judicial Forgiveness" is our unable-to-pay-it-back gift from God for pardoning our sin. This type of forgiveness hinges on admitting we have done wrong, telling God we are sorry, and turning away from our sin (Psalm 32:5, 1 John 1:9, Luke 24:47, Acts 2:38; 5:31). This forgiveness is rooted in and given by God.

Psychological Forgiveness
Letting go + Extending grace = psychological forgiveness

"Psychological Forgiveness" involves letting go of our contempt and revenge and extending grace to the one who hurt us. Letting go.

When God calls us to let go of the hate it is because hate hurts. Someone once said, "Hate is like acid. It destroys the vessel that holds it." Letting go of hate doesn't mean releasing the yearning for justice;

we were made to want things righted. We let go of the hate and grab hold of God's character that He will one day exact perfect justice. Until that day, letting go of hate means releasing the poison that is killing us. The primary New Testament Greek verb for forgiveness is aphiēmi, which means to "let go, give up a debt, keep no longer."[13]

For most of us however, letting go is difficult. In *The Secret Life of Bees,* Sue Monk Kidd explained that people would often choose death over forgiveness any day of the week. Perhaps because letting go of our hate feels like a part of us is dying.[14] Remember Bilbo Baggins in *The Fellowship of the Ring*? The prospect of releasing that wretched ring seemed ludicrous to him. Yet, Gandalf prodded Bilbo to release his grasp. Unrelenting, Bilbo insisted that the ring was his. The magnetic pull tantalized Bilbo beyond reason despite the fact that the ring was hurting him, destroying him, killing him. Gandalf persisted to invite Bilbo to open his grasp because he understood the seductive pull, yet he wanted better for him.[15]

But how can we get past this mountain of pain, resentment, and rage? How can we let it go? Releasing the vice grip on our wrath can be eased as we remember that bitterness stands in between us and God. A river filled with pollution can't flow freely. We are unable to swim in the waters of intimacy with our Father when green garbage bags of resentment are mucking up the stream. It takes time to clean up the river, but ridding it of waste allows the streams of living water to flow freely from within.[16]

When we cease counting the numbers of injustices,
When we let go of obsessing about the wrongs done to us,
When the name of the one who wronged us is safe on our lips,
When toxic words come to an end,
like an eagle ascending higher than the honking horns and traffic jams…
   the wind carries us
     and we fly above the fray and
       we are free to
         SOAR.

Extending Grace

The other side of the Psychological Forgiveness coin is the face of grace. It means extending goodness to the very person who has hurt me. Imagine a funeral where a grieving man picks at his food and listens to people swap stories about his beloved dad. Over on the other side of the Fellowship Hall, standing in the corner, a group of fearful brothers murmur, "What if our brother holds a grudge against us and pays us back for all the wrongs we did to him?"[17] After the funeral, the brothers email an earnest letter. They write,

> *Dear Joseph,*
> *"Your father left these instructions before he died: "This is what you are to say to Joseph: I ask you to forgive your brothers the sins and the wrongs they committed in treating you so badly." Now please forgive the sins of the servants of the God of your father."[18]*
> *Love,*
> *Reuben, Simeon, Levi, Judah, Issachar, Zebulun, Bilhah, Gad, Asher, Dan, Naphtali, and Benjamin*

A glow in the distance announces the break of day as Joseph turns on his laptop and clicks on his inbox. The email from his brothers is waiting. He reads their words.

Joseph weeps.[19]

As Joseph sits on his Adirondack chair facing the Nile, he writes in his prayer journal and heavy tears dampen the pages. His brothers arrive and they throw themselves down before him.

"We are your slaves," they say.

Joseph replies: "Don't be afraid. Do I act for God? Don't you see, you planned evil against me *but God used those same plans for my good,* as you see all around you right now—life for many people. Easy now, you have nothing to fear; I'll take care of you and your children." He reassured them, speaking with them heart-to-heart.[20]

How could Joseph not only let go of the wrong done against him, but also extend grace to the very people who tried to murder him?

Perhaps in part, it is because he realized the lesson that became the theme of his life and the theme of the book of Genesis: God intends that the years of hardship His people faced be used for their good and for His glory. Lamentations 3:33 tells us that He does not *willingly* bring affliction or grief to the children of men. When He does allow pain, it is not meaningless pain. It is purposeful pain.

The person who molested your client, or brother, daughter, sister…did not have their best interests in mind. BUT GOD intends to bring good out of the evil of the molestation.[21] God never would have allowed the evil unless He could bring good out of it. Bringing good out of evil is one of God's favorite things to do. It's His modus operandi.

Joseph realized this and he became unburdened by resentment toward his brothers and was able to extend grace to them. Joseph knew that even in a vile prison, "the Lord was with him; He showed him kindness"[22] and God would only allow that which could be used for Joseph's best. That's how we can extend grace to the very people who intend us harm.

But what about Cloe …

who, at fourteen years of age, was abused by her teacher, and her teacher now caught, admits the abuse? Should Cloe let go and extend grace to her former teacher? And the teacher's church…should they forgive him and allow him to work with the youth? Or then there is Josh, whose teenage sister molested him when he was a little boy, but his sister has never admitted the abuse. Does forgiveness mean letting Josh's sister spend time with his now young son?

This is what the third type of forgiveness, Relational Forgiveness, speaks to.

```
Relational Forgiveness
(Letting go + Extending grace) + (Repentance +
Restoration) = Relational Forgiveness
```

Relational forgiveness is all about the restoration of relationship or reconciliation between the victim and the one who perpetrated the abuse. BUT while Relational Forgiveness is the destination we are hoping to arrive at, some people who sexually violate others do not repent. Relational forgiveness arrives on the scene when the person who violated realizes her sin and takes action to change her behavior before the victimizer and victim enter into a connecting relationship again. This kind of forgiveness is talked about in Luke 17:3, "If your brother sins, rebuke him; and *IF* he repents, forgive him." Notice the stipulation attached to relational forgiveness.

> When one forgives, one does not open a jail cell door but has an affective, cognitive, and possibly behavioral transformation toward the injurer; one can forgive and see justice realized…In forgiving , the injured party may give up the qualities of resentment or even hatred but not necessarily enter into relationship with an untrusted offender.[23]

Letting go and extending grace to the person who hurt us is always required. But if Josh's sister does not admit to having committed the abuse, reconciliation is blocked. David and King Saul illustrate this kind of block to reconciliation. After years of King Saul being hot on the kill-David-trail, the shepherd boy spared the life of and confronted the "Lord's anointed."[24] In response, King Saul said he was sorry. However, the two men were *not* reconciled (1 Samuel 26:25). David needed to brush away any flecks of bitterness clinging to his heart but reconciliation did not occur.

When the one who perpetrates abuse truly repents, with God's help, we are fashioned to let go of our loathing, extend grace, and engage in relational forgiveness. By pushing open the doors of relational forgiveness, we surrender our soldier-like resolve and set a caged dove free.

So What Does It Look Like?

Nearing the end of the semester in trauma class, counseling students were asked, with crayons in hand, to draw a picture of forgiveness. Apologies over the lack of artistic abilities abounded, yet their creations were remarkable as one would expect in a room full of counselors-to-be. One young woman drew raindrops and explained that forgiveness is like a cloudburst because it often includes a lot of tears in the process and because it is life-giving. Others drew people holding hands or making eye contact, things hard to do when forgiveness has not been offered. Another drew a flag – a symbol of "claiming" forgiveness; while one drew a woman on her knees praying, stating that there is just "something about the kneeling posture." Another student attempted to draw something to resemble music, simply and wisely mentioning that "when I'm holding onto bitterness, I can't sing."

We'd like to post these forgiveness pictures on the walls of our survivor groups, churches, homes, and our hearts as reminders of the hues, shapes, and textures of forgiveness.

And now for a real-life picture….

New Melodies

I (Tammy) counseled a woman for a couple of years who had been horrendously abused.

As a little girl, she recalled men placing paper money in the hands of her father and being forced to go with these men so they could do to her what should never be done to a child. She begged her father not to make her go, yet her father's refusal to relent is etched firmly in her mind. Her father was a leader in his church. For a long time we talked about the abuse and the effects on her adult life. And then one day, along our journey together, she sensed God had been pursuing her. He wanted her to *let go* of all that hate. The task before her loomed large and loud.

We arranged to meet for several hours one afternoon in my office. With lots of people praying, this courageous woman verbally stated out loud before God and me, the litany of remembered offenses her father and others had done to her. And then with me as her witness, one by one, she stated, " I forgive _____ ."[25]

That afternoon she used a whole box of tissues.
That afternoon I saw a scandalous portrait of freedom.

Here, forgiveness and freedom were completed with the act of letting go, as the father of this woman had died, and restoration of relationship was no longer an option. Learning to sing again after years of being bitter and voiceless is difficult, painful. But letting go is like going from a type of chronic emotional bronchitis to being able to sing arias and cavatinas.[26] So even though she couldn't be in relationship with her father any more, she began to sing the melody of a woman set free.

Pictures of Relational Forgiveness for heinous crimes are lean and spare. So, we end this chapter with a Relational Forgiveness portrait. For the record…

> God's people need more of these images.
> More artwork to hang on the wall.
> More music to play.
> The playlist is too short.

Rain Down

MAY HE COME DOWN LIKE RAIN UPON THE MOWN GRASS, LIKE SHOWERS THAT WATER THE EARTH. IN HIS DAYS MAY THE RIGHTEOUS FLOURISH, AND ABUNDANCE OF PEACE TILL THE MOON IS NO MORE.

Psalm 72:6-7

Just when I (Hannah) was beginning to believe that the reconciliation well was dry, I read an article about the country of Rwanda. You may recall that in 1994 there was a genocide that took place in this small country, killing about a million of its citizens, (one out of every eight Rwandans), mostly Tutsi minorities. One report claimed that 77 percent of the Tutsi were eliminated during this slaughter, primarily by two Hutu militias.[27] Machetes were used to rape and kill people in village after village. Years following this mass genocide, more than 110,000 men and women guilty of these crimes filled Rwanda's overcrowded prisons. What you may not know is that recently tens of thousands of them were released, and old wounds have been re-opened. The country was festering and bleeding with hate oozing everywhere.

Bishop John Rucyahana, chairman of Prison Fellowship Rwanda, returned to his home country after spending some time in exile in Uganda and some time studying in the United States. No news report could have prepared him adequately for what he would see when he returned: bodies in shallow graves, corpses in schools and churches. Bishop John was filled with bitterness and a desire for revenge.

Like most Tutsi survivors, Bishop John had lost many members of his extended family in the genocide. Even after the establishment of some semblance of order, and after John had begun preaching to the Hutus in the prisons, another family member was killed: his niece, Mado.

> As Bishop John tells the story, he is mindful of his audience. "Can you bear to hear how they killed her?" he asks. "Can you bear it with me?" He pauses tenderly before he begins the story, as if to give his listeners the choice of whether to journey into the pain with him or to turn back. Then, he speaks of the unspeakable:
>
> "They stripped her naked, used machetes to peel the skin off her arms from shoulder to wrist, gang-raped her, and cut off her head. They then raped her mother, killed her and her brother also." The story is too much to bear; but it is a story true to the experience of many of the people of Rwanda, where one out of every eight people was killed.[28]

Still, Bishop John felt called to forgive the Hutu people, and to preach the love of Jesus Christ to them. He knew he needed to let go, and to extend grace, in order to represent his Lord well. He explained that he couldn't wait for the pain to go away to forgive his enemy. Just as Jesus didn't wait to forgive until His pain was over. Bishop John and Deo Gashagaza (who also lost more than a dozen family members) used a program called the Umuvumu Tree Project to "prepare prisoners to repent and prepare surviving victims and their families to forgive." Deo had prayed and fasted for three days, asking God for strength to overcome his anger and depression. Both of these men now engage victims and their families, as well as offenders in this long process of reconciliation:

> In the prisons, Bishop John makes clear that he is not coming on behalf of prosecutors, who have a file against them. "That is not my area," explains the Anglican bishop. "That is the area of the government. There is another file I am dealing with, the divine file down there … the conscience file. The conscience has written a record of what you have done … So whatever the conscience is telling you to put right today, God appeals you to put right."

> Recently, after he preached that message in a prison in Ruhengeri, a prisoner came forward in tears. "Bishop," said the prisoner, "the file from the government prosecutors accuses me of having looted, having destroyed property, having killed people's cows, but the divine file, the conscience file, has a file much heavier than the prosecutors'." "Why? What is that file?" John asked him.

> "Five of us killed and attacked a family. We killed all of them. None of them survived, and nobody saw us. Nobody accused any of us, but the file you are talking about has brought me to justice. I'm sorry." Overcome by tears, the man could not continue. Later, he went back and "upgraded" the prosecutor's file to reflect God's file.[29]

As if that weren't inspiring enough, many of these men then ask for help to display their remorse and as a result, have begun building houses for their victims. An entire village of 60 houses were built. The Bishop explained,

"The hands once used to kill are now being used to bless...
The perpetrators who have repented are also gathering under
the same roof as their victims to praise and worship God.[30]

This picture of gathering under the same roof to worship God is an
image of the ultimate restoration of the Kingdom of Heaven. Our
Father, who is in Heaven ...Your kingdom come. Your will be done,
on earth as it is in Heaven.[31]

May we boldly invite the only One who *is* the perfect marriage of
justice and grace into our journey so that He might help us to live
freely and fully in the life of forgiveness. May we understand that
by allowing justice to take its course, we are simultaneously offering grace to all those in need – the ones who are hurting others and
need to be stopped, the ones who have been hurt, and need to be
comforted, and the ones who have been covering the sin, and need
to be enlightened.

Oh God, rain down Your justice and Your grace ...

We want to want to forgive.

Flying above the Fray

forgiving incalculable suffering

DISCUSSION STARTERS

1. Draw a picture of your personal journey of forgiveness.

2. You order your favorite Gingerbread latte at your local hang-out and pull up a chair with the Dixie-Chicks. The conversation stumbles into forgiving evil. You respond...

3. Have you ever been told to forgive too quickly? Has anyone ever said to you to just "get over it?" What do you think might be God's perspective on quick forgiveness?

4. Who is the most difficult person for you to forgive? What are you afraid might happen if you do forgive?

5. As you read the story of the people of Rwanda, what stirred in you? What's He saying to you about this whole forgiveness thing?

I will refresh the weary and satisfy the faint.
Jeremiah 31:25

We develop so many of the same symptoms
that plague our clients,
only we are better than they are at denial.
Jeffrey A. Kotter

As fish are caught in a cruel net,
or birds are taken in a snare,
so men are trapped by evil times
that fall unexpectedly upon them.
Ecclesiastes 9:12

The three most common narcissistic snares
in therapists are the aspirations
to heal all, know all, and love all.
John Maltsberger & Dan Buie

Praise be to the Lord, to God our Savior,
who daily bears our burdens.
Psalm 68:19

The most important strategy in your personal life
is to have one. (A personal life that is).
Karen Saakvitne & Laurie Pearlman

Hitting the Wall

vicarious traumatization

About the Eighteenth Mile

I (Tammy) teach a graduate course on trauma and as we trudge through the effects of abuse, about midway through the semester, inevitably several students begin to feel a little like Eeyore. They become a little pessimistic, overcast, and discouraged. During this stage in the semester, some students seem to take up residence in the southeast corner of the Hundred Acre Wood, an area labeled "Eeyore's Gloomy Place." Stomachs ache after devouring a few too many stories about abuse, perpetrators, and long-term effects.

Hearing about evil in "this dark world" is difficult because we were made for a different world. Sometimes, however, the difficulty for students is that they "get" class content all too well due to traumatic experiences in their formative years.[1] First-hand experience of traumatic experiences during formative years is common for veteran therapists as well. Several authors surveyed mental health professionals and found that 30 percent of therapists reported abuse histories.[2] It impacts me when my students hurt. I realize some of them may be considering personal abuse during their formative years in a deeper way for the first time. And even for those who don't know first-hand abuse, it's hard to listen to evil. Consequently, I work hard to make the class a safe place so that folks are able to acknowledge that look-ing at evil is difficult.[3] However, a few years ago, my semester felt ex-tra burdensome. My students were adjusting to the heaviness of the trauma material but I felt like *I* had loaded my belongings in a white and orange U-Haul truck and moved into Eeyore's Gloomy Place. In addition to the trauma class I was teaching a Social Problems course that contained a lot of heavy material, and in between, I was writing about shame, powerlessness, and betrayal; watching trauma movies; reading trauma books before bedtime (which I tell my students never to do as trauma literature is a poor sedative!); counseling some folks who were dealing with pretty heavy concerns; and to top it off, I was conversing with Hannah for hours a week about abuse.

I. H.I.T. T.H.E. W.A.L.L.

The term "hitting the wall" is often used by runners to describe what happens between the eighteenth and twenty-fifth mile of a marathon. About that time, a long-distance runner's legs stiffen and hurt, and every ounce of energy is required to lift each leg as each and every muscle screams, "Don't go any farther! Quit now!" The athlete's body is depleted of energy-containing fuel.

In similar fashion, as trauma therapists listen hour after hour to the incessant barrage of incest stories and tales of uncles, brothers, sisters, fathers, pastors, and mothers who molest innocent children and trusting teenagers, their bodies scream, "Don't go any farther! Quit now!" Too often, trauma therapists can begin to jog alongside survivors into the land of despair, leaving a trail of empty emotional and spiritual fuel tanks in ditches along the side of the road.

The common aftermath of a therapist hitting the wall has been coined vicarious traumatization (also called compassion fatigue). The word "vicarious" means participating in an event secondhand, and consequently, tasting the experiences of another. In the context of trauma therapy, an overload of secondhand experiencing refers to the cumulative effects on the therapist as a result of doing trauma work with survivors of abuse (e.g., child or adolescent abuse, domestic violence, rape).[4] It occurs among those working specifically with trauma survivors (e.g., trauma therapists, emergency medical workers, critical incident workers, rescue workers).[5] As caregivers bear witness to dark stories voiced from survivors of abuse, many caregivers eventually see humankind through a "trauma lens."[6]

Hitting the wall can be a valuable experience when it becomes a red flag which helps us recognize our limitations and the type of race we are in. Trauma work is most commonly a marathon and not a sprint. Therefore, in order for trauma caregivers to press on as they journey with survivors, pacing, refreshment, and restorative activities are vital. In this chapter, we discuss the unique effects experienced by caregivers who work with trauma survivors and we encourage regular rest times. We stand on the sidelines as trauma therapists run by and offer cheering support and spiritual Gatorade for parched throats.

Sunshine and Thunderstorms

During the writing of this chapter, I (Tammy) combed my library for a chapter on the JOYS of counseling. *The cupboard was bare.* I thought perhaps it was just my predilection toward selecting books focusing on the unsmiling side of counseling, so I did some research. But the well was fairly dry there, too. Hmm… the drought of chapters, books, or seminars on the satisfying moments in soul care says something, doesn't it? Nevertheless, over the years of working in a Christian counseling center, secular university counseling centers, a mental health center, and my present private practice, many rich moments and eternal times jump up and down for attention.

I remember the death of two children in a car accident that led their mom to counseling. The grief eventually brought up abuse issues as well. As we waded through the valley of the shadow of death, I got to talk with her about the Good Shepherd. Eventually, this woman, her husband, mother, and father came to church, and fell in love with *Yahweh Rophe: The Lord who Heals.* I am thankful for countless other divine days, too. An afternoon spent with a woman forgiving evils done to her, praying with a man as he relinquished his grip on pornography, witnessing a college student choose life instead of death, laughing together over new-found peace, leading survivors of trauma one step closer to Jesus… This is what I was made for. The grace and mercy of God have rained down during many encounters with His precious people.

At the same time, the journey with survivors includes difficult days. Just as marathoners may run in scorching heat, frigid cold, or drizzly days, caregivers face inclement weather. Survivor stories expose caregivers to the elements of human atrocities. Experiencing downpours of graphic descriptions of cruelty, violation, and savage assaults are part of the weekly forecast. Unannounced touchdowns of disclosures, memories, and flashbacks are common.[7] Sometimes, apparent aids in the storm, such as the legal or mental health systems, have leaky roofs and add greater frustration.[8] In their notable book, *Trauma and the Therapist,* Laurie Pearlman and Karen Saakvitne explain that vicarious traumatization mirrors posttraumatic symptoms that clients reveal.[9]

Over time, trauma can press down on caregivers like soaking wet clothes during a heavy rain. As the rains pelt us and the winds blow, our therapy boat is tossed to and fro and on certain days, we wonder, *Will the rain ever stop? And where is a safe harbor?* Perhaps these questions were on the minds of the disciples the overcast evening Jesus compelled them to get in a boat…

Water Walking

Jesus received the news that His cousin and beloved co-laborer was brutally killed by Herod. The ache on Jesus' heart must have been wide and deep. In response, He "withdrew by boat privately to a solitary place"[10] but the crowds were hot on his trail. Even though He sought a secluded place to speak with His Father, He had "compassion on them and healed their sick." And then, with a few loaves of bread and a couple of fish, He fed the crowd of thousands until they "were satisfied."[11]

Satisfied
 atisfied
  tisfied
   isfied
    sfied
     fied
      ied

It matters to Jesus that His people are truly *satisfied*.

After the feeding of the thousands, He "*made* the disciples get into a boat" so they could go without Him to the other side of the Sea of Galilee. The Greek word for "made" is "compelled." All-knowing Jesus, aware that a storm was ready to pound on the disciples, directed them, urged them to go *into* the storm. And a fierce tempest it was.[12]

After a whole night of fighting the winds and the waves, Jesus arrived on the fourth watch. The fourth watch of the night was between 3 and 6 a.m.

Note to self:
Jesus didn't come on the first watch.
Jesus didn't come on the second watch.
Jesus didn't come on the third watch.
On the pages of the book of Mark, we read that Jesus came on the *fourth* watch.

Jesus doesn't always come when we want Him to. If it is hard to get your mind around Jesus' delay, notice what comes next. Even after all that straining… Jesus *almost* didn't stop to rescue them. "He saw the disciples straining at the oars, because the wind was against them. Shortly before dawn he went out to them, walking on the lake. He was *about to pass by them*."[13] The Commander of the Coast Guard saw a sinking ship and He was ready to motor on by.

Perhaps Jesus was not going to stop because He knew the suffering of the storm would teach them what no dry days could do. Perhaps the storm was intended to reveal and remind the disciples of their desperate need for their Savior. We may never know until we get to

Heaven why He was about to pass them by or why He seems to pass us or our clients by during certain phases in the monsoons of life. But one thing we do know. When the disciples cried out, "immediately" Jesus said, "Take courage! It is I. Don't be afraid."[14] When they cried out, He didn't pass them by. Jesus doesn't always alter our clients' circumstances or our circumstances, but He responds to the cries of His kids instantly and He offers Himself—"It is I"—without a moment's hesitation.

In Matthew we learn that it was at this point during the battering of the storm that Peter says to Jesus, "Tell me to come to you on the water."[15] And Jesus says "Come."[16] So Peter got out of the boat and began to walk on water. "But when he saw the wind, he was afraid and, beginning to sink, cried out, 'Lord, save me!'" And then comes that word again: *immediately.* Immediately, Jesus reached out His hand and caught him.[17]

Trauma caregivers are asked to swing their legs out over the boat's side and walk on stormy waters. We have been called to listen to things that our ears were never meant to hear. But like Peter, we are created to keep our eyes fixed on Jesus, because when we focus our attention on the winds and the waves, we sink into the turbulent waters. Bearing the weight of trauma is something we are incapable of doing. The evil is too much, too big. This is one reason why it is absolutely necessary that, as caregivers, we "pray without ceasing," asking Him for the grace to see Him even in the tsunamis of traumatic events. Even when we can't understand.

Selfless Self-Care[18]

One of the ways we care for clients is by caring for ourselves.[19] We aren't talking about the North American obsession of *Give me another latte, new outfit, latest techie toy, pair of shoes for every occasion, it's-all-about-me* kind of self-care. Jesus gave up food, sleep, time away, and private retreats in order to love people.[20] So did His disciples. Yet at the same time, He called them away to quiet places, praying places, restorative places.

214

One of the ways trauma caregivers care for themselves is to follow Socrates' advice to "know thyself." However, this summons is not so that we can live in introspective land. Every caregiver has been hurt, disappointed, or grieved to one degree or another along the journey, and recognizing and wrestling with our woundedness can serve to free us up to serve others. J. D. Guy said it well: "The wound of personal distress may itself render the therapist more empathic, sensitive, and effective in treating the psychic pain of others."[21] Paul said it even better:

> Praise be to the God and Father of our Lord Jesus Christ, the Father of compassion and the God of all comfort, who comforts us in all our troubles, so that we can comfort those in any trouble with the comfort we ourselves have received from God.[22]

Pain can be a powerful teacher. Blind spots abound when we are unwilling to look into our rearview mirror.

> The psychotherapist who has never struggled with intense feelings of vulnerability or existential predicaments may have difficulty understanding (let alone feeling empathic toward) a client for whom these are overwhelming concerns. At the other extreme, the severely distressed practitioner who harbors little hope for happiness or well-being in his or her own life is unlikely to be encouraging of such hopes in the lives he or she counsels.[23]

In the movie *Neverwas*, Zachary's past was affecting his personal life and therapy practice. Zachary's father lived in bleakness, a life void of joy, and yet, paradoxically, his father penned a widely acclaimed children's book, brimming with hope, about a magical kingdom named *Neverwas*. Prescription drug addiction and depression ushered Zach's father to Millwood, a residential psychiatric institution. However, after his father's release, Zach found his father hanging from a tree.

Years later Zachary, a promising psychiatrist, left a prestigious position to work at Millwood in an attempt to unravel the confusion surrounding his father's sadness and suicide. In his new psychiatry role at Millwood, Zachary met Gabriel, a patient who had been in Millwood with Zachary's father years before. While Gabriel was not in touch with much of reality, in a fatherly way, he advised the troubled psychiatrist that he needed to find and wrestle with his life losses.[24]

Some of us caregivers spend a lot of time running from what we have lost. Running comes in many shapes and sizes. We may try to fix others when we couldn't fix family members during our formative years. We abuse chemicals. We stay so busy accomplishing by writing books, being a well sought-after speaker, renowned therapist… Often, these activities become attempts to muzzle our past, present loneliness, and heartaches.

There is a mixed bag of research on the subject of whether a personal history of trauma inclines a caregiver toward vicarious traumatization. Some research has revealed that caregivers who have a history of personal trauma are more likely to be weighed down by secondhand hurt,[25] while other studies have not found this to be the case.[26] It appears that we need more study in this area. However, based on my (Tammy's) observation of hundreds of counselors-in-training, how we are doing with "our stuff" affects how our clients are doing with "their stuff," regardless of what our stuff may be. And even if a caregiver has been given the gift of growing up in a healthy home, hearing trauma stories hour after hour will take its toll.

Of course this happens in areas other than trauma as well. Several months ago, I (Hannah) was sitting with more clients than usual who were struggling with disordered eating and body image. In the midst of this, I became aware one day that I had gone almost all day without eating and felt secretly victorious about this! It was a feeling reminiscent of an almost decade-past struggle. I immediately told a few close friends that I was feeling this way, and they lovingly spoke truth into my life and prayed for me. The Lord refocused my mind on where it needed to be, which equipped me then to love my clients more effectively. This experience reminded me of that classic, often-forgotten truth that *I am not bulletproof.* Many counselors may choose to specialize in an area from which they have grown personally, which is why I am privileged to walk with many clients who struggle with eating disorders. But it is important for me to remember that I'm one meal away from going back to the empty well of a love affair with food. I must be vigilant. And sometimes that means setting up some practical boundaries, like informing Pastor Laura (our beloved counseling center receptionist) when I'm "maxed out" on clients wrestling with eating problems. Or sometimes I ask her not to schedule some of my trauma survivors back to back. This is one of the ways I try to protect myself so I can care for God's people over the long haul.

We can learn a little about self care from dirt. Yes, dirt.

Friends of mine (Tammy's) live on a peaceful stretch of land outside the bulging metropolis of Winona Lake, Indiana. They have lots of tall trees, a brook, cattle, and a crazy white goat named Dudley who thinks he is a horse sometimes. Cindy and Joe rent out a piece of the property to a farmer during the summer months. Several years ago, we were sitting on the back deck and I noticed the corn growing wildly high. Confused, I asked, "Wasn't something else growing there last year?" Joe gave me the I-don't-know-what-you're-talking-about look. But after a moment of exceeding joy over my befuddlement, he said that soybeans grew in the same location the previous year. After I thought about the need to plan another get-back-at-Joe scheme, I asked, "Why the rotation of crops?" My farming friends explained that land needs rest. Corn removes certain nutrients from the dirt, so in order to keep from exhausting the soil, crops are alternated each year. Ultimately, the soil benefits from the rest and the crops grow better.

Similarly, hearing about evil hour after hour robs the body. One of the ways I am learning to replenish and pace myself is to rotate serious counseling, writing, and teaching hours with times of laughter. It is important that I plan periodic respites from the serious side by watching movies and reading books that are not trauma-related. I have grown to LOVE long belly-laughs with trusted friends, and of course, plan mischievous ways to one-up Joe! Time outs must be deliberate, as many well-intentioned folks cheer us on for our high-speed endeavors. This makes pacing difficult, but it is primarily our running around that can drown out the steady call of the Shepherd who wants to lead us by still waters.

Howard Macy explains,

> We fool ourselves, though, when we simply blame others, for often it is our own weakness that upgrades requests to the status of 'demands.' Surely some people do pressure us, but more often we twist our own arms with our pride, our lust for activity, or our insatiable need to please others. The things we choose to do are, by and large, worthy enough, but we must learn that we can be tyrannized as easily by the good as by first-rate wickedness. If we are to establish stillness in our lives, then we will have to say no to some good things and to some nice people in order to have it. Ironically, it is waiting for God, which we so seriously jeopardize with calendars crammed full, that can help us learn what to take up and what to turn away.[27]

A checklist to help us check some things off our life list may be helpful too.

Raceday Checklist

There are plenty of tips to help marathon runners stay in the race. Eat a proper diet, taper, don't wear brand new socks, trim your toenails (kind of makes sense, doesn't it?), drink plenty of water the day before the race... and the list goes on. It is important that we caregivers discover what helps us keep in the race and what brings rest to our souls. A study of 200 trauma therapists (mostly women) revealed that restorative activities for them included

discussing cases with colleagues,
    attending workshops,
        spending time with family or friends,
           traveling,
              vacation,
                hobbies,
                  movies,
                    socializing,
                      exercising, and
                        limiting their caseloads.[28]

Another study of 100 psychologists (mostly men) found that for them,

              taking vacations,
            engaging in social activities,
          emotional support from colleagues,
        friends and family,
      reading,
     consultation,
    workday breaks,
   nature time,
  seminars, and
safe places to process vicarious trauma.[29]

We would also add,
    connecting with godly people,
    expressing our creativity in our garden,
    card-making,
    painting,
    pottery,
    making God a priority in this dark world, &
    praying with a team of people.

Deliberately choosing restorative activities can lead us to lie down in green pastures. Trauma work is too heavy for us, and we cannot do it alone. Knowing our limitations is part of self-care. Rest may look different for different people, but rest we must.

In fact, do you know that some runners experience remarkably faster times when they take walk breaks? During a marathon, periodic pauses allow different muscles to be used, thus allowing greater endurance and, ultimately, improved race times. Jeff Galloway explains,

> When a muscle group, such as your calf, is used continuously step by step, it fatigues relatively soon. The weak areas get overused and force you to slow down later or scream at you in pain afterward. By shifting back and forth between walking and running muscles, you distribute the workload among a variety of muscles, increasing your overall performance capacity. For veteran marathoners, this is often the difference between achieving a time goal or not.[30]

Even if you have no plans in the next year to do a triathlon or a 26.2-mile marathon, the need for rest times, whether during long-distance competitions or long-term care-giving, is striking.

Rest is also a theme peppered throughout Scripture. God rested: "By the seventh day God completed His work which He had done, and He rested on the seventh day from all His work which He had done."[31] God offers rest to His people in His new covenant with them: "For I satisfy the weary ones and refresh everyone who languishes."[32] In the New Testament, we see Jesus, God's son, making similar declarations to His people and to us. He says radical things like, "Come to Me, all who are weary and heavy-laden, and I will give you rest,"[33] and, "If anyone is thirsty, let him come to me and drink."[34] Rest is important to God. Yet it so often seems unimportant to us.

I (Hannah) had a teacher in high school who used to say, "If you want to work hard at something, work at resting." I may not remember a lot of what my teachers in high school said but this idea has really stuck with me all these years. *Work at resting.*

Psalm 46:10 states, "Be still and know that I am God." Some translations put it this way: "Cease striving and know." So many of us have interpreted this to be a good-tip-from-God kind of verse.

Correction: These words are a command. This is God's way of saying, "Enough!" Rest isn't just some random gift that God offers because He's nice. He commands us to rest because He knows that we need it—*He made us to need rest.*

I am not good at resting, as a general rule. Busyness is probably one of the areas in my life I struggle with the most. I have hurt many that I love because projects and *something else* became more important. There's always *something else,* isn't there? I have hurt God more than anyone because of this. I'm sorry, Father.

What about you? When you have fifteen minutes to spare, do you feel a desperate need to fill it with a task? Welcome to the club. Brothers and sisters, let us consider that when we work without resting, we are working to meet our own needs, and we are writing our own stories instead of realizing that we are characters in His. And in His story, we must rest.

Work at resting.

If you think this is a common symptom just among our fast-paced, Western, technological, instant-gratification culture, that's not entirely true. Busyness did not start with cell phones and laptops and conference calls and deadlines. Busyness has been amped up by all the "time-saving devices," but struggling with overwork has been going since the Old Testament days.

Moses had a problem with overwork, and God taught him a lesson through none other than an in-law. We read in Exodus 18 that Jethro, Moses' father-in-law, came to visit him and was bringing Moses' wife and kiddos. The first few verses sound like a delightful family reunion of sorts, in which Moses and Jethro share with each other what God has been doing in their lives, and they rejoice with one another.[35]

And then *it* came about.

Literally.

221

"It came about the next day that Moses sat to judge the people, and the people stood about Moses *from the morning until the evening.*"[36]

Uh-oh.

"Now when Moses' father-in-law saw all that he was doing for the people, he said, 'What is this thing that you are doing for the people? Why do you alone sit as judge and all the people stand about you from morning until evening?'"[37]

Moses offers an excuse. Jethro responds:

> *"The thing that you are doing is not good.*
> *You will surely wear out,*
> *both yourself and these people who are with you,*
> *for the task is too heavy for you;*
> *you cannot do it alone."*[38]

Jethro proceeds to offer Moses a different way of doing things: first and foremost, to pray over these disputes, and also to teach and delegate this work to others that he can trust.[39]

For those of us who struggle with wanting control (all of us), this can be quite a difficult thing—trusting others to do the work in the way *we* want them to. But something comforts me about knowing that Moses was like me in this way and that he could learn obedience and trust.

May God give us the grace to respond as Moses did:

"So Moses listened to his father-in-law and did all that he had said."[40]

Dirt, Pestilence, Joe, & the Word of God

And finally, there is one more vital issue that we as therapists need to consider when running the race with trauma survivors.

Remember Joe, Tammy's friend who knows a lot about dirt? After Joe explained how crops need to be alternated each year to give the soil rest, he added another farming tip. He told me that planting the same seed in the same field year after year allows crop enemies to get a foothold. So rotating crops not only lets the ground rest, but it also thwarts disease and insect infestations.

The Enemy of this world is working to get a foothold into caregivers' lives. The pages of Job reveal that Satan is agitated and roaming,[41] while Peter refers to the Devil as a roaring lion who is on the prowl.[42] Paul points us to the *real* battle: "For our struggle is not against flesh and blood, but against the rulers, against the authorities, against the powers of this dark world and against the spiritual forces of evil in the heavenly realms."[43]

Like pestilence on a plant, Satan desires to gnaw away at the character of God and prompt us to question His goodness. The Enemy's sleight of hand trick is intentionally done to persuade us that God is the enemy. But Satan is the Deceiver (Genesis 3:1-5; John 8:44). And while Joe fights off plant pestilence through alternating crops, we must fight, too—but our fighting is of a different kind.

> We do not wage war as the world does. The *weapons* we fight with are not the *weapons* of the world. On the contrary, they have *divine power* to *demolish strongholds*.[44]

The Greek word for "weapons" doesn't refer to defensive-tactic weaponry. Instead, these are weapons designed to be used in an offensive attack, like a battering ram.[45] We demolish or "pull down or destroy"[46] the Enemy's discouraging ways through the forceful weapon of God's truth. The Greek word for "stronghold" is the idea of a military castle or fortress or "anything on which someone relies."[47] The more I sit with hurting and hurtful people, I am increasingly aware of my need for His Word to be hidden in my heart and on my lips when He leads me to speak into the lives of clients. After a day of abuse stories, I need His Word because it is mighty and strong[48] in providing comfort, strength, endurance, and perspective as well as attacking the lies of the enemy.

It is amazing what you can learn from dirt, bugs, pestilence, Joe, and the encouraging Word of God.

Running with Perseverance

The long and short of it is that "trauma is contagious"[49] and as Oswald Chambers once said, "the sheep are many and the shepherds few, for the fatigue is staggering, the heights are giddy, and the sights awful."[50] In our own strength, this marathon is too difficult, too long, too dangerous. Of this race Paul speaks into the trauma caregiver's soul:

THEREFORE, SINCE WE ARE SURROUNDED
BY SUCH A GREAT CLOUD OF WITNESSES,
LET US THROW OFF EVERYTHING THAT HINDERS
AND THE SIN THAT SO EASILY ENTANGLES,
& LET US RUN WITH PERSEVERANCE
THE RACE MARKED OUT FOR US.
LET US FIX OUR EYES ON JESUS,
THE AUTHOR & PERFECTER OF OUR FAITH,
WHO FOR THE JOY SET BEFORE HIM ENDURED THE
CROSS, SCORNING ITS SHAME, & SAT DOWN AT THE
RIGHT HAND OF THE THRONE OF GOD.
CONSIDER HIM WHO ENDURED SUCH
OPPOSITION FROM SINFUL MEN, SO THAT
YOU WILL NOT GROW WEARY & LOSE HEART.

Hebrews 12:1-4

Hitting the Wall

DISCUSSION STARTERS

1. What does it look like when you feel buried in the blizzard of trauma stories?

2. Who in your world gets what you hear on a regular basis?

3. What is restful for you? When is the last time you had a good belly laugh? What does "playful" look like on you?

At the profoundest depths of life,
people talk not about God but with Him.
D. E. Trueblood

True prayer is focused on the relationship
with our Father, not an answer.
The deepest prayer wants God alone—
all of God—more of God—only God.
Calvin Miller

I could not quiet that pearly ache in my heart
that I diagnosed as the cry of home.
Pat Conroy

Stretched Out
praying for survivors

Who Will Pray for Us Now?

AS FOR ME, FAR BE IT FROM ME THAT I SHOULD SIN AGAINST THE
LORD BY FAILING TO PRAY FOR YOU.

1 Samuel 12:23

My (Tammy's) mom died on Mother's Day evening. Barbara Schultz taught me more about talking to God than any storybook, seminar, or sermon. Conversing with God was the thread in the fabric of her life. She prayed with such fervor, like she was her Daddy's most loved child. As is true for praying people, my mom learned to call on God because she sensed her enormous need for Him. Her illness forced her to give up speaking to women's groups and teaching first graders and brought her instead to a quieter ministry—a ministry vital in its quietness. She spent her days praying for people.[1]

The night my mom died, I began calling loved ones to share the news of her death. I spoke to Lori, who knew my mom because of my mom's visits to Indiana. Lori, who does not know Jesus yet, frequently came by my home even when I was not there to talk with my mom. Lori knew that my mom enjoyed her, and often, after some conversation, my mom would ask Lori if she could pray for her. That's the way my mom loved Christians or non-Christians—

she prayed for them. So, the night of my mother's death, I recall Lori's grief-filled question on the phone, "Who will pray for us now?" My friend's query echoed the words lodged in the heart of my brother and me, and so many others who knew my mom—*Who would pray for us now like my mom?* She took seriously the words in the twelfth chapter of Samuel—she did not want to sin against the Lord by failing to pray for loved ones.

My mom's steadfast commitment to pray for others in grueling situations got me thinking—isn't that what clients need, too? Don't they need someone who will cover them in prayer and plead on their behalf? A graduate education in counseling is a hefty privilege. There are so many issues to learn about when it comes to people's problems and healing. However, if advanced education fails to teach caregivers to depend on God for life-changing healing from addictions, mental illness, and broken relationships, and instead, graduates become more reliant on themselves, well, this training is **FLAWED**.

Author Terry Wardle penned these words:

> Too many Christian counselors do not help clients meet the Lord during the counseling session. The conversation is limited to words spoken between the professional and the broken person. Granted this is valuable and an important part of foundational work. But if inner healing is to occur, the dialogue must shift from the caregiver talking with the client to a *broken person dialoging with the Living God.*[2]

Theologian and author Richard Foster explains, "If we truly love people, we will desire for them far more than it is within our power to give them, and this will lead us to prayer."[3] Survivors of abuse need far more than caregivers. Loving survivors through talking to God is the crux of our attention in this chapter.

Lives on the Line

You remember King Herod the Great? He was the guy who decreed that all the baby boys be slaughtered in Bethlehem and surrounding areas at the time of Jesus' birth. Like the words penned in Dante's *Inferno*, Herod had "no sting of conscience."[4] Herod the Great had a grandson named Herod Agrippa I who was like an unpinned grenade waiting to go off. He was a chip off his grandfather's old toxic block. Some grandparents pass on antique clocks, treasured pictures, beloved books. Herod passed on an inheritance of evil.

At the beginning of Acts 12, grandson Agrippa had "James, the brother of John, put to death with the sword."[5] This murderous act pleased the Jews and Herod liked riding the crest of popular approval, so he tossed Peter into a maximum-to-the-max security prison.[6] Since imparting justice wasn't on Herod's to-do list, it was only a matter of time before Peter would likely be executed, too. It was a hopeless situation. Then a three letter word[7] arrives on the scene in verse five. The word isn't worth many points in the game of Scrabble, yet it meant everything in Peter's life. **BUT**. "So Peter was kept in prison, but the church was earnestly praying to God for him."[8] The church knew Peter's life was on the line, so they resolutely prayed for him. The Greek word for "earnestly" is *ektenēs*, which translates as "stretched out" and "intent."[9] *It is a portrait of continuous and urgent pleadings before God.* It is what my mom did for me during the trials of my life. This is what caregivers are meant to do on behalf of survivors who are in prisons of fear and hate and in the shackles of addictions. Caregivers who love God were designed to do the kind of praying that gets that clients' lives are on the line.

And to our cries, God responds and does the impossible. In Acts 12:6-7 we read,

> The night before Herod was to bring him to trial, Peter was sleeping between two soldiers, bound with two chains, and sentries stood guard at the entrance. Suddenly an angel of the Lord appeared and a light shone in the cell. He struck Peter on the side and woke him up. "Quick, get up!" he said, and the chains fell off Peter's wrists.

Despite heavy chains falling to the floor, no guard heard Peter walk right out the prison door.

Peter's story reminds us that survivors need far more than what our education, experience, intellect, and empathy can offer. *They need the God of Heaven.*

Yet the lingering question that continues to bite its fingernails and tap its anxious foot in the story of Acts is: **What about James?** Weren't people earnestly praying for him, too? How come Peter was rescued and James wasn't? Why bother praying when praying seems like a game of Russian roulette?

We have walked with survivors who prayed as children for the abuse to stop, yet the abuse kept marching on. And then they ceased talking to God. We have also prayed earnestly for many survivors to stop going down certain destructive, dead-end roads, yet with their pedal to the metal, they 'keep on truckin'. God doesn't always do what we ask Him to do.

Leave it to Luke to place an answer-to-prayer story and an unanswered-prayer story side by side in Scripture. God doesn't avoid sharing chronicles that leave us wondering and wrestling. Frankly, we do not know why Peter was rescued and James was not. Maybe the events happened quickly without a lot of room to pray. Maybe people did pray for James but they prayed with little expectation or double-mindedly. Or maybe people did pray earnestly and God chose not to answer this request for a reason unknown to us this side of Heaven.[10] What is certain is that God calls us to pray. There are the Peters and James in this world with their very lives on the line, desperate for praying people.

What God does let us know is that evil King Herod Agrippa, who seemed so powerful at the beginning of the chapter, was "struck down" by an angel of the Lord and was "eaten by worms and died" by the end of the chapter.[11] We do know that someday, all those who seem to get away with evil acts on this earth will need to answer to the almighty God.

When it comes to prayer, there are some other things that we know to be true. We do know that we want to belong to the kind of church

Peter belonged to—the kind of church that prays all night long when needed. We do know that we want to be the kind of caregiver, professor, wife, daughter, husband, son, friend, sister, brother who prays our way through the prisons of life on behalf of loved ones. We do know that one of the reasons we are called to pray is because God answers prayer. But we also pray so that we might be able to submit and receive God's answer, whatever it might be.[12] We do know that true healing from sexual violations or from any other form of trauma will come about on the heels of recognizing we need God. Although much is shrouded in mystery about prayer, these are some things we do know to be true.

Coming Home

AND THE END OF ALL OUR EXPLORING

WILL BE TO ARRIVE WHERE WE STARTED.

T.S. Eliot

A few years ago, after my (Tammy's) class grades were submitted, house was cleaned, presents were bought, and bags were packed, I sat waiting in the Fort Wayne, Indiana, airport, waiting to go northward for Christmas. I'm a creature of habit in many ways. When I land in Chicago for a brief layover, I buy a Starbucks venti skim chai and I listen for the familiar accent of Winnipeggers milling around our departure gate. It is there I begin to hear the sounds of home. At the end of the two-hour ride, when the plane begins its descent, my eyes fasten to familiar sights of a snow-bitten city blanketed with warm memories. As soon as I can get through customs, I come bursting through the doors and a white-haired man with a broad grin on his face and arms open wide awaits me. "I'm so glad you are home," my dad says.

Perhaps if upon my Winnipeg arrival I received a tongue wagging about how long it has been since I had been back to the city I grew up in, or I was greeted with a "Not Welcome!" sign, then I might not want to come back to the place that was my home for so many years.

Still, a lot of us can't wait to get out of Dodge even when our spiritual homes are sweet and there is no place better. We want more. What we have is not enough. Like the prodigal son, we pack our bags and hit the road. We take off in our jet planes and are unsure when we will come back again.[13] Henri Nouwen shares that leaving becomes our inclination.

> Yet over and over I have left home. I have fled the hands of blessing and run off to faraway places searching for love... Somehow I have become deaf to the voice that calls me the Beloved, have left the only place where I can hear that voice, and have gone off desperately hoping that I would find somewhere else what I could no longer find at home.[14]

Eventually, though, many of us get tired of the pigsties in the distant countries we reside in: the trough of self-sufficiency, the pigpen of control, and the hovel of bitterness. Yet even when we "get" that there is an urgent need to talk with God, and even when we grow weary of our pigsties, sometimes it still takes us a long while to come home. Ambivalence clouds our homecoming.

> I love Jesus but want to hold on to my own independence even when the independence brings no real freedom. I love Jesus but do not want to lose the respect of my professional colleagues, even though their respect does not make me grow spiritually. I love Jesus but do not want to give up my writing plans, travel plans, and speaking plans, even when these plans are often more to my glory than to the glory of God.[15]

In the story of the prodigal son, it says he eventually "came to" his senses. He realized he didn't need to live with the pigs. He wanted to come home because he was made for home. Home was the place he belonged.

Even when our prayer relationship with God is "still a long way off"[16] and the only words available are "Help" or "Hey, God," with a broad grin and arms open wide, He comes running and says, "I'm so glad you are home."

It's good to arrive home. As we begin to settle into where we are meant to live, breathe, and exist with Him, dimensions change. He comes running and says, "I'm so glad you are home."

Futility of Formulas: HOW to Pray...

So what's the secret? What are the specific steps to praying for our clients? In other chapters, we have mentioned our veiled (maybe not-so-veiled) antipathy toward sure-fire steps. Yet if you walk through your neighborhood Christian bookstore, plastered on countless covers are rock-solid, take-it-to-the-bank pledges to freedom:

Five Steps to Better Self Esteem,
    One Week to an Obedient Adolescent,
        Ten Days to Mucho Money
            Minutes to a Massive Church[17]
                And the list goes on and on…

These pitches make us a tad uncomfortable. Ok, a lot uncomfortable. Don't get us wrong. Advice and steps can be very helpful. Throughout Scripture, advice is offered and steps are lovingly laid before us when it comes to confronting, building tabernacles, selecting elders, and even approaching our Father who is in heaven. When it comes to *praying for survivors*, we crave wisdom gleaned from seasoned men and women of prayer who know what it means to labor for others. We are most assuredly not saying praying for clients should be marked by willy-nilly petitions or that you should do whatever you want. BUT, there's something about one-size-fits-all prayer formulas to freedom that raises the hair on the back of our necks and elevates our uneasy thermometers.

In his book *Searching for God Knows What,* Donald Miller has this to say about looking for recipes in the Christian cookbook of life:

> [P]erhaps, formula books, by that I mean books that take you through a series of steps, may not be all that compatible with the Bible. I looked on my shelf at all the self-help books

I happened to own, the ones about losing weight… the ones about getting rich, the ones about starting your own pirate radio station, and I realized none of them actually helped me all that much. All the promises of fulfillment really didn't work… It made me wonder, honestly, if such a complex existence as the one you and I are living can really be broken down into a few steps. It seems if there were a formula to fix life, Jesus would have told us what it was…

My friend at Bible college believes the qualities that improve a person's life are relational, relational to God and to the folks around us…

To be honest, though, I don't know how much I like the idea of my spirituality being relational. I suppose I believe this is true, but the formulas seem much better than God because the formulas offer control…; The trouble with people is they do not always do what you tell them to do. Try it with your kids or your spouse or strangers at the grocery store, and you will see what I mean. The formulas propose that if you do this and this and this, God will respond. When I was a kid I wanted a dolphin for the same reason…

I have come to believe the sooner we find this truth beautiful, the sooner we will fall in love with the God who keeps shaking things up, keeps changing the path, keeps rocking the boat to test our faith in Him, teaching us to not rely on easy answers, bullet points, magic mantras, or genies in lamps, but rather in His guidance, His existence, His mercy and *His love.*[18]

Scripture is devoid of formulas, yet filled with the call to pray. And if that weren't enough, throughout the pages of our favorite book are pictures of praying people.

Prayer Pictures

Months after I (Hannah) was a degreed counselor, but far from knowing what on earth I was doing some of the time, I was scheduled to meet a female client. I didn't think we would connect. She seemed emotionally guarded and intelligent. Emotions I understand, but I was intimidated by her intellectual brawn and I worried that she wouldn't respect me and what I saw as my relative lack of intellect. I considered transferring her to an extra clever counselor. (How insecure could I be?)

One morning I was sitting with my journal, Bible, and coffee and I began to pray through my day that was ahead. I prayed specifically for each of the clients that I would be seeing that day. I prayed for *her*. Oh Lord, how can I help her? In my desperate insecurity before the Lord, it was like something happened: I was tapping in just a little bit to how *He* feels about her. It's like He was opening up my eyes and my heart to this vast ocean of love that He wanted to show her, and for now, He was showing it to me.

An idea came to me that, looking back, I believe was the prompting of the Holy Spirit. I went to the back room of my house and picked up the children's book *You Are Special* by Max Lucado and stuck it in my bag. *Really, Lord? You want me to read this highly intelligent woman a KIDS' BOOK?*

It was 3 p.m. and she came into my office. I don't remember all that she talked about that day, but I know we were discussing a handful of people in her life who had treated her poorly. There were quiet moments, and there were a lot of unanswered questions. Her head had been down for a long time, and she finally looked up for a moment and asked, "Does He think I'm special?"

You know where this is going. Within a few moments, I told her that this morning it had seemed strange but important for me to bring and read a story to her. She looked at the title, and offered a half-smile. I read to her while she cried. To this day, tears fill my eyes as I remember this moment. He was there. We were both listening

235

intently. And I think we both walked away feeling loved by Him, feeling so special to Him.

Was this moment not a prayer? Two of his daughters sitting in a room together, asking questions, feeling the pain of not having answers, and finally being willing to look up long enough to hear His response.

I learned that day in a most vibrant and colorful way that so much of my prayer time for my clients is about listening: listening to His heartbeat for each person. It's about being open to what He is up to in their lives and wanting to be a part of it.

Recently I heard one of my friends give voice to a thought that I can't get out of my mind. He said this: Imagine if you were going to have lunch with the most important person in the world. Would you do all the talking?

Prayer Penguins

FOR THIS REASON, SINCE THE DAY WE HEARD ABOUT YOU,
WE HAVE NOT STOPPED PRAYING FOR YOU.
Colossians 1:9

Remember when penguins got *really* popular? A few years back, during a cultural field experience trip to El Paso, Texas, and Juarez, Mexico, Tammy, myself (Hannah), and three other graduate assistants stayed at Tammy's Aunt Betty's house. On most mornings the five of us would get up early and go for a prayer walk. (Correction: Tammy is always up early. The four of us made ourselves get up to go with her.) On one particular morning, one of the girls was aching over a loved one in prayer and she began to cry. We all stopped, and the four of us surrounded her and prayed for her and her loved one. At the end of this special prayer time, as the cars whizzed by on this El Paso street, someone commented that our huddle made us look like a small group of penguins, standing close together.

And then it just sort of hit us. Penguins have to huddle close to physically survive bitter temperatures.[19] Likewise, believers need to huddle close together in prayer in order to spiritually survive.

When I (Hannah) began my graduate work at Grace College, I had just moved in with a couple of girls that I basically didn't know: Ashley and Laura. We were embarking on one of the greatest challenges of our lives, and the last thing we wanted was to make more friends. All three of us had collected some quality girlfriends in our days and were in serious romantic relationships at the time. Little did we know that God had a different idea.

It was in that semester that a particular class changed our lives forever: Ethics and Legal Issues in Counseling, taught by Tammy. Yep, that's right. *Ethics.* Ok, so it wasn't learning about the "duty to warn" or dual relationships that changed our lives. It was Tammy, and the way she prayed at the beginning of class each week. Not just a thirty-second quickie. It was like she was *going* to connect with her Father In this time, and she invited us along for the ride. I remember stepping out of the classroom one week because the *prayer time* had impacted me so greatly. Late in the semester, our classes were packed and this prayer time became shorter. Ash, Laura, and I, who had begun to pursue intimacy with one another despite our original plan, began to feel like something was missing. What was it?

PRAYER. We needed some Tammy-style prayer in our lives. So one night we decided that we were going to pray together. Out loud. It was so awkward and uncomfortable at first, but has become one of the safest places for us to be.

We've pretty much prayed together every week since then. And it has changed everything.

Laura moved. Then Ashley moved. But thanks to three-way calling, we almost never let a week go by without catching up and praying on the phone. We believe that prayer is the glue that keeps our friendship together.

We pray for each other's marriages, families, clients, and personal walks with God. We know that when we walk into the counseling room, we are walking into a spiritual battle for someone's soul, and we need each other, behind the scenes, praying.

If You Can Prayers

PRAYER IS AN EXPRESSION OF WHO WE ARE...
WE ARE A LIVING INCOMPLETENESS.
WE ARE A GAP, AN EMPTINESS THAT CALLS FOR FULFILLMENT.
Thomas Merton

There are too many days when I want to pray on behalf of the clients I care for but my whispers to God are meek and timid, filled with doubt. On these days, when evil looms large on the horizon, the list of clients mesmerized with meth is long, and client relationships have run amuck, my prayer life frequently mirrors the words of the father of the demon-possessed son, who said to Jesus, "*If* you can do anything for him."[20]

Despite this father's little faith, Jesus, the best of counselors, responded with words that elicited faith rather than a rebuke. Jesus did not stomp out the smoldering wick that was waiting to be ignited.

"If you can?" said Jesus. "Everything is possible for him who believes."

So the father responded, "I do believe; help me to believe more, Jesus."[21]

Maybe you see his prayer as a giant contradiction, but we think it is a great prayer.

> Help me to believe more, Jesus.
> Help me to believe more, Jesus,
> that you are the healer of my clients.
> Help me to believe more, Jesus, that without you,
> all my "brilliant" counseling is just words..
> Help me to believe more, Jesus,

that you love my client more than I could ever love her.
Help me to believe more, Jesus,
that you will never love me more than you do right now.
We do believe. Help us to believe more, Jesus.

Prayerless Striving

Do you want to try something radical? We mean really radical.

`Radical: definition: marked by a considerable departure from the usual or traditional.`

There was an entry in Philip Yancey's thought-provoking book *Prayer: Does It Make Any Difference?* by a lawyer who worked with Bishop Desmond Tutu in South Africa. He spent his time investigating genocide in Rwanda, as well as in twelve other countries, specializing in human trafficking, slavery, illegal detention, torture, and helping widows and orphans. He wrote about how prayer became the lifeblood of their work.

> From the very beginning, I believed we needed reminders that the work of justice is God's work, and that God is on our side in the battle for justice. Otherwise, we might get overwhelmed by the enormity of the evil we confront. I feared a slide toward what I call *prayerless striving*. So every day our entire staff begins with thirty minutes of silence, in which we encourage prayer and meditation. We don't talk, we don't work. We sit at our desks and pray. In addition, every day we get together at eleven o'clock and spend thirty minutes praying for each other and the cases we're involved in. Our staff members often report this is the most meaningful part of their day.[22]

So we got to thinking, imagine if caregivers who worked with survivors began the day with thirty minutes of silence, and later in the day, spent thirty minutes praying for other caregivers and the clients they see. Imagine all the productivity we would be losing. Imagine all the eternal productivity we would be GAINING. Imagine!

Stretched Out
praying for survivors
DISCUSSION STARTERS

1. If you were to draw a picture of the time you spend being with Abba, what would it look like? What are the colors and textures in this picture?

2. Is there a Peter or James in your life on whose behalf He is wooing you to be stretched out in prayer?

3. What is your "If you can" prayer? Tell Him. He'd love to hear.

4. Would you be willing to stop your day and spend thirty minutes praying for your clients?

God conquers not in spite of the dark
mystery of evil, but through it.
Ravi Zacharias

Joy is a mystery because it can happen
anywhere, anytime, even under the most
unpromising circumstances, even in the
midst of suffering. Even nailed to a tree.
Frederick Buechner

A joyful heart is good medicine.
Proverbs 17:22

Most people live dejectedly in worldly
sorrow and joy; they are the ones who sit
along the wall and do not join the dance.
Soren Kierkegaard

You turned my wailing into dancing;
you removed my sackcloth and clothed me with joy.
Psalm 30:11

Break forth, shout joyfully together,
you waste places of Jerusalem;
for the Lord has comforted His people,
He has redeemed Jerusalem.
Isaiah 52:9

a shot of

H$_2$O

Powerful, gentle, life-giving, destructive, colorful[1], and transparent are adjectives that paradoxically describe water. Its sensations soothe, refresh, energize. Water surrounds and is in us. We drink in the sounds of water flowing through shiny silver faucets, trickling brooks, waterfalls, waves, fountains, RAIN. It's the background noise for sleep. Lengthy, hot showers, bubble baths, hot tubs bring comfort. We dive, splash, score goals, ski, float, paddle, race, surf, soak in rays beside it. Deep-colored creatures that make water their dwelling place mesmerize onlookers.

Drip,
   Drip,
      Drip.
Gushing. Downpours.

Seashores and cloudbursts share the scent of summer. Deep, shallow, wide, winding, puddles. Shades of azure, teal green, light blue, our reflection, His reflection. I AM the Living Water.[2]

As we tour the sounds, sights, and scent of water, we realize there are not enough pages to contain the beauty, mystery and the depth of description.[3] It is the same with the vast sea of joy. We are eager to splash wildly and other times, sit quietly on its shore. Glimpses of joy are captured in unplanned moments, in the midst of tears yet for many of us, this thing called joy remains elusive and unfamiliar.

Maybe you have skipped ahead to this chapter. Perhaps you needed a break from the heavier side of this book and the heavier side of life. Or maybe, just maybe, you are clinging to the promise that joy comes in the morning after a long night of tears.[4] Father, may the words of this chapter lead us to refreshing pools of waters. May we have the courage to dive in with abandon.

Oceans in Elevators

OH, GIVE ME BACK MY JOY AGAIN;
YOU HAVE BROKEN ME—NOW LET ME REJOICE.
Psalm 51:8 NLT

"We need a shot of joy," said my friend who was planning a women's retreat. "It's been a hard winter for many of the women." I (Tammy) sat still listening as if there were a rare butterfly before me, not wanting it to fly away, as her yearning for a weekend of joy fluttered. When she asked me if I was willing to speak about joy, my emotions were mixed. Like a captain of a ship spotting a lighthouse in a storm, I was drawn in the direction of this topic. Yet, I reminded her of the themes that take center stage in my counseling, speaking, and writing…suffering, angst, walking with travelers through the valley of the shadow of death. I told her that people don't usually make appointments with me to talk about the joy they are experiencing! Her gracious invitation remained steadfast.

It hadn't occurred to me to swim free-style, full-throttle after joy. I too often wade where joy is only marginal. Yet while sipping a chai with my friend, memories flooded my mind. When I was a little girl, there were times when I would cup my mom's sad face in my hands and pray that God would take her depression away and never, never let it come back. But her depression returned. Perhaps that's part of the reason I work with sad people. Still, when her depression lifted, my mom knew a kind of joy I have rarely seen in others. She knew both the interior of sunless days and beams of light. So, the retreat topic made me thirsty for more than a shot, and instead for an ocean of joy where others and I could swim.

With hopes of deep waters before me, I asked God to give me glimpses of joy and the visual capacity to see. Then, a call from my sister-in-law came. My brother's health had continued to decline. He had lost a hundred pounds and now he had a blood and heart infection. My dad was flying to be with him and I needed, wanted, to go too. So I went, and on Valentine's Day, my dad and I spent the morning with my brother in the hospital. Dad began reading to my brother and I left for a brief walk around the still pond adjacent to the Brandon, Florida, Regional Hospital. As I rode the elevator, my soul was concerned, quiet, tender, contemplative, but before I reached the ground floor, five middle-aged African American women got on. One woman appeared to be the patient and the remaining four were visiting friends. These women were drenched in broad grins and generous laughter and their high spirits poured into that elevator. One woman looked at me and said, "Happy Valentine's Day" and another woman turned to me and said, "I love your earrings." I felt like a little girl at a party who batted open the piñata and treasures rained down on me. Their cheer buoyed me up.

They walked on down the hall, arms around their patient friend, giggling and talking. And then I realized God had placed the ocean shore smack-dab in this undersized hospital elevator. I bounded down the hall, "You ladies are cool waters of joy," I voiced. More smiles and I was surrounded by a group hug. The woman who was a patient looked at me intently and said, "It is joy from Jesus." I told her that I already knew that and they were an answer to prayer as I had asked my Father for sightings of joy and their splashing about got me wet! Gratitude in the shape of tears filled my eyes.

Maybe you have a yen for what these women have too. Not the gilded and perfumed but inwardly lacking kind-of joy to which many

Christians accede. Rather, a thirst for the absurd kind of joy that refuses to break in hospital wings, prison cells, and the hearts of survivors. We are not talking about a celebration of evil abuse but a radiance that shimmers even in the midst of the vilest circumstances. How is this possible? Let's dive in and see.

In

GOD HAS MADE ME FRUITFUL *IN* THIS LAND OF MY SUFFERING.
Genesis 41:52 [Emphasis added]

I love digging in the dirt. There's nothing like ripping out those incessant weeds who are bullying my flocks, gaillardias, daisies, poppies, and black-eyed Susans. When those weeds are out of there, my perennials flex their muscles and show their stuff. Digging deep in Scripture brings me delight too.

> **Question:** Recently, when I put my foot
> on the edge of my shovel
> and pushed down,
> what do you think I unearthed
> when it came to the circumstances
> surrounding the New Testament guys
> who wrote about joy?
> **Answer:** There was a lot of dirt
> going on in their lives too.

Paul wrote Philippians and used the word joy 16 times in four short chapters, more often than any other letter in Scripture. But this apostle wasn't lying on the sands of the Mediterranean Sea, sipping raspberry iced tea as he penned these words. Rather, he wrote this joy treatise while he was in a bleak, Roman jail, chained to guards 24/7, awaiting a trial by Caesar. Think about it. What would you write about if you were unfairly doing time? In this grim setting Paul wrote, "Always be full of joy *IN* the Lord. I say it again—Rejoice."[5] Paul wasn't saying that prison was great. But somehow joy washed over Paul *IN* the middle of his jail cell.

Along comes the apostle John. When he wrote the book of Revelation, he was ninety years old, living in exile on the Island of Patmos. John, one of the original twelve disciples, one of the close friends of Jesus, knew he was going to face death soon.[6] Yet, in a Patmos prison, he painted pictures of heaven, where joy will never end. He wrote to buoy the despairing Christians living in the time of Nero that there is a better world coming. A place where evil will reign no more.

> Then I saw a new heaven and a new earth…I saw the Holy City, the new Jerusalem, coming down out of heaven from God, prepared as a bride beautifully dressed for her husband… It shone with the glory of God, and its brilliance was like that of a very precious jewel, like a jasper, clear as crystal…The city does not need the sun or the moon to shine on it, for the glory of God gives it light, and the Lamb is its light.[7]

And then there is the time Jesus spoke about joy. He and His men left the upper room after they shared the Passover meal, a lamb. Jesus would pray throughout the night, sweat drops of blood, be arrested by a mob led by Judas and experience an agonizing crucifixion. But just before this brutal death, on His trek to the Garden of Geth semane, Jesus explained to His disciples the way to have *complete* joy.[8] When I read the word complete, I ran as fast as I could to my Bible Dictionary.[9] The Greek word is *plēroō* which means to be filled to the brim, to be liberally supplied.[10] Jesus didn't promise a Dixie cup worth of joy. He promised a whopping, 64-ounce, Super Big Gulp kind that is running over the brim of the container.

On the road to the cross, Jesus made the promise that complete joy is possible during the month of April, when the grape vines were in bloom. He said, "I am the vine; you are the branches. If a man remains *IN* me and I *IN* him, he will bear much fruit."[11]

Gardening 101 tells us that the vine is the whole plant – stock, roots, branches, and leaves. When Jesus says, "I am the vine; you are the branches," He wants us to realize that we were made to be attached to Him. We are part of the vine. If we were sitting on a Chicago street, having a Jamba Juice with Jesus, He might say:

Don't try to make it on your own.
    Hold tightly to Me.
        Embed yourself in Me.
            Sink yourself into Me.
                Be rooted in Me.

In other words, cling to Me like a rider on a runaway horse.

When I (Tammy) head out to the garden, my indoor cat Jack, clad in his big fur coat, loves to tag along. Most of the time, he wanders close behind me or he sits in the wheelbarrow shade, his favorite UV ray protector. But from time to time, Jack hears a bird, or sees something rustling in the neighbor's bushes and before you know it, Jack is gone. I get a little nervous thinking he could wander into the street because, while cats are exceedingly clever, Jack isn't street-savvy. Jesus gets concerned when we stray, as well. He knows we are prone to wander and we get in trouble when we roam. Perhaps that is why He says eleven times in the fifteenth chapter of John to "abide" or "remain" *In* Him. But He doesn't only tell us to remain close to Him so we will steer clear of trouble or so that we bear lots of fruit. "I have told you this so that my joy may be in you and that your joy may be complete."[12] Jesus let us know that our proximity to God impacts our revelry.

Still, there's something else. Remaining involves more than being conscious of God or maintaining a connection. The language in Scripture that depicts our relationship with Him is shamelessly romantic. In a heart carved on an oak tree in the forests of heaven are the words, "I am my lover's and my lover is mine."[13] If you gathered all the affection of the most passionate lovers in history, all their tenderness, kindness, devotion, affinity, and romance would only be a vague image of God's passionate desire for you. Joy draws breath in this knowing.

So what's the gist of joy? Absent of the carnival ride and cotton candy variety of joy that is sold on many a church street corner, this brand is weathered, deep, and it ripples outward. This genre of joy is aware of the upthrust of Providence—knowing that God brings good out of rubble. Joy remembers that the searing pain of prison, acid-like-words, and soul-bruising blows by abusers, do not equal an uncaring God. Joy stands near her God because there is nowhere else she would rather be than in the arms of her Lover. This joy is not unacquainted with sorrow. There are days joy has tears streaming down her cheeks. Red eyes and tissues in hand yet seized with the truth that someday, joy will be flavor of the day, every day. Joy is rooted *In* the black soil of truth so that the weeds, torrential downpours of life, and pruning are designed to make us look more like Jesus, the master Gardener.[14]

Two men in prison, one man on the way to the cross, were wooed by God to pen or voice words about joy. Seems like most often, the price of admission to this class of cup running over joy is harvested *IN* the land of our suffering.

Red Colored Joy

Poneloya is a beach community on the west coast of Nicaragua. It was our destination on the last day of being with the Nicaraguan people before coming home. The students were acting in a play for the teenagers in the village on the topic of God-type self esteem that's not so much about self and instead about being one of His kids.

While the students were acting, it was my (Tammy) job to hand out red t-shirts to the smaller children who were playing close by. We brought large army bags full of hundreds of t-shirts. Bags and bags of red because of a little mistake. Our Grace College mission statement is *Character, Competence, and Service.* These words were supposed to be rainbowed on the back of the t-shirts. *Supposed to be* is the operative phrase. Somewhere along the line, the logo got printed: *Character, Competence, and Character.* Oops. There must have been a rush on Character this year. Anyway, because of this printing mistake, hundreds of t-shirts were stuffed into bags that made their way to Poneloya.

As I started handing out the t-shirts, children began crowding around me. All these children, speaking in Spanish, with desperate looks on their faces, were begging me for a shirt. And the crowds kept coming. Pretty soon, moms with lots of children came. Teenagers came. Hundreds flocked around this non-Spanish speaking woman passing out red t-shirts, who was trying to tell the people that there were enough t-shirts for everyone. Quite a scene…a middle class, American woman trying to convince impoverished people that there will be enough. In English no less. Cultural Sensitivity 101 here I come!!

A brand new t-shirt may not be a big deal to most Americans, especially in a foreign language and with an incorrect logo to boot. But in Poneloya, it was like I was passing out hundred dollar bills. New t-shirts or new anything did not come along that often. These gifts were clutched tightly as the recipients smelled them, breathing in the fresh aroma of new.

Before long, there was a sea of red in Poneloya. All these brown-skinned people were wearing Grace College t-shirts. It was one of the most beautiful pictures I have ever seen. A mistake at a Midwestern American Christian college clothed throngs of Nicaraguans that day.

I continue to digest the lessons my Nicaraguan family taught me during our time spent there. We witnessed many without shirts, shoes, or running water. Still, among some of the Christians, we witnessed contrasts side by side. Revelry amongst the ruins. Rejoicing amidst the rubble.

Without excuse for our American excess, I witnessed Nicaraguan Christians who reflected Paul's words while he sat in a prison. "I have learned to be content whatever the circumstances. I know what it is to be in need, and I know what it is to have plenty, I have learned the secret of being content in any and every situation, whether well fed or hungry, whether living in plenty or in want. I can do everything through him who gives me strength."[15]

Confession (well, sort of): The interpretation of this passage has often been a burr under my saddle. I have heard people recite these verses who have little awareness of hurt and anguish. People who have refused to wrestle with pain and have used this verse as whitewash over dark fences. In contrast, authentic joy is bereft of amnesia. Joy in the resurrection of Jesus came only after He went through the hell of the cross. I think that this was one of the reasons I was so drawn to my Nicaraguan friends. They lived both delight and devastation, yet their moods failed to vacillate like the stock market because they refused to focus on their lack without seeing the bigness of God.

Devoid of denial over his difficult circumstances, rather, Paul, in the midst of prison, kept his eyes on Him. Circumstances that could have determined his mood and made his prison existence misery did not. Frankly, I have a long way to go when it comes to keeping my eyes on my vertical God versus my horizontal circumstances. I too often fail to put my spiritual glasses on and I grope around in the dark. Sometimes though, when I allow Him to lift my chin so my gaze is on Him, I catch glimpses of the red t-shirt kind of joy worn in a little town in Nicaragua one January afternoon.

Not Like

My thoughts are NOT LIKE your thoughts.
Your ways are NOT LIKE my ways.
Just as the heavens are higher than the earth,
so are my ways higher than your ways
& my thoughts higher than your thoughts.

Isaiah 55:8-9

Several decades back, two sisters in their fifties and their eighty-something-year-old dad spent their time helping Jews escape Hitler's execution spree. But they got caught and landed in a concentration camp. During their time in that hell on earth, their dad became ill and died in a lonely hospital corridor and was buried in a pauper's grave. Eventually, these two sisters were sent to Ravensbruck where prisoners were called by their numbers instead of names, starvation thrived, roll call roared at 4:30 a.m. and late prisoners were savagely beaten, and physician visits required women to strip in front of male guards. Then, one sister died. The camp was filled with ceaseless suffering. Shortly thereafter, out of the blue, a clerical error happened. Corrie Ten Boom was released one week before all women her age were killed.[16]

Professor and author Lewis Smedes once said that, "only the heart that hurts has a right to joy." Corrie Ten Boom experienced ongoing atrocities and yet when she spoke to crowds after her release, her words were bubbles floating upward and outward, like the carbonation of joy. She told her audiences, "faith is like radar that sees through the fog, the reality of things at a distance that the human eye cannot see." She "got" suffering and she "got" joy, experiences that seem like curious companions.

I once asked a carpenter friend about his favorite tool, the one he cannot live without. The nail gun was his reply, the younger brother to the hammer. When it comes to matters of the kitchen, many master chefs explain that the chef's knife is their favorite tool. You can slice, dice, chop, and mince faster than a speeding bullet.[17] But when it comes to matters of a joyful heart, it seems, the furnace of affliction is God's most frequent tool. "See, I have refined you, though not as silver; I have tested you in the furnace of affliction" (Isaiah 48:10). Corrie Ten Boom understood this. She lived extreme forgiveness as a rejoinder to extreme wickedness and she maintained this was her secret to a life resonating joy.

C.S. Lewis wrote in *Mere Christianity,* "If we really want to learn how to forgive, perhaps we had better start with something easier than the Gestapo."[18] C.S. Lewis' advice is wise. Said another way, in the words of Mountain Climbing 101 first tenet: Don't start at Mt. Everest. Start at Indiana-size mountains (well, they are not really mountains per se, but you get the idea). It seems Lewis was suggesting that we need to develop forgiveness muscles, starting off with lower altitudes and less treacherous topography. But occasionally, God directs us to higher altitudes, like in the case of Corrie, who started out forgiving the Gestapo and the members of the Third Reich. Letting go of her hate changed everything.

If Hannah and I had power like God for a day, would we allow kids to be sexually abused? *Not likely.* Abuse is evil. Yet, what God allows and the way God thinks is not the same as we think. His thoughts aren't even like the way we think. And His methods, His agenda, and the way He works to bring good *out of* evil in our lives, well, it is not like our ways. Not even in the same ball park.

Corrie could not, in her own strength, take off her backpack of hate that was loaded down with the memories of those who committed barbaric cruelty to her sister, father, other loved ones, and herself. Yet as she asked God for His strength to forgive, she was freed up for God's bigger and higher plans. After being released from prison, this single, Dutch clockmaker in her fifties, spent the rest of her days travelling to prisons, churches, schools, sharing the message that swimming the rivers of joy involves letting go of our hate. Imagine the bigger and higher plans He has waiting for us if we relax our grip and let the hate float away. More joy than we ever dreamed.

Daddy's Little Girl

Joy is so hard to describe, but it is one of those things that you know when you see it …and if you're well-acquainted with sorrow, you can spot fake joy from a mile away, can't you? It seems that somewhere in the recipe for joy, a heaping spoonful of identity really brings out the true taste. Knowing who you belong to in the deepest places of your heart brings healing, identity, and true joy. Brennan Manning tells this story about a woman he met from the midwest after speaking at a retreat. A woman who finally gets a taste for true joy:

> I will never forget a retreat experience years ago…On one particular night, the line extended well beyond midnight and after finishing, I went straight to bed, not even taking my clothes off I was so exhausted. About three o'clock in the morning, I heard a rap on the door and a squeaky little voice;
>
> "Brennan, can I talk to you?"

I opened the door to find a seventy-eight-year-old nun. And she began to cry.

"Sister? What can I do for you?"

We found two chairs in the hallway and her story began.

"I've never told anyone this in my entire life. It started when I was five years old. My father would crawl into my bed with no clothes on. He would touch me there and tell me to touch him there; he said that's what our family doctor said we should do. When I was nine, my father took my virginity. By the time I was twelve, I knew of every kind of sexual perversion you read about in dirty books. Brennan, do you have any idea how dirty I feel? I lived with so much hatred of my father and hatred of myself that I would only go to Communion when my absence would be conspicuous."

In the next few minutes, I prayed with her for healing. Then I asked her if she would find a quiet place every morning for the next thirty days, sit down in a chair, close her eyes, upturn her palms, and pray this one phrase over and over: Abba, "I belong to You."

It's a prayer of exactly seven syllables, the number that corresponds perfectly to the rhythm of our breathing. As you inhale – *Abba*. As you exhale – *I belong to you.*

Through her tears she agreed: "Yes, Brennan, I will."

One of the most moving and poetic follow-up letters I've ever received came from this sister. In it she described the inner healing of her heart, a complete forgiveness of her father, and an inner peace she'd never known in her seventy-eight-years. She concluded her letter with these words:

A year ago, I would've signed this letter with my real name in religious life—Sister Mary Genevieve. But from now on, I'm Daddy's little girl.[19]

Do You Hear What I Hear?

Let me make one thing crystal clear. I (Hannah) don't sing. I mean, not the kind of singing with a mic, on stage, on the radio, or in a back alley for that matter. People would run for the hills with their hands pressed over their ears if I did. But joy was made to be expressed.

If you check out the majority of contemporary song lyrics, they're about a guy who is smitten by a girl or a girl who is love-struck with a guy who rescues her from a lonely heart. Of course, you can express a lot of other emotions by way of song. From street music to country western, classical, and jazz, all deliver their emotions and messages that were made to be conveyed. Songs express something from the depth of who we are and how we are feeling in a way that spoken words cannot.

How do you decide what music to listen to? Perhaps it has something to do with your ... joy? I don't know about you, but when I come to realize that everything I'm listening to is sad and depressing, it's the obvious signal that there is something going on inside me. Something has robbed my joy; something is not at peace. The music I'm listening to tells me something about my joy in a way that nothing else can.

But it may not be time to change the CD just yet ... if you realize something is going on inside that is robbing your joy, it's not all bad to listen to music that validates your pain and gives your sorrow room to breathe. Do not be so quick to just listen to something that may just bring some "cheer." Scripture says, "Like one who takes off a garment on a cold day, or like vinegar on soda, is he who sings songs to a troubled heart."[20] Forced cheer, like fake joy, is not helpful. Often it is all about the timing.

I grew up in a musical family. All my family members (except me) play an instrument well, and have great voices. One of our favorite pastimes is sitting together as a family engaging in song. Whether singing Christmas carols before we open presents, or folk songs around a bonfire (including some of dad's originals), we love the history of song that brings us together! Even *happy birthday* has its own six-part harmonious flair!

So when my dad wrote me a song for my eleventh birthday, and then later added a verse and sang it on my wedding day, it touched deep wells of joy that are hard to express. This wasn't just Daddy singing me a lullaby until I fell asleep, although he had done that plenty of times. This was years of history with a person. This was the man who, once after I had an awful break-up, just held me and prayed for me, and later got out his guitar and led the family in a rendition of "When you're down"[21]: a cheesy-sounding moment, but truly perfect in its timing. They were simple and truthful words to soothe a heart tempted to believe lies, sung by people who have lived out those truths.

When you're down
And there's no one to be found
Just look around,
He's standing by.

He loves you so, He loves you so
Yes He does, my Lord loves you so.

When your foe whispers in your ear
and he tells you there's no one to hear
Just stand your ground,
Refuse to fear, just refuse to fear.

Start to praise the Lord, start to praise the Lord
Bless His name, bless His holy name.

He loves you so, He loves you so
Yes He does, my Lord loves you so.

So when that same man walked me down the aisle at my wedding, danced with me, and sang to me, there was a deep joy – buried in the same places with my deepest sorrows where he had also been present. Remember when we prayed for this day, dad? Remember when you danced with me at a wedding two days after that one break-up and whispered to me through my tears that this day *would* come?

That's a lot like my Heavenly Father, also. A dad who meets us in the pit, in the dark and grimy places – and because He has gone there with us, we can stand on top of the mountain with Him too, sometimes even looking up at Him from the valley and feel joy just to know He's there. And when we remember that He is there and that He is good and has always been there, we start to remember the Song.

New Song

Giving voice to song is a theme between God and His chosen people. Remember those Israelites fleeing Egypt and miraculously getting across the Red Sea only to watch the bad guys be swallowed up in the body of water they had just walked through? Chapter fifteen of Exodus is like reading out of a hymnal – it is practically all song! Moses and the rest are thrilled at what God has done, and you get the feeling when you read it that they just can't help themselves but rejoice![22]

So maybe it's no surprise when Moses is at the end of his life, and the Lord instructs Moses to write a song[23] and teach it to the Israelites as a witness to what God has done. God knows that once in the promised land and once they find comfort, they will stop crying out to Him and they will turn to other gods, but there will always be this song.

And the song will haunt them. Many years down the road when God's people have committed spiritual adultery and left Him behind for other gods, God condemns their unfaithfulness and yet still offers restoration. He speaks through His prophet Hosea, "Therefore, behold, I will allure her, bring her into the wilderness and speak kindly to her, then I will give her her vineyards from there, and the valley of Achor as a door of hope. *And she will SING there as in the days of her youth, as in the day when she came up from the land of Egypt …*"[24]

God had not forgotten the song they used to sing, and He wanted to hear it again. It sounds as though God had missed her voice, the voice of His bride, His people. And He misses our voices when we stop singing. And He longs for the day when He hears it again, and even more for the day when, face to face, it is known that the voice can never fade again; the music never has to die. He has even let us know in advance that the song awaits: "And they sang *the song of Moses*, the bond-servant of God, and the song of the Lamb, saying, 'Great and marvelous are your works, O Lord God, the Almighty; Righteous and true are Your ways, King of the nations.'"[25]

What About Now?

When you are walking in the hot coals of life, it is certainly hopeful to remember that heaven's cooling oceans are awaiting us. But does that mean that our joy gets put on hold until then? Look at Tamar – she lived a desolate life, right? How can you find joy in the waste places, the desolate, dry, thirsty ground?

Somewhere along the line, we have developed a picture in our minds that joy is a feeling that comes and goes, that joy is demonstrated in smiles and good cheer. That may be true sometimes, but if joy is anything of the substance we've written about thus far, the stuff that is developed in the trials of life, it can not possibly be a fickle emotion and it certainly doesn't require a bright affect.

Sometimes joy is simply … gratitude. And gratitude is a perspective, a stance on life that chooses to see things, to really notice the value of an object, or a person. Gratitude is not denial, but an acknowledgement that God has a plan that we can not see right now. When I do not know when the check is coming, it is being grateful for the things I can afford. When I am sick, it is talking about it honestly, but stumbling into gratitude when I realize I can still put one foot in front of the other.

For most, gratitude begins as a discipline. It is a choice to dedicate some portion of my time to acknowledging what is good. A couple of years ago, I (Hannah) was taking a class on the topic of prayer[26] and given an assignment – I don't remember what the number was exactly – but we had to keep a list of things we were grateful for every day. I have not stopped that assignment – not because I'm that much of an overachiever, but because I realized that it provided me with something I desperately needed. I gained a perspective shift in which I was seeing the blessings of God and feeling uniquely loved by Him even on the days that were really hard. Here are some of my favorites:

1. The wind and the way it felt on my tear-stained face.
13. Pink toenail polish & silver hoop earrings: the simplest things that make me feel oh so feminine.
21. Dropping gas prices.
22. Hooded sweatshirts.
57. Sundays.
58. Toasted turkey & cheese sandwiches.
80. Having enough time.
92. Being invited to write a book.
93. Crushed ice.
106. A night off – here's to sitting on my kitchen counter while eating supper, spilling my yummy coffee on a good book, and hearing the sound of a dishwasher in the background.
127. Being set free.
159. HEALING. Thanks for picking out that place in South Bend – the sights, the sounds. Thanks for walking with us through that park. Thanks mostly for showing me your sad heart – the heart that hurt deeply for the LITTLE GIRL who learned how to be seductive to get noticed, to get "love." A fresh new wave has begun, hasn't it? Thanks, Father!
212. Sexuality.
216. Long talks at Steak & Shake with a good friend, a plate of cheese fries, and a clock that does not own us.

248. Best Meal EVER: Salmon Picatta at the Grand Lux Café in downtown Chicago.

324. Every winter that I survive the roads.

335. Being able to be ugly with Him. Gross hit-the-steering-wheel-and-weep-and-swear prayers.

426. Slogging through the Betrayal chapter.

482. AC in my car – it's been YEARS since I've started a summer this way! Thank You!

531. The rain that poured just as Brian got on one knee …

594. Tea on a cold day.

640. Sleeping in on a Tuesday.

715. The leaves are raked. Free at last!

723. Three hours in an emergency room with my love, eating pop-tarts and watching HGTV & political news.

But enough about the way He loves me … how does He love you? Let us count the ways! The Enemy wants to keep us blind from the blessings of God because when we can't see the ways He's loving us, we start to think that maybe He just doesn't … and our joy gets robbed. So I dare you to start a list …

Drip …
  Drip …
    Drip …

(The sound of God's blessings being poured out on your life).

A Shot of Joy

DISCUSSION STARTERS

1. What would it look like for you to dive into the ocean of joy, even in your land of suffering?

2. What are the words of the new song that God is writing in your life?

3. Would you be willing to take a shot at a gratitude list to God? If so, how about if you tell God five things you are thankful to Him for... right now.

GOD CAN TAKE ANY MESS, ANY MISHAP,
ANY WASTAGE, ANY WRECKAGE, ANY ANYTHING,
AND CHOREOGRAPH BEAUTY & MEANING FROM IT.
Mark Buchanan

LET ME KNOW THEE, O LORD, WHO KNOWEST ME:
LET ME KNOW THEE AS I AM KNOWN OF THEE.
O THOU THE VIRTUE OF MY SOUL, MAKE THY ENTRANCE INTO IT,
AND SO FIT IT FOR THYSELF, THAT THOU MAYEST HAVE AND
HOLD IT WITHOUT SPOT OR WRINKLE. THIS IS MY HOPE…
Augustine, Confessions, Book X, Chapter I

I WILL MAKE RIVERS FLOW ON BARREN HEIGHTS,
& SPRINGS WITHIN THE VALLEYS.
I WILL TURN THE DESERT INTO POOLS OF WATER,
& THE PARCHED GROUND INTO SPRINGS.
I WILL PUT IN THE DESERT THE CEDAR
& THE ACACIA, THE MYRTLE & THE OLIVE.
I WILL SET PINES IN THE WASTELAND,
THE FIR & THE CYPRESS TOGETHER,
SO THAT PEOPLE MAY SEE & KNOW,
MAY CONSIDER & UNDERSTAND,
THAT THE HAND OF THE LORD HAS DONE THIS,
THAT THE HOLY ONE OF ISRAEL HAS CREATED IT.
Isaiah 41:18-20

the great Exchange

Date Palms

Sleeping Beauty, the Ugly Duckling, Pinocchio, the childhood sagas of characters transformed—a woman trapped in deep sleep becomes a loved princess, an outcast animal becomes a stunning swan, and a wooden boy becomes real. Movie land is mesmerized by rags to riches and hoodlum to healed epics too. Broken-down horses, cars, toys, and boxers morph into something different, something better. Audiences whoop and holler over the protagonists' ability to prevail over suffering and grasp depth of character. Perhaps if they can persevere, and they can change, maybe we can too.

Sometimes against-the-odds stories even take place in the world of trees. For example, many years ago, dense 80-foot-high date palm forests marched across southern Israel[1] but eventually these towering forests virtually vanished. Nevertheless, during an archaeological dig in 2005 on Masada[2], three 2,000 year-old[3] date palm seeds were unearthed. Someone got a bright idea and soaked the seeds in warm water. Growth hormones and enzyme-rich fertilizers were added to the mix and then these ancient seeds were planted in an Israeli kibbutz. Expectations were low, but five weeks later a small shoot elbowed its way to the surface. A two-thousand-year-old seed is en route to becoming a Judean date palm tree.

Maybe you are thinking the transformation of a two-thousand-year-old seed into a tree is novel and maybe even remarkable but I'm not in botany class so **B.I.G D.E.A.L!** But if you can keep following the bread crumbs just a little longer there is a metamorphosis just around the corner. You see, in ancient Israel, the date palm was a staple due to its shelter, shade, medicinal properties, and concentrated food energy source.[4] Palm trees symbolized grace and elegance to the Hebrew nation.[5] Not coincidentally, the daughter of King David was given the Hebrew name for date palm: Tamar. Princess Tamar was destined to provide shelter, shade, and nourishment to those who came near. She was designed to stand tall in grace and elegance, but instead she was raped and lived a desolate life.

Hannah and I have lived with the story of Tamar for several years. Her bleak life has plagued our thoughts and prompted us to ponder. Scripture does not provide a front row seat to the story of her life after she was raped, but what we do know is that Tamar is not alone. There are countless survivors of sexual trauma who become pinned down in desolate. Why do some get stuck after the abuse while other survivors break free and live fruitful lives?

For some, life includes extra measures of grueling. But like buried 2000-year-old seeds that come bursting to life in the form of graceful Judean date palms, God loves to move into a world of sorrow and bring the broken hearted beyond desolate and into meaningful and buoyant living. Against the backdrop of torment, He shows Himself to be the Healer of the hurting.

This chapter is not about cosmetic changes or quick fixes. The motif taking center stage in the hospital wards of life is an extreme makeover from the inside out. For transformation ushers us into the land of beyond. As Arundhati Roy poignantly stated, "Not only is another world possible, she is on her way. On a quiet day, I can hear her breathing."[6]

Extreme Makeover

MERE IMPROVEMENT IS NOT REDEMPTION.

C.S. Lewis

Years ago my dear friend Kimbo and I (Tammy) planted a garden in her outside-the-city-limits back yard. We were so ambitious. We dreamed of all the money we would save on the delicious vegetables we would grow. We talked about the zucchini casseroles we would make and how everyone would rave about what good cooks we were (without anyone knowing the main ingredient!). Well, we weren't so good at watering, and we kind of forgot to weed a lot. Consequently, our plot didn't *exactly* look like the cover of *Better Homes and Gardens,* but all was not lost. Along the way, I learned a valuable lesson about composts.

Kimbo had this big bin where the family dumped lawn clippings, small sticks, soft plant clippings and kitchen scraps. And then, after some time,[7] rich soil-like material called compost appeared! When you think about it, this garbage-to-compost extreme-makeover is kind of mind-blowing. Throw-away organic material (things that were once living) becomes transformed into a medium that helps vegetables (when you water them), flowers, and grass grow! That's what God does too. He loves to take broken-down people who are deemed garbage and transform them into something beautiful. For a glimpse of God's brand of extreme makeover, let's revisit Tamar's story and a passage in Isaiah.

Ashes, Ashes, We All Fall Down

TAMAR PUT ASHES ON HER HEAD...

2 Samuel 13:19

...TO BESTOW ON THEM A CROWN OF BEAUTY INSTEAD OF ASHES...

Isaiah 61:3

When I (Tammy) was eleven years old, we received one of those middle-of-the-night phone calls. Our 100-year-old downtown church, where my dad pastored, was burning to the ground. A man who hated the Jews lit a match and set our church building aflame. A sign in the church yard read, "Welcome to our Jewish friends," the source of this man's red-hot rationale. Overnight my dad's sermons and books, our grand church organ, wooden church floors and pews, the place of much ministry and memories were converted to ashes.

Wearing ashes in the ancient world was a visual picture of a soul devastated by the fires of life. It was an expression of violation, deep sorrow, grief, repentance, humiliation, [8]or a symbol of the death of someone or something. Tamar put ashes on her head in place of a covering a princess would wear.[9] Ashes expressed death in a way words were found wanting. Yet, paradoxically, it is in the ashes of life where some of God's finest works come forth. In Isaiah 61:3, we read that God wants to comfort all who mourn, "and provide for those who grieve in Zion--to bestow on them a crown of beauty instead of ashes."

There is a time to grieve.[10]At times, we need to wear our grief, like Tamar's ashes, when we have been violated.[11] Yet, at some point, God gently says, "You give me your scars, the evil done to you, your pain, hurt, the ashes you are wearing, and I will give you something exceedingly better." To the grief-stricken, the God of the Universe extends a "crown of beauty." Instead of a life of desolation and abuse as our identity, to all those who know Him He offers a crown of declaration: You are My daughter. You are My Son. Children of the King of Kings you have been given a royal lineage no one can rob. As speaker and author Beth Moore wisely said, "If you are not royalty, He is not King."[12] Despite Amnon and every other perpetrator's actions that bring great grief, He asks us to relinquish the ashes of self-hate, the ashes of Turkish Delight, and the ashes of bitterness. Like a trapeze artist who swings high above the ground and releases the security of the bar in his hands to fly toward the next, there comes a time when He wants us to emerge from the gloom and let the ashes of abuse go. While freedom from the infernos of abuse is not a promise extended, in the midst, God offers the Great Exchange.

Tears

(TAMAR) PUT HER HAND ON HER HEAD AND WENT AWAY,
WEEPING ALOUD AS SHE WENT.
2 Samuel 13:19

...THE OIL OF JOY FOR MOURNING...
Isaiah 61:3

As Tamar left the one who violated her, she not only wore ashes and a ripped royal robe, she wept aloud. Psalm 102:9 says, "For I eat ashes as my food and mingle my drink with tears." Her tears seemed endless; it is the kind of sobbing the violated understand. And to the cries of Tamar and all others who know the angst of mourning, He offers a third exchange. Give Me your wailing so I can bless you with the oil of gladness.

In ancient Israel, anointing someone with oil was the customary treatment of an honored guest.[13] To the Tamars of this world, He saves the most favored seat with the placecard designation, "Most Honored Guest." As the music starts, He invites those who have worn ashes, degradation, and mourning to put our dancing shoes on so we can swirl on the floor with our King and as Lewis Freedman said, "You can't be afraid of stepping on toes if you want to go dancing."[14]

Ripped Robes

(TAMAR) TORE THE ORNAMENTED ROBE SHE WAS WEARING...
2 Samuel 13:19

...THE GARMENT OF PRAISE FOR THE SPIRIT OF HEAVINESS...
Isaiah 61:3

As Princess Tamar exited the "house of her brother"[15] clad in her "richly ornamented robe,"[16] she ripped her royal robe. To the daughter of King David and others who know sexual violation, God offers new clothing and the garment of praise. How is it possible to swap torn attire donned with ashes for royal robes and singing? It is humanly impossible. So God does for us Tamars "what we cannot do for ourselves."[17] He asks us to release the familiar outfit of outcast and pauper so He can dress us in fine, regal linens and He gives us a new song.[18]

One thing is certain: This is not a quick costume-change style of transformation. This kind of redesign comes only by the touch of the Great Physician who speaks the language of transformation and offers the touch of freedom. The same Physician who allowed the violation to occur delivers a rock solid guarantee that He would never have allowed the scorch of the flames unless He can bring beauty.

Instead

...THAT THEY MIGHT BE CALLED TREES OF RIGHTEOUSNESS,
THE PLANTING OF THE LORD, THAT HE MIGHT BE GLORIFIED.
Isaiah 61:3

Someone once said that the most important part of a sentence follows the "but." We can have beauty, new garments, and the oil of gladness, *BUT* the offer of an extreme makeover is companioned with a choice.

It is not beauty **AND** ashes.
It is not the oil of gladness **AND** mourning.
It is not a garment of praise **AND** a spirit of despair.

In the wisdom-filled book of Isaiah, He uses the word "instead" and asks us to make Him an exchange. The Hebrew word for instead is *tachath*, which means "in place of, in exchange or return for."[19] A trade is waiting in the wings.

I have a 1995 Honda Accord named Betsy. Over the years, each of my cars has been dubbed "Betsy" once they get *that* age. Come to think of it, people might start calling me Betsy any time soon. Betsy has been a good ole car. She carried me over the highways and byways during my doctoral program and she has brought me back and forth to Winnipeg many times. Yep, Betsy has served me well, but lately she has been wearing down. Her clutch has seen better days and her get up and go has, well, you know, got up and went. The time is coming that I need to trade Betsy in for a newer model, but it is unlikely she will be worth that much in the deal.

There is an exchange waiting for the Tamars of this world too. Still, it may be difficult for some of us to trust that God is not a shady shyster waiting with a lemon in the used car lots of life. And while our ashes, rags and tears are heart-rending, they are familiar. Stepping into the land of unknown is a vulnerable pilgrimage, but He calls us to trust Him and to choose to let the familiar go.

On the days we choose to trade, He paints one more picture in verse three of Isaiah 61. "They will be called oaks of righteousness, a planting of the Lord, for the display of His splendor." You are no longer a brittle bush, blown about by the winds of this world. You are a mighty oak tree. I planted you. I water you. I pour out my warm sunshine over you. And when people see your brawny branches and the shade you offer, they will know that this spindly little twig turned mighty oak tree, well, only God could have done that. This is possible because another tree held the bloody body of the Son of God for you and me.[20]

Out of the devastating rubble and ashes, God loves to take the shattered and make us strong.

Magnum Opus:
A Great Work, especially a Literary or Artistic Masterpiece[21]

THE PARADOX IS INDEED THAT NEW LIFE
IS BORN OUT OF THE PAINS OF THE OLD.
Henri Nouwen

So when the Master Artist takes a torn and tattered canvas and splashes paint with colors from the sunset and shades from the sea, what does the exchange of beauty for ashes, joy for mourning, and garments of praise for a spirit of heaviness look like? Join us for a walk through the art gallery halls of transformation and enjoy our friend Adam, one of His remarkable magnum opuses. We include the *before* canvas so you would see the staggering transformation in the *after* artwork.

> When I met my neighbor he was in his driveway playing with WD-40 and some matches. Eruptions of fire seared the sky as my eyes went wide with wonder. I was immediately enamored both with the fire and much more so with the young man who I had the deepest hopes of befriending. He attended church on a more than weekly basis. When he said I could hang out with him, my nervous and awkward body language in no way communicated the somersaults and leaps of joy my heart was professing. The more I got to know him, the more I felt like the luckiest kid in the world.
>
> We would often race to the nearby mower shop. Out of breath but full of life, we would purchase soda-pop for fifty cents. He often bought me my favorite kind and we shared much laughter as I guzzled orange, bubbly sweetness. It was in the backyard that he taught me how to play football as a first and second grader which began in me a love for the game. His marks upon my young life were indelible as I grew up to be the captain of the football team in high school and remain, to this day, a vociferous fan of the game.
>
> He had a deep voice and whiskers and he taught me so many things: *he was so much like a man, but I had never met a man like him.* I wanted to grow up to be him.
>
> My mom and dad trusted him. His mom and dad trusted him. His church esteemed him.
>
> If anyone had something bad to say about him, "he would never hurt anyone…" my tiny voice would have professed, "He is my hero!"
>
> Then he began to watch pornographic films with me while masturbating. Soon he began to require that we act out the

movies. I did not have categories within my mind to define the depth of violation that I experienced, but I knew something had gone wrong in the world. It began with exposure and fondling and progressed toward increasingly invasive and damaging behavior. So too did the verbal and emotional abuse have a progression. He started by telling me that I was the only kid in the neighborhood who he could share those sexual encounters with because I was the only one who could keep them secret. As time progressed and his violation of my body became endemic in our relationship, he dehumanized me by making me eat dog food. Other days he would threaten that if I told anyone his dog would tear me to shreds. He threatened the lives of my parents and sister if I ever told anyone. He snapped rubber bands in my open eye. I learned to cooperate with the sexual abuse so as to avoid violent sexual assault which only further perpetrated the message that I was to blame and buried the secret under landfills of shame.

The last day I was within touching distance of him was a day that he became so enraged that he placed me in his garage and pointed a gun at me. He drug me upstairs and told me to undress. While he left the room I crumpled on the floor to my knees in his room naked and prayed a simple but passionate prayer, "Help." He entered the room and the phone rang. He ran down the hall to answer the phone and I threw some of my clothing on and scrambled home.

That was the last day that Adam was sexually abused, but nightmares went on for years and anger boiled up as people around him failed to respond properly to his violation. Eventually, he found "life" in what seemed like a beautiful sexual relationship with a woman – what an irresistible salve to a broken heart and a broken body: the Turkish Delight of consensual sex. Unfortunately, this type of sex is like placing ashes on our head and ripping our robe. It's a visual way of saying, *My soul is devastated and desperate in a way I can't describe, and I surely don't deserve God's design for sex in my life, so I'll just rip that idea to shreds and wear this one instead.*

For a time, Adam lived a desolate life. He dressed in the ashes of sexual sin and ripped robes. His tears "were his food day and night, while they said to him all day long, 'Where is your God?'"[22] And then one night on his college campus while crossing a field to the library, he heard God's offer of exchange … I (Hannah) recently asked our dear friend to share more about the exchange that God offered him that night on the field, and how he has lived out his Beauty for Ashes. He said it like this:

> Because of Jesus - I am no longer a slave to bitterness and hatred.
>
> Because of Jesus - I was set free to reach out to people with love instead of hiding as a prisoner within self-erected walls of shame and self-contempt.
>
> Because of Jesus - the song of my heart sings of hope rather than despair.
>
> Because of Jesus - I am no longer afraid to sleep and dream at night.
>
> Because of Jesus - I am no longer afraid to be alone with my thoughts and memories.
>
> Because of Jesus - I was stirred to contact and offer forgiveness to my perpetrator.
>
> Because of Jesus - I was offered the courage and conviction to speak to hundreds of people about the unmitigated, unadulterated, indisputable, irrefutable hope that is found in Him.
>
> Because of Jesus - I am training to become a child psychologist.
>
> Because of Jesus - I am a child of the King.
>
> Because of Jesus.
>
> Because of Jesus.
>
> *Praise be to Jesus.*

And because of Jesus - on the days when shame creeps back in, when fears begin to overwhelm, when lies and half truths begin to distract, when unbelief and cowardice cause me to squirm, when I of all people need to remember and practice the very things I have been inclined to preach, when the stain of sin bleeds dark and foul...there is forgiveness and grace and hope in abundance for this wayward man.

The type of trauma Adam experienced leaves many others bitter, brooding and steeped in sin: the ingredients for a desolate life. Instead, Adam is a quiet and humble man, wise beyond his years. A young man, with an old soul, who lives to tell others about the large love of Jesus.

Strong in the Broken Places[23]

THERE ARE SOME THINGS YOU LEARN BEST IN CALM,
AND SOME IN STORM.
Willa Cather

You can learn a lot about healing the next time you get an orange glow-in-the-dark cast for your broken arm. Almost immediately after the bone in your arm breaks, your body tries to put itself back together again. That's because our bodies were designed to fuse together after broken bones. And with proper care, the healing site can sometimes become even stronger than before the break.[24]

Broken hearts can become even stronger after the trauma too.

I (Tammy) spoke in an impoverished country about beauty-instead-of-abuse-ashes. Following the seminar, a woman (we will call her Sally) in her forties waited, shifting her weight from foot to foot, like a kid outside the principal's office. A heaviness was inseparably wedded to her like an illness that would not heal. In a hushed voice, Sally asked if we could talk. With the help of a quiet room and a translating friend, she voiced a secret that had never found its way to words before that day.

When Sally was eleven years old, as she sauntered homeward one evening, down an unfrequented road, she passed an abandoned building where a group of teenage boys were milling about in the distance. Before this young girl's fear burst into flames, the teenagers grabbed and dragged her into the deserted building. Weeping through each word, she recalled a brutal rape on a cold cement floor and sounds of harsh laughter in the background. The raping voices proclaimed her dead and then disappeared. Yet, Sally survived.

Over the years, hardships continued to grow higher like piles of brick in a construction site, but somewhere along the way, Sally came to know Jesus. With conviction in her voice and tears streaming down her face, she told me Jesus did not allow her to die that night in that broken down building. Sally was now working in a crisis pregnancy center and her fervent passion was to help save the lives of babies. What came next in our conversation is difficult to put words to. It was like a collective-watershed-God-moment that washed over and drenched us. We realized that her devout passion to protect unborn babies arose out of the ashes of her rape as she knew what it was like to be left to die and she knew what it was like to be given the opportunity to live.

That day this dear woman cried buckets of tears. Where was God when Sally was raped? In Genesis 28:16, Jacob spoke the words, "Surely the Lord is in this place and I did not know it." Jacob was never out of God's presence, but for a time his surroundings shouted God's absence. Surely the Lord was there in the midst of Sally's darkest hour. Without ironing away every wrinkle and placing suffering neatly in its proper drawer so that the mysteries are smoothed away, He was there. He was there in the anguish over the evil done to Sally and His Son was interceding on her behalf.

In the midst of Sally's great grief, as the truth of God's love and purpose for her life embedded into the substance of her soul, she started smiling not only with her mouth but with the look in her eyes and the upright angle of her shoulders. She resembled a yellow poppy opening wide to the sun as she grasped the truth that He never left her. For a sizable part of her life, she breathed the belief that she was the sum total of that discarded and crumpled little girl left to die on a carpetless floor. That day, in the tiny room, God impressed upon her being that He never left her and He had purposed her to protect little ones from evil. This was her life calling, birthed in her painful past, growing into His redemptive future. That day, as He was mending the wounds of a little girl, He was making this beautiful and courageous woman stronger in the broken places.

Confession Time

Unfortunately, some people never get to experience the *strong in the broken places* part of the story.

For several years, Hannah and I have struggled with the final words in Tamar's story. "And Tamar lived…a desolate woman" (2 Samuel 13:20). Absent of any happily ever afters, bereft of corner-turning events, devoid of an upbeat ending, Tamar lived the rest of her days in desolation.

Several times in the process of writing this book, I (Hannah) have dreamed about what Tamar's life could have been like. I wonder about the people she would have ministered to, the children she would have nurtured. I wonder about the people whose lives were a little more windswept and exposed because they didn't get the shade they were supposed to from this one Royal Date Palm: Tamar. But sadly, like Tamar, there are a myriad of children, teenagers, women, and men in Central Asia, Nicaragua, South Korea, Mexico, Ukraine, and in the pew sitting next to you on Sunday morning who know too well, the first hand effects of rape and child sexual abuse. Tamar's story holds up a mirror to our world where sexual violence is not infrequent. A world where many are desolate. This truth should cause us to become enraged and saddened. But if that is all it causes, we have missed the central point.

On a plane heading toward France, I (Tammy) was reading *The Gospel of Ruth* by Carolyn Custis James. She penned words that I underlined, circled and then starred. My evident markings prompted the man sitting next to me to comment that it must be a very important point that I was reading. And he was right! Carolyn was writing about the life of Ruth but the truth she penned applied to Tamar as well. She explained that while stories in Scripture can tell us volumes about the character of one of God's people, these life stories are even more importantly designed to tell us something about the character of God. "Whenever we study God's Word, our main quest is always to discover what he is telling us about himself. If we marginalize God or make someone else the focal point, we will always miss the main message of the book. Always."[25]

For several years, we had a difficult time seeing more than the desolation of Tamar's life. We empathized with her sorrow, her aloneness, her shame, her anguish, and the contemporary plight of many worldwide. But we were missing something central. Our eyes were fixated on the trauma of Tamar's life and we were blinded from seeing more.

Eugene Peterson once said, "The gospel offers a different view of suffering. In suffering we enter the depths, we are at the heart of things; we are near to where Christ was on the cross." Tamar stood near the suffering of Jesus. Tamar's story painted in distressed hues, reveals her need, our need, and your need for the resurrected Savior. Tamar's story was never designed to be a stand-alone story. Her story was intended to make us aware of our hunger for something more. For someone more.

Please don't hear us say that we are in any way minimizing the trauma of abuse. The events of Tamar's story were never meant to be trivialized or forgotten. They were meant to be embraced and understood, but they were not meant to be the end of the story. Similarly, the crucifixion of Jesus without the resurrection of Jesus is an unfinished story. It is incomplete and bereft of the main point. We were not designed to live forever in the day after the crucifixion. The crucifixion is indeed a central chapter in The Story. However, the Crucifixion and the Resurrection are not either/or stories. They are both/and stories. So too, each of us was designed to be a partaker in stories of sorrow *and* stories of redemption. We were made for both stories.

Dreaming...

So what about you? As we have wondered about Tamar, we have also been curious about you, the reader. What could God possibly do to redeem the abuse, the shame, the addictions, and the desolation of your own life? What would you look like Beyond Desolate? And for those who care for a multitude of survivors, you who are weary on many a day, what does it mean for you to live beyond desolate in the caring journey? What would happen if you would allow Tamar's story to be your rallying cry to step into the sadness of those who have been ravaged so that we will learn something about the character of God who is well acquainted with our grief and the One who longs to be our Redeemer?

Don't read over this too fast. We're serious. Close your eyes and dream for a moment. Think BIG. Dare to dream for a moment or two. What might God want to do? How could He use your rags and your rage and turn them into something glorious and glad?

You see, Tammy's full name is Tamra. It's the same word that "Tamar" comes from: Date Palm: a place of shade and nurturing. Tammy could have stayed in the desolation of her own life: the secrets, the shame of abuse, the fear, and the desperate attempts to look like none of those things. But God called her to the Great Exchange, and it was an offer she couldn't refuse ... for very long. I have watched up close and personal as Tammy lives beyond desolate imperfectly but she walks in the direction of living the life for which she was made – the life identified in her name. She has certainly been the shade on a scorching hot day in my life for several years, and I know I am not the only one who would say that. Many of us think of her as "mom" and we know life just wouldn't be the same without her. God has used her to call me, and so many others, to live beyond desolate, to exchange our ashes for beauty, and she has given us an example of what that looks like, living it out day after day. We thank you. Our parents and spouses and children thank you. Because you accepted the offer, our lives have also been changed.

Still, while we are grateful for the ongoing transformation work in Tammy, the testimony on her lips is not centered on her and the same goes for my (Hannah's) story. And to this end, Tamar's story included on the pages of Scripture is a desperate signpost pointing in the direction of a suffering Savior who died for the desolate. Tamar's story serves as one more reminder about how much we need Jesus in this world where suffering happens every day. Jesus is the hero in her story and the hero who wants to bring good out of evil and hope out of the darkest night in your life too. A Savior who has no desire to erase all your wounds, but a Savior who has intended a life beyond desolate for you.

So, are you dreaming big yet? He dreams so much bigger for us than we ever could. So go for it.

He wants to exchange …

Your **depressing** playlist for a dance! mix

Your **FETAL POSITION** for cartwheels

Your **NIGHTMARES** for the sweetest of dreams

Your **INSOMNIA** for deep rest

Your **HARD HEART** for one that is Alive!

Your **fat jeans** for your party shoes

Your starvation for a **feast**

Your RAZORS for a **TRUMPET**

Your salty tears for sweet laughter

Your **bitter conversations** for life words

Your Running shoes for Slippers

Your CONSTANTBUSYNESS for a hammock

Your isolation for D-E-E-P C-O-N-N-E-C-T-I-O-N

Your empty tank for one that OVERFLOWs

Your LONELY HOUSE for HIS HOME...

Your HeLL for His Heaven

I AM MAKING EVERYTHING NEW!
Revelation 21:5

the great Exchange

DISCUSSION STARTERS

1. What does desolate look like in your life?

2. What's it like to be in the hands of the Master Surgeon? What is the texture and feel of His hands?

3. Describe some time when God has taken some of the ashes of your life that have been swept to a dark corner of a room and transformed these throw-aways into something beautiful.

4. How might God use your makeover SO THAT His desire, His story is accomplished in your life? Who might need the shade of your tree so they might experience His gentle breeze?

endnotes

Birth

1 See Birth (2009).

2 See Darwish (2008).

3 See Kristof & WuDunn (2009).

4 Ephesians 2:10.

5 Globally, the vast majority of victims of abuse are female. However, recent Catholic priest scandals, among others, have raised awareness that abuse is well-known to a myriad of males as well. Also, research about the epidemic of child sexual abuse of boys in Muslim countries is making its way to the light of day. For example, in Afghanistan it is common for men to take boys aged nine to fifteen as their "boy players." These young boys are garbed in makeup and girls' attire and required to dance for middle-aged men. Many married men keep these boys "for pleasure" because, they argue, they can't see women, who are clothed in hijabs (coverings from head to ankle), but they "can tell which boys are beautiful." This culturally-sanctioned child sexual abuse of boys is prevalent and has unimaginable consequences. [See Brinkley (2010, August 29). See also Qobil (2010, September 7).]

6 Thanks to Chad Hacker for reminding us that sometimes even when certain language is not exclusive, extra invitations need to be sent out so men feel welcomed to the table.

Tamar: A Desolate Woman

1   2 Samuel 13:1-22.

2   Absalom and Tamar's mother was named Maachah, and their father was David. Absalom was Tamar's biological brother, while Amnon was Tamar's half-brother.

3   2 Samuel 13:2.

4   2 Samuel 13:3-4.

5   2 Samuel 13:5.

6   2 Samuel 13:1: "the **beautiful** sister of Absalom, son of David." Every word in Scripture is there for a reason. God found it important to mention Tamar was beautiful.

7   See 1 Samuel 13:14.

8   Anna Salter is one of the foremost experts regarding sexual offenses. When it comes to answering the question why King David might not have detected Amnon's slick moves, one possible reason is based on an explanation by Dr. Salter: "We don't recognize these people as predators, because we think sex offenders are monsters and surely we would recognize a monster, wouldn't we? That nice young minister who runs all the youth programs, the one with the crooked smile and the thatch of brown hair over his brow, the one who visits the elderly and gives the poor money from his own funds. Surely not him. He could not be a child molester with ninety victims while he's still in his twenties. That good-looking, polite young man who just wants to see the motorcycle for sale in the back yard. Surely he couldn't be a rapist with a knife in his back pocket waiting for you to turn your back to pull the cover off." However, in her book, Mr. Morgan, a knife-wielding rapist of an adult and children explains: "I lived a life of a chameleon or a salamander, changed colors with the wind. I didn't just live a double life. I lived multiple lives. Whatever life the situation called for, I lived it. If I hung around Christian people and I knew that they were Christian, then my actions and my mannerism were similar to theirs. And I adapted to whatever

the situation required. If I hung around people who cursed and used vulgar language and smoked dope, then I adapted to that situation. I could feed back to people what I thought they wanted to see and what I thought they wanted to hear." Offenders bank on the fact that people won't read through their deception. [See Salter (2003), pp. 5, 35-36.]

9   While perpetrators are adept at lying, denial was also a theme in David's role as a father. Steven Tracy explains, "After the rape, when Amnon's predatory deviancy was public knowledge, David did absolutely nothing... Later on, when unavenged Absalom asks for Amnon to go with him to the sheep shearing, David allowed Amnon to go, precipitating his murder (2 Samuel 13:24-29). Later on, when Absalom began to steal away the hearts of the people, which ultimately resulted in civil war, David was oblivious to his son's growing rebellion (15:1-14). David's failure to embrace the truth of Absalom's bitterness cost the lives of at least twenty thousand soldiers (18:7), as well as Absalom's life (18:14-15). It also led directly to ten royal concubines being publicly raped (15:16; 16:22). David did not protect because he did not want to be disturbed with the truth" [See Tracy (2005), p. 59.]

10 See 2 Samuel 11-12.

11 2 Samuel 13:10.

12 Leviticus 20:17.

13 Only about a third of women victims are raped by a stranger. [See Salter (2003), p. 81.]

14 2 Samuel 13:13.

15 For many in this culture, rape was a crime of theft against the family. The specific victim was incidental. [See Featherman (1995), p. 133.]

16 Deuteronomy 22:25.

17 See Fontes (2005).

18 One option is 1-800-656-HOPE. This is the number for the Rape, Abuse & Incest National Network. 24 hours a day, seven days a week. Free. Confidential.

19 See Kardam (2005), pp. 34, 40. Kardam sheds light on a former Turkish law that promotes rapists marrying their rape victims: "The practice of marrying girls to their rapists was also reinforced in a way by the former penal code in Turkey which stated that when the rapist gets married to the woman he raped, his penalty is suspended, and when he remains married for five years then the penalty is absolved." In many countries around the world, perpetrators of rape may be excused for their crime if he marries his victim. [See United Nations Children's Fund Innocenti Research Centre (2001).]

20 Deuteronomy 22:28-29.

21 2 Samuel 13:14. Please understand the gist of this violation was not about sex. Rapists habitually blame the sexual offense on stress, alcohol, a strong sex drive, or the victim, or sometimes suggest that it "just happened." However, rape is most frequently calculated and well-planned, and it may involve anyone and anything as a means to gain power and control.

22 2 Samuel 13:15.

23 2 Samuel 13:17.

24 2 Samuel 13:20.

25 "The question of succession to David's kingdom is a theme just below the surface of this text" [See Arnold (2003), p. 565.]

26 2 Samuel 11:24-25.

27 For a good majority of history, rape was determined a crime against the woman's father, husband, or brother instead of as a crime against the victim. [See Smith (2004).]

28 2 Samuel 13:21.

29 2 Samuel 13:37.

30 2 Samuel 13:20.

31 See Blue Letter Bible (1996-2008f).

32 "Nothing in all creation is hidden from God's sight" (Hebrews 4:13).

Aftermath of Abuse

1 See Frisbie, Berner, Myers, & Sharzer (2004).

2 See Allen (2005); Briere (1996); Briere & Elliot (2003); Browne & Finkelhor (1986), pp. 66-77; Chu (1998); Elliot & Briere. (1992), pp. 391-398; Langberg (2003); Romano & De Luca (1999), pp. 55-78.

3 See Putnam (2003, March), pp. 269-278.

4 See Salter (1995).

5 See Courtois (1996), p. 91.

6 See Terr (1991).

7 See Ford and Courtois (2009) for an in-depth study of complex trauma and complex traumatic stress disorder responses.

8 See Hunter & Gerber (1990), pp. 79-89.

9 See Hopper (2011).

10 An excellent book marking the journey of individuals coming out of sex trafficking reflects the trek of transformation in the name change from "victim" to "victor". [See Grant & Hudlin (2007).] The identity as "Overcomer" is another consideration derived from Revelation 12:11 ASV. "And they overcame him because of the blood of the Lamb, and because of the word of their testimony; and they loved not their life even unto death."

11 "He who has an ear, let him hear what the Spirit says to the churches. To him who overcomes… I will also give him a white stone with a new name written on it, known only to him who receives it" (Revelation 2:17).

Cesspools of Shame

1 See Hugo (1862), p. 34.

2 2 Corinthians 7:10.

3 See a variety of sources, including Allender (1995); Finkelhor & Browne (1985); Fontes (2005); Hunter (1990); Lisak (1994).

"[S]hame, not guilt, is now the prominent emotion troubling Western culture" [Parker & Thomas (2009), p. 214.].

4 See Feiring, Taska & Lewis (2002).

5 See Sanderson (2006).

6 See Fontes (2005).

7 See Finkelhor & Browne (1985).

8 See van der Kolk (2007) chapter titled "The complexity of adaptation to trauma self-regulation, stimulus discrimination, and characterological development."

9 See Bender, Mosier, Smith, Weinstein, Weinstein & Sant (1997).

10 See Kettlewell (1999), p. 60.

11 See Finkelhor (1979).

12 See Salter (1995), p. 185.

13 Another common ploy is to entice victims by offering gifts. On July 29, 1994, little seven-year-old Megan Kanka was enticed to enter the adjacent home of Jesse Timmendequas. He pledged a puppy to this little girl. He then viciously raped and murdered her. Timmendequas had sexually abused two other children but had only served six of his ten years in prison prior to raping and killing Megan. Megan's parents never knew of his past. In 1994, Megan's Law was enacted in New Jersey. [See Smith (2004), p. 126.]

14 See Fontes (2005), p. 139.

15 See Shelley & Stoecker (2005).

16 See Gupton-Pruett (2009).

17 See Allender (1995), p. 68.

18 See Sanderson (2006), p. 325.

19 See Briere (1996).

20 2 Samuel 13:3.

21 See Dewey, Hahn, McArthur, & Schumacher (1994).

22 Psalm 119:94.

23 Leviticus 26:13.

Allegiance Divided

1 See Malcolm Muggeridge's account of a conversation with Svetlana Stalin as cited in Zacharias (1994), pp. 26-27.

2 See Ambivalence (2002).

3 See Freyd (1997), p.63.

4 See Lawson, Drebing, Berge, Mincellett & Penk (1998).

5 Exodus 1:8-14.

6 Exodus 1:8-22.

7 Exodus 4:29-31.

8 See Exodus 3:12, 3:18, 4:23, 5:1, 5:3, 7:16, 8:1, 8:20, 8:27, 9:1, 9:13, 10:7, 10:8, and 12:31. Peter Enns explains, "Worship is the appropriate response to God's love for them. It is also the ultimate reason for which He is bringing them out of Egypt... The point of the Exodus is not freedom. It is about God calling His own people back to Him in order that they might enter into a relationship" [See Enns (2000), pp. 133, 144-145.]. Michael Card also reasons, "The goal of deliverance is always worship... The object of their freedom was not simply their emancipation. The purpose was the worship of God" [See Card (2005), p. 23].

9 Exodus 14:10.

10 Exodus 14:11-12.

11 See Enns (2000).

12 See Allender (1995). See also Finkelhor & Browne (1985).

13 See Sheinberg & Fraenkel (1999, May/June).

14 See Berendzen & Palmer (1993).

15 Ibid, p. 21.

16 See Russell (1999), p. 293.

17 Ibid., p. 358.

18 Ibid., p.138.

19 Ibid., p.140.

20 See Yuksel (2000), pp.153-162.

21 See Kettlewell (1999), p. 178.

22 Exodus 15 and 16.

23 "For I am the Lord, who heals you" (Exodus 15:26b).

Never Trust Again

1 King David *gets* betrayal. See Marva Dawn's examination of this passage: "Our English words don't reveal the poignancy of these Hebrew expressions. The first word for 'friend' implies an intimacy often used to describe the relationship of a woman and her husband. The profound closeness that once existed with the beloved has been violated. The second word comes from a very signifying deep knowing and involving the idea of revealing or discovering. This friend is one to whom the poet has disclosed his hidden self, the most profound truths of his being. Yet this is the one who attacked him, who has violated the covenant that knitted them together" [See Dawn (1998), p. 47.].

2 See Newton (2007).

3 Ibid.

4 See French (2007, June 14).

5 See The 'monsters' among us.

6 See Finkelhor & Browne (1985).

7 See Sanderson (2006).

8 See Mcalinden (2006).

9 See Frawley-O'Dea & Golder (2007), p. 18.

10 See Salter (1995), p. 74.

11 2 Samuel 13:5-8.

12 See Keller (1986).

13 Ibid., p. 14.

14 Ibid., pp. 11-12.

15 We're not kidding. Maybe it's not one of the most flipped-to books of the Bible, but it's a stellar one nevertheless.

16 Ezekiel 34:2-3.

17 Ezekiel 34:2-5a.

18 See Jamieson, Fausset & Brown (2000).

19 Ezekiel 34:8, 10.

20 See Rosenthal (1999), p. 23.

21 Ibid., p. 27.

22 Ibid., pp. 34-35.

23 "During this time of coming to terms with the loss of meaning, church can seem at best irrelevant and at worst painful. Messages that used to comfort or inspire, worship that used to uplift, seems no longer to be in tune with their needs and present reality. To attend worship may be to experience a great sense of alienation. In this process, first of coping with the loss of meaning, and secondly finding new meanings through the pain, the abuse survivor is likely to be able to be more hindered than helped by comforters who can only remind the person of the old meanings, the old explanations and beliefs. Those are the very things whose loss she is grieving, and if she is to return to them, it must be in a way that takes account of her life experiences, which integrates them somehow into her worldview." See Parkinson (2003), pp. 167-168.

24 See Zarra (1997), p. 92. If you are a leader of a church, and especially if you are going through a situation like this at your church, chapter 7 in this book specifically highlights steps a congregation can take which include (1) healing of the lives of the victims, (2) repentance, reparation, and eventual restoration of the perpetrator, and (3) rebuilding of trust and oneness in the church community. Also check out chapter 11 in Parkinson (2003). The chapter is called "When Ministers Sin" and provides important information for the disciplinary process.

25 See Corcoran (2005), p. 327.

26 See Clark (2009).

27 Ibid.

28 1 Samuel 2:22-25.

29 1 Samuel 3:11-14.

30 See Tozer (1961).

31 See Ponton & Goldstein (2004).

32 See Rossetti (1995).

33 See Kane, Cheston & Greer (1993).

34 See Gartner (2007), pp. 85-100. See also chapter titled "The Struggle of Faith" in Parkinson (1997), pp. 161-176 and Rossetti (1995).

35 See Matchan (1992, June 8).

36 See Gartner (2007), p. 98 .

37 See Gartner (2004).

38 See Altson (2004), p. 14. I (Hannah) started reading this biography while we were on a book weekend escapade in Michigan. I started reading it in bed one night. I don't recommend that, but if you can stomach it, it has a powerful message you should read. It's a quick but important read, which is why we include pieces of her story in this chapter.

39 Ibid., pp. 52-53, 65-66.

40 For example, bridegroom/bride (Isaiah 61:10, 62:5; Hosea 2:16, 19-20; Revelation 19:7-9), brother/sister (Mark 3:35), shepherd/sheep (Ezekiel 34:11-15; John 10:1-18; Luke 15:3-7; Hebrews 13:20), Father (Psalm 68:5; Isaiah 9:6; Ephesians 4:6; Romans 8:15; Galatians 4:4-6), mother (Isaiah 49:15-16), friend (John 15:15; James 2:23; Proverbs 22:11), master/bondservant (Matthew 25:14-30; Luke 19:11-27; Acts 16:17; Revelation 22:3), potter/clay (Isaiah 64:8; Jeremiah 18:4-6; Ephesians 2:10).

41 "Certainly God is neither masculine nor feminine, but more than all our words can ever connote" [See Dawn (1998), p. xiii.].

42 See Kennedy, Howsam, Bloye, & Curtis (2005).

43 Job 23:3.

44 See Altson (2004), pp. 127, 145.

45 Ezekiel 34

Anguish Unvoiced

1 See Hammel-Zabin (2003).

2 See Summit (1983). Frequently at seminars on abuse, folks ask me, "Tammy, why don't they tell?" And my answer is that there are many, many reasons why people don't disclose abuse. Some of these reasons are described in this chapter. Perhaps there are as many reasons for not telling as there are people. This brings us to the the important fact that it is vital to ask the client about the circumstances, events, beliefs, and feelings that stopped him or her from telling. Not telling is teleological (i.e., There is a reason he or she didn't tell.).

3 See Fisher & Rivas (2001), p. 44.

4 See Kettlewell (1999), p. 23.

5 See Silverman (1999), p. 225.

6 See Dalenberg (2000).

7 One brave man who read this chapter shared that as a teenager, he didn't tell about the abuse because he pondered, "Who would have believed me?" His perpetrator was the revered jock, president of the this-and-that club, and he was just the non-athletic kid next door. This "great guy" would never do such a thing. The abuse was one blow. Not being believed was one more blast that he didn't feel he could take. Our friend's words illustrate that there are so many reasons people don't tell. The task of the counselor is to listen for the reason that hushed the person we journey with and to applaud the courage that has swelled up inside so that she or he can speak now.

8 See Lovett (2004).

9 See Finklehor & Browne (1985); Lovett (2004); Sgroi (1982); & Summit (1983).

10 See Hardy (1891), p. 203.

11 Ibid., p. 205.

12 See Fine, Head, Wilson, & Sharp (1998).

13 See Fisher & Rivas (2001), p. 283.

14 2 Samuel 13:19.

15 See Malchiodi (2003).

16 See Kardam (2005).

17 See Hammel-Zabin (2003).

18 See Card (2005).

19 See Murphy (2005), p. 3.

20 See Teacher & Powell (1994), p. 73.

21 See DeSalvo (1989), pp. 120-125.

22 See Terr (1990).

23 Ibid., pp. 533-546.

24 See Schulkind (1985), p. 69.

25 See Farber (2006).

26 See Fontes (2005).

27 See Gilligan & Akhtar (2006).

28 Every situation must be looked at individually. When children are in danger, extraordinary wisdom is needed to discern a means of bringing the child to safety within a given culture.

29 See Brown (2009), pp. 166-182.

30 Thanks Mukhabbat for our many conversations about culture. You have opened my cultural eyes wider. Thanks for reminding me that culture is a central ingredient in understanding people but culture alone is incomplete. At the same time, when we close our eyes to culture, we miss seeing the colorful hues of our brothers and sisters next door and around the world.

31 See Foote (1994), p. 14.

Unrequited Love

1 See May (1988), p. 3.

2   Isaiah 30:1, 12. The Hebrew word for rely is batach, which means to "feel safe, to set one's hope and confidence upon." The Hebrew word for "depended" is sha'an, which means to "lean upon, to rest upon, to support oneself." These words help us to understand the essence of addictions: attaching, trusting, and hoping in anyone or anything other than our God. See Blue Letter Bible (1996-2011).

3   Emphasis added. [See Eldredge (2007), pp. 80, 93.] Also, Gerald May wisely differentiates between objects or people we are deeply connected to and those to which we are addicted: "The difference is freedom. We care deeply about many things and abhor many others, but with most of these we remain free to choose the depth and extent of our investment. They do not become gods. Remember, then, that true addictions are compulsive habitual behaviors that eclipse our concern for God and compromise our freedom, and that they must be characterized by tolerance, withdrawal symptoms, loss of willpower, and distortion of attention" [See May (1988), p. 37.].

4   See Lewis (2001a), pp. 125-126.

5   See Corey (2009). It should be noted that Freud later acknowledged the inadequacy of his "pleasure principle," identifying other forces that motivate us and help us make decisions. This updated theory can be further explored in his work *Beyond the Pleasure Principle*.

6   As I (Hannah) was perusing the Internet, I ran across this on a blog: "I largely agree with those who say heaven and hell are mostly metaphors for how someone approaches living in this world. On one level, at least, the metaphor seems to be speaking about attachment. If you are emotionally and psychologically attached to things and can't step back from your attachments, then it's going to be hell for you. After all, everything is transitory, and you will suffer—sometimes greatly—when things change. On the other hand, if you can let go of attachments as spontaneously as a child lets go of someone's hand, then this world can be something of a heaven for you. Its transitory nature will often delight you, rather than constantly threaten you. You will be psychologically

and emotionally free to enjoy the moment, to take delight in things great and small, even though all things come to an end." I liked it, although I don't agree with all of it, I thought I would share it with you. It underscores this whole idea of addiction and attachment. See Sunstone (2008, May 6).

7 See Jantz (1995), p. 67.

8 See Knapp (1996), p. 104.

9 See Corbin, Bernat, Calhoun, McNair, & Seals (2001); Glover, Janikowski & Benshoff (1995); Kang et al. (1999); Moncrieff et al. (1996); Quinn (1994); and Wilsnack, Vogeltanz, Klassen & Harris (1997).

10 See Dube, Anda, Whitfield, Brown, Felitti, Dong & Giles (2005).

11 See Abbey, Ross & McDuffie (1994), pp. 97-123. It is important to note that while drinking alcohol at the time of the assault in-reases a woman's vulnerability to assault, the perpetrator remains morally, legally, and spiritually responsible for the assault.

12 See Widom & Hiller-Sturmhofel (2001).

13 To the cycle of chemicals being used to cover abuse issues, is added the fact that substance abuse programs are often brief inpatient stays in which patients detoxify, get chemical addiction education, and prepare for twelve-step programs when released. This is an important component; however, underlying abuse issues may be missed. Added to this mix is the fact that trauma education is a missing component in many graduate schools. Thus, many medical and mental health professionals are not qualified to detect trauma issues. [See Duncan (2005), pp. 275-277.]

14 See Jantz (1995), p. 54.

15 See Cohn (1996), pp. 1-16.

16 See Costin (2007), p. 39.

17 See Andersen (1990).

18 See Costin (2007), p. 42. Since boys' bodies are often and typically the apparatus for developing self-esteem through physical

performance, this is especially significant in regards to sexual abuse. When one's body has been damaged in abusive ways, men can often become passive, avoiding all things male, or on the opposite extreme, hypermasculine, seeking to "prove" their strength or competence [See Andersen, Cohn & Holbrook (2000), p. 63.]. For the man who has become more passive and who values more feminine traits and qualities, obsession with the body and thinness (a typically female quality) can take place. Interestingly, there is a higher rate of homosexuality among males with eating disorders than females [See Bramon-Bosch, Troop & Treasure (2000).]. On the other extreme, a man who has become hyper-masculine may be more likely to struggle with *muscle dysmorphia* or an increased and unhealthy level of obsession on muscle-building/weight gain. In short, male *and* female victims of sexual abuse have experienced a terrible trauma of the body (as well as mind and soul), and it makes sense that body dissatisfaction and eating disordered behavior present themselves as both a way to respond to the abuse and a way to punish or alter the body in such a way that abuse might not ever transpire again.

19 See Doctor & Shiromoto (2010). Basically, there were bank robbers who held employees hostage for six days in 1973 in Stockholm, Sweden. The victims in this instance became emotionally attached to the robbers and defended them when it was all over. Criminologist and psychiatrist Nils Bejerot coined the term "Stockholm syndrome" in a broadcast covering this event, a phrase he was using to describe the psychological response of loyalty in an abducted hostage regardless of danger.

20 See McKinley (2005), p. 12.

21 See D'Onofrio (2007).

22 See Conterio, Lader & Bloom (1998).

23 See Austin & Kortum (2004); Froeschle & Moyer (2004); Haines & Williams (2003); and White, Trepal-Wollenzier & Nolan (2002).

24 See Conterio, Lader & Bloom (1998).

25 Ibid.

26 See Harrison (1998), p. 17.

27 See Babiker & Arnold (1997), p. 1.

28 See Klonsky & Muehlenkamp (2007).

29 See Schneider (2007).

30 See Russell (1999).

31 See Kluft (1990), pp. 11-34.

32 See Ropelato (2008).

33 See Hallman (2008), p. 56.

34 See Yuan & Yuan (2011), p.11.

35 The male who was sexually abused by another male may fear that he is homosexual; the female survivor who was abused by a male, or the male survivor who was abused by a female, may fear heterosexual sex, as it is reminiscent of the childhood sexual abuse [See Sanderson (2006), p. 352.].

36 See U2. (1987).

37 Ibid.

38 David Sheff wrote a hard-to-put-down-book about his life as father to Nic, his beautiful boy who entered the dark cave of addiction to meth. David followed his son in the cave and tried to pull him out. In the cave, David became aware of his own addiction [See Sheff (2008).].

39 See Bell (2007), p. 73.

Requited Love

1 Hosea 2:14.

2 Hosea 2:3.

3 See Crabb (2001), p. 96.

4 See Piper (1982).

5 See May (1988).

6 See Hubbard & Wiseman (1989), p. 84.

7 Hosea 2:15.

8 See Alighieri & Carlyle (1849), p. 3.

9 This idea is also detailed in Scripture in passages like Psalm 6:6-10, 34:17-18, 38:8, and 42:7; Proverbs 28:26; Isaiah 38:12-13; Matthew 9:36; Romans 7:15-20; 1 Corinthians 8:2; 2 Corinthians 12:9-10; and others.

10 See Manning (1999), p. 68.

11 The lyrics for the chorus of "Grace Like Rain" reflect this idea too. See Agnew (2003).

12 See Yancey (2000), p. 280.

13 2 Corinthians 12:9.

14 See Manning (1999), p. 23.

15 Exodus 16:17-18.

16 See Nouwen (1995).

17 See Allender (1999), p. 169.

18 Genesis 2:18.

19 Hosea 2:13; 13:6.

20 Galatians 6:2.

21 Galatians 6:5.

22 See Geisel (1949), pp. 42-44.

23 See Manning (1999), p. 31.

24 See Burroughs (2004). If you can step back for a moment from the lack of ethics in this description of advertising, it provides an inside look at the way our "drug of choice" works.

25 See Bruce (1952).

26 John 14:2-3.

Indomitable Hope

1 See Marvin & Darabont (1994).

2 Rachel Fox read the title of this chapter and kept thinking, *Abominable Hope*. Like the abominable snowman, she said. She got the words mixed up. Yet her misreading sheds light on the way many survivors perceive hope: It's abominable.

3 Ecclesiastes 3:11.

4 See Eldredge (2007), p. 20.

5 See Hope (2003).

6 See Solnit (2006), p. 5.

7 See Moody (1994), p. 63.

8 See Guthrie (2005), pp. 154, 156.

9 John 1:5.

10 See Merton (1999), p. 186.

11 2 Corinthians 4:7.

12 2 Corinthians 12:9.

13 See Blue Letter Bible (1996-2008h).

14 See Blue Letter Bible (1996-2008i).

15 Genesis 28:16; Deuteronomy 31:6, 8.

16 See Blue Letter Bible (1996-2008g).

17 2 Corinthians 4:16-18.

18 See Wolff (1988).

19 See Burton & Burton (1969).

20 2 Samuel 13:20.

21 See Tozer (1961), p. 99.

22 Ibid., p. 102.

23 Lamentations 3:19-24.

24 Exodus 16:17.

25 Nancy Guthrie underscores the biblical words that point our gaze to the future. "The biblical descriptions of heaven include a long list of 'no mores.' It is almost as if the biblical writers, in their struggle to describe what heaven will be, find that describing what it will not be is more instructive. No more night, no more time… No more separation—only eternal togetherness with those we love. No more sun or moon, as Jesus will be the only light we need. No more marriage, as we'll be forever wed to our Bridegroom, Jesus. No more time, as time will no longer be defined by minutes or hours, but only by the richness of Jesus' presence. God knows which 'no mores' will mean the most to those of us who hurt. No more sorrow. No more crying. No more pain. No more curse. No more death. 'No more' encapsulates some of heaven's sweetest gifts" [See Guthrie (2005), p. 174.].

Marching Down Memory Lane

1 Dialectic: Debate or discourse.

2 See Schultz (2000, August); and Schultz, Passmore & Yoder (2003).

3 See Conte (1993); Elliott (1997); Herman (1997); Martinez-Taboas (1996); and van der Kolk, McFarlane & Weisaeth (1996).

4 See International Society for the Study of Dissociation (ISSD) (2005).

5 See Loftus (1993); Loftus & Ketcham (1994); and Yapko (1994).

6 It is interesting to note that delayed memories have been documented throughout this century for survivors of a variety of traumas including natural disasters, combat soldiers during war, victims of kidnapping and torture, concentration camp survivors. See Madakasira & O'Brien (1987); Wilkinson (1983); Shonnenberg & Blank (1985); and Kinzie (1983), pp. 311-319. It is important to consider why the subject of delayed memories has become controversial when associated with delayed memories of CSA versus other types of trauma.

7 Polemic: "A controversial argument, especially one refuting or attacking a specific opinion or doctrine." See Polemic. (2003).

8 See Van der Kolk (1997), p. 2.

9 See Bremner & Narayan (1998); and Bremner, Scott, Delaney, Southwick, Mason, Johnson, . . . Charney (1993).

10 Dissociation: Blank spaces in memory that can last from minutes to years that is not caused by ordinary forgetting.

11 See Steele & van der Hart (2009).

12 See Courtois, Ford, & Cloitre (2009).

13 2 Samuel 13:17.

14 See Briere & Lanktree (2012).

15 Ibid.

16 See Volf (2006), p. 79.

17 Ibid, p. 26.

18 Ibid, p. 108-109.

19 See Courtois, Ford, & Cloitre (2009), p. 95.

20 See Steele, van der Hart, & Nijenhuis (2005).

21 Luke 22:54-62.

22 Matthew 26:31-35.

23 John 21:13-19,

24 See Smith (2008).

25 1 Peter 3:15.

26 Matthew 25: 14-30.

27 See Spitzer & Avis (2006), p. 182.

28 See Wright, Crawford & Sebastian (2007).

29 See Himelein & McElrath (1996); and McMillen, Zuravin & Rideout (1995).

30 See Smith (2002), pg. 17.

31 Ibid, p.48.

32 Ibid, pp. 7-9.

33 Ibid, p. 147.

34 See Arnold (2003).

35 Genesis 28:16.

36 Joshua 4:1-9.

37 1 Samuel 7:12.

38 Psalm 126:3.

39 See Church (1905).

Prayer Mosaic: The Language of Lament

1 See Mosaic (2005).

2 See Tiegreen (2007), p. 2.

3 See Dearman (2002), p. 429.

4 See Lament (2011).

5 See Card (2005), p. 17.

6 Ibid, p. 98.

7 See Peterson (2005), p. 11.

8 See Hallesby (1994), p. 18.

9 This is a question that was pondered for a couple of hours over coffee and tea with our good friend, Keri. Thanks for sharing your "watermelon" with us, Keri!

10 As Andrea Dworkin quipped, "Incest is boot camp [for prostitution]" [See Dworkin (1997).].

11 See Rivers (1997), p. 142.

12 The prayer of this little girl echoes the desperate petition of King David: "My heart is in anguish within me; the terrors of earth assail me. Fear and trembling have beset me; horror has overwhelmed me. Oh, that I had the wings of a dove! I would fly

away and be at rest—I would flee far away and stay in the desert; I would hurry to my place of shelter, far from the tempest and storm" (Psalm 55:4-8).

13 See Parkinson (2003), p. 161.

14 See second definition from Doka (1989), p. 4.

15 See Lewis (1964), p. 22.

16 Habakkuk 1:2.

17 See Card (2005), p. 21.

18 1 Samuel 30:4.

19 See Sittser (2003), p. 57.

20 2 Samuel 13:19.

21 2 Samuel 13:20.

22 See Card (2005), p. 20.

23 2 Samuel 13:20.

24 See Parkinson (1997), pp. 169-171.

25 See Altson (2004), pp. 136-137.

26 See Allender (1995), p. 135.

27 Genesis chapter 32.

28 Genesis 32:26.

29 See Card (2005), p. 78.

30 Ibid., pp. 80-81.

31 Sri Ramakrishna, a prominent Hindu, noted, "There can be as many Hindu Gods as there are devotees to suit the moods, feelings, emotions, and social backgrounds of the devotees" [See Hinduism gods (2011)].

32 Romans 1:16.

33 See Card (2005), pp. 24-25.

34 See Ponton & Goldstein (2004).

35 See Macy (1999), p. 95.

36 See Yancey (1988), p. 237.

37 See Macy (1999), p. 96.

38 See Foster (1992), p. 24.

39 See Yancey (2006), p. 89.

40 "For there to be harmony in music, the composer needs to use both the treble clef and the bass clef. The treble clef provides the melody. The bass clef brings depth to the music. Without the bass clef, the melody line can sometimes seem shrill or simplistic. The bass without the melody is sonorous and tuneless… For worship to be sensitive to survivors of sexual abuse, and those who have experienced many other forms of suffering, there needs to be a greater recognition of the bass clef in life—that if God brings victory it is neither easy nor cheap for the believer" [See Parkinson (2003), p. 175.].

41 See Card (2005), p. 109.

Flying Above the Fray

1 See Milchan, Grisham, Nathansham, Lowry & Schumacher (1996).

2 See Linde, D. (1999). The Goodbye Earl music video won both the Academy of Country Music and the Country Music Association Video of the Year awards in 2000.

3 See Shults & Sandage (2003), p. 12.

4 See Bass & Davis (1988), p. 348.

5 See Herman (1997), pp. 189-190. See also Miller (1991), p. 131. Alice Miller shares her antipathy towards the idea that forgiveness is a part of the healing journey. She stated, "In recent years I have been sent many books… describing different kinds of therapeutic intervention. Without a single exception, all these authors presume that forgiveness is a condition for 'successful' therapy. This notion appears to be so widespread in therapeutic circles that it is never called into question—something urgently needed. But for-

giveness does not resolve latent hatred and self-hatred but rather covers them up in a very dangerous way."

6   See Smiley (1991), pp. 354-356.

7   See Bury the hatchet. (n.d).

8   Jeremiah 31:34. See also Isaiah 43:25.

9   Idioms, Cambridge International Dictionary of. *The Free Dictionary*. 1998. July 24, 2008 <http://idioms.thefreedictionary.com/bury+head+in+the+sand.

10 See Seibold (2001), p. 295. Within the family, the fires of quick forgiveness may also be stoked if husbands of survivors become uncontrollably infuriated at the perpetrator over their wives' abuse. Survivors may be inclined to cover the rage toward the individual who abused with shallow forgiveness so that husbands will not think the hurt runs as deep. See Holeman & Myers (1997).

11 See North (1987), p. 502.

12 See Tracy (2005). See also Tracy (1999).

13 See Blue Letter Bible. (1996-2008a). See also Matthew 6:12, 18:21.

14 See Kidd (2002).

15 See Osborne, Sanders, Warsh, & Jackson (2001).

16 John 7:33.

17 Genesis 50: 15.

18 Genesis 50:16-17.

19 Genesis 50:17.

20 Genesis 50:19-21, *The Message*.

21 Extending grace to those who hurt us is described in 2 Corinthians 2:7, "Now instead, you ought to forgive and comfort him, so that he will not be overwhelmed by excessive sorrow." The Greek word for forgive used in this verse is "Charizomai," which means to "do something pleasant or agreeable (to one), to do a favor to, gratify." See Blue Letter Bible (1996-2008j).

22 Genesis 39:21. The Lord demonstrated that beautiful Hebrew word, Hesed. The loving-kindness of God.

23 See Freedman & Enright (1996).

24 1 Samuel 26:9.

25 See Everett Worthington's *Five steps to forgiveness: The art and science of forgiving*. Step1: Recall the Hurt, Step 2: Empathize, Step 3: Offer the Altruistic Gift of Forgiveness, Step 4: Commit Publicly to Forgive, Step 5: Hold on to Forgiveness. Dr. Worthington has something wise to say on this topic. He researched the topic of forgiveness for years. Then his mother was brutally murdered by thieves who used a crowbar on his defenseless mom. Then Dr. Worthington was brought face-to-face with what it means to forgive the men who killed the woman he loved.

26 "Aria" is an 'air or melody; an elaborate melody sung solo with accompaniment, as in an opera or oratorio.' [see Aria (n.d.).] "Cavatina" is 'a simple song or melody, properly one without a second part or a repeat, an air.' [see Cavatina (n.d.).]

27 See Human Rights Watch (1999).

28 See Larson (2008).

29 See Larson (2008).

30 Firsthand accounts have been written in recent years about what is happening in Rwanda. People who have experienced evil upon evil are forgiving. A country that has been so corrupt and broken is rising out of the ashes. A country where forgiveness is now a national policy. I don't know about you, but I want Rwanda in my own soul. See some amazing reads—Larson (2009) & Rucyahana (2007).

31 Matthew 6:9-10.

Hitting the Wall

1 Susan McCammon wrote an excellent chapter on ways to set the tone in a class about trauma. She explains the need to inform

students about topics that will be discussed, giving choice to not attend as well as alternative assignments. She discusses making referrals available for students who may have trauma issues surface [See McCammon (1999, pp. 105-120.].

2 See Follette, Polusny & Milbeck (1994).

3 See Lee (1989). In this article, the author decribes the impact of teaching about violence on the students and upon herself as the instructor. She explains that students "were saturated with the topic and visibly moved. Even class members who did not identify as survivors were concerned, angered, scared, and wanted to see things change, especially on the issue of pornography. As a teacher, it is always difficult to end such a session without feeling anxious about the aftereffects of such an intense morning on students. One survivor of violence said she would have liked 'a few extra moments at the end of the session to reach out to others for support—even just time to sit in the silence or tears.' At this point, prose, poetry, music, and a session on self-defence could be especially empowering" (p. 544).

4 See Saakvitne (1995), p. 281.

5 See Trippany, Kress & Wilcoxon (2004).

6 See Neumann & Gamble (1995).

7 See Pearlman & Mac Ian (1995).

8 See Schauben & Frazier (1995).

9 See Saakvitne (1995), pp. 281-282.

10 Matthew 14:13.

11 Matthew 14:14, 20.

12 Matthew 14:24 says the storm "buffeted" the disciples. The Greek word for buffeted is to be "harassed" or "distressed."

13 Mark 6:48.

14 Mark 6:50.

15 Matthew 14:28.

16 Matthew 14:29.

17 Matthew 14:30-31.

18 Thanks to wise Gwynne Shaver for this heading and some wise ideas to chew on regarding selfless self-care.

19 Caring for ourselves. We have a good model of this important practice in Jesus. On many occasions He withdrew from the crowd to a quiet place (Luke 4:42; Mark 6:46).

20 See Matthew 4:1-2, Luke 4:1-2, Mark 3:20, Luke 6:12-16, and Mark 6:30-34. Jesus gave of Himself constantly but He was not hurried or a workaholic.

21 See Guy (1987), p. 15.

22 2 Corinthians 1:3-4.

23 See Mahoney (1991), p. 351.

24 See Ekhart, Lorenz & Stern (2005).

25 See Trippany, Wilcoxon & Satcher (2003). See also Pearlman & Mac Ian (1999).

26 See Follette, Polusny & Milbeck (1994).

27 See Macy (1999), p. 50.

28 See Pearlman & Mac Ian (1995).

29 See Saakvitne & Pearlman (1996). This book is an excellent resource for caregivers. It provides loads of wisdom for caregivers struggling with vicarious traumatization, practical suggestions, and some excellent classroom/seminar experiential activities. While their view on spirituality and a higher power appears to differ from ours, there are many nuggets of truth that can be mined.

30 See Galloway (2005).

31 Genesis 2:2.

32 Jeremiah 31:25.

33 Matthew 11:28.

34 John 7:37.

35 Exodus 18:7-12.

36 Exodus 18:13 (emphasis added).

37 Exodus 18:14.

38 Exodus 18:17-18.

39 Exodus 18:19-23.

40 Exodus 18:24.

41 "One day the angels came to present themselves before the Lord, and Satan also came with them. The Lord said to Satan, 'Where have you come from?' Satan answered the Lord, 'From roaming through the earth and going back and forth in it'" (Job 1:6-7).

42 1 Peter 5:8.

43 Ephesians 6:12.

44 2 Corinthians 10:3-4 (emphasis added).

45 See Kellemen (2007).

46 See Blue Letter Bible (1996-2008d).

47 See Blue Letter Bible. (1996-2008e).

48 See Blue Letter Bible. (1996-2008b).

49 See Herman (1992), p. 140.

50 See Chambers (1995), p. 30.

Stretched Out

1 Excerpt adapted from Peugh & Schultz (2005), p. 1-3.

2 See Wardle (2001), pp. 198-199.

3 See Foster (1992), p. 191.

4 See Alighieri & Carlyle (1849).

5 Acts 12:2.

6 Two guards were chained to Peter, one on each arm. Two more were stationed outside the door or the gate of his cell.

7 The Greek word for "but" is only two letters.

8 Acts 12:5.

9 See Blue Letter Bible. (1996-2008c).

10 Jesus did not always get what He asked for, either. Before Jesus' death, He prayed for Simon Peter that his faith would be strong. "Simon, Simon, Satan has asked to sift you as wheat. But I have prayed for you, Simon, that your faith may not fail. And when you have turned back, strengthen your brothers" (Luke 22:31). Yet Peter's faith did fail. Big time. The famous three strikes. But Peter was not benched for the rest of his life. Satan did sift Peter like wheat, but the sifting brought about a humbled man, a stronger-in-the-broken-places man. We don't always see the beauty God loves to bring out of the ashes of unanswered prayers. But sometimes, as in the case of Peter, we do.

11 Acts 12:23.

12 See Fung & Fung (2009, May).

13 Yeah, I (Tammy) was listening to internet radio and John Denver songs were playing while I was writing this section.

14 See Nouwen (1993).

15 Ibid., p. 39.

16 Luke 15:20.

17 Well, we kind of made these titles up but you get the picture.

18 See Miller (2004), pp. 10, 12-15.

19 "Emperor Penguins huddle together for warmth, with those on the outside of the huddle being cycled through to the inside and then back to the edge so they don't spend too long at the exposed periphery." See Drisdelle (n.d.).

20 Mark 9:21-24 (emphasis added).

21 Mark 9: 23-24.

22 See Gary (2006), p. 110.

A Shot of Joy

1 See State Water Resources Control Board Clean Water Team (n.d.).

2 John 10:4

3 Thanks to my artistic friend, Cindy Bryan, who gave me the idea of water with all of its hues, shapes, and elegance. I love your affinity for God's artistry. I love you.

4 Psalm 30:5.

5 Philippians 4:4 NLT

6 See Lotz (2005).

7 Revelation 21:1, 2,11, 23.

8 John 15:11.

9 Actually, I clicked my online Bible Dictionary. Less exercise.

10 See Blue Letter Bible. (1996-2009b).

11 John 15:5.

12 John 15:11.

13 Song of Solomon 6:3.

14 Romans 8:29.

15 Philippians 4:11-13.

16 See Ten Boom, Sherrill & Sherrill (1971).

17 Well, that is what the advertisement said.

18 See Lewis (2001b).

19 See Manning (2009), pp. 45-46.

20 Proverbs 25:20.

21 Written by Joe Hermiz (Hannah's dad). Performed by the Hermiz boys (Joe and John) in a club near you ... in the '70s.

22 Of course, in their true Israelite/human fashion, they are complaining by the end of the chapter about not having any water.

But who of us has not been like this? I know sometimes I'll be driving in my car singing to God or just telling Him how grateful I am, and all of a sudden I'm grumbling (to say it kindly) because someone is driving too slow, or because I make a turn only to find out they're *still* working on Argonne Road! When are they ever going to complete that job?

23 Deuteronomy 31:19-20; 32

24 Hosea 2:14-15, emphasis ours.

25 Revelation 15:3, emphasis ours.

26 Thanks Roger Peugh for this life-changing assignment.

The Great Exchange

1 See Kalman (2005, June 12).

2 Masada is the mountaintop overlooking the Dead Sea where years before Romans laid siege to a group of Jews.

3 Carbon dating confirmed the date of these time-worn seeds, plus or minus a margin of error of 50 years. This places the seeds during or just before the Masada revolt. See Kalman (2005, June 12).

4 All rolled into a one and a half inch date, vitamin A, C, E, K, Riboflavin, Niacin, Vitamin B6, Vitamin B12, Calcium, Iron, Magnesium, and a heap of other healthy stuff abounds. See *iloveindia.com* (n.d.).

5 See Judean date palm (n.d.).

6 See Roy (2003, January 27).

7 Composting can take a few months to a couple of years depending on the type of materials you use, temperature, moisture, and amount of air. See Lambeth (2009, January 16).

8 See Eager (1913).

9 Other examples of individuals in Scripture who wore ashes: Job sat in ashes in response to the death of his family. The entire na-

tion of Nineveh, even the animals, wore sackcloth and ashes as a reaction to Jonah's proclamation of God's judgment upon them.

10 Ecclesiastes 3:4.

11 Anne Lamott captures the importance of grieving like this: "After a while it was like an inside shower, washing off some of the rust and calcification in my pipes. It was like giving a dry garden a good watering. Don't get me wrong: grief sucks; it really does. Unfortunately, though, avoiding it robs us of life, of the now, of a sense of living spirit." See Lamott (1999), p. 72.

12 See Moore (1999).

13 Luke 7:46, 2 Samuel 12:20.

14 Lewis Freedman was an Emmy and Peabody award winner, television producer and program executive for CBS and PBS.

15 2 Samuel 13:8.

16 2 Samuel 13:19.

17 See Oswalt (2003), p. 651.

18 Revelation 5:9.

19 See Blue Letter Bible (1996-2009a). Copyright ©1995-2009 by the American Academy of Orthopaedic Surgeons.

20 Thanks to Tiberius Rata, a wise Grace Seminary Old Testament professor and friend who reminded us that all the blessings of Isaiah 61 are possible only because of Christ's life and sacrifice (See Luke 24:44).

21 You may remember the nurturing mother spider in *Charlotte's Web,* who upon death's door, told Wilbur that her offspring were her greatest work of art. You can learn a lot from kids' books!!!! See White (1980), p.144-145.

22 Psalm 42:3.

23 See chapter 34 of Hemingway (1929) on being stronger in the injured places of our lives.

24 Of course this depends on a lot of things like nutrition, the severity of the break, proper casting, the immobilization of the limb, and the type of bone broken. See Surgereons (2007, October).

25 See James (2008), p. 31.

references

Abbey, A., Ross, L. T., & McDuffie, D. (1994). Alcohol's role in sexual asault. In R.R. Watson (Ed.), *Drug and alcohol abuse reviews: Addictive behaviors in women.* (pp. 97-123) Totowa, NJ: Humana Press.

Agnew, T. (2003). Grace like rain [Recorded by T. Agnew]. On *Grace Like Rain* [CD]. Memphis, TN: Ardent Records.

Alighieri, D., & Carlyle, J. A. (1849). *Divine comedy: The inferno.* New York, NY: Harper.

All About Religion. (2002-2011). Hinduism Gods. Retrieved from http://www.allaboutreligion.org/hinduism-gods-faq.htm

Allen, J. G. (2005). *Coping with trauma: Hope through understanding* (2nd ed.). Washington, DC: American Psychiatric Publishing.

Allender, D. B. (1995). *The wounded heart: Hope for adult victims of childhood sexual abuse.* Colorado Springs, CO: NavPress.

Allender, D. B. (1999). *The healing path: How the hurts in your past can lead you to a more abundant life.* Colorado Springs, CO: WaterBrook Press.

Altson, R. (2004). *Stumbling toward faith.* Grand Rapids, MI: Zondervan.

Ambivalence (2002). In *The American heritage dictionary online.* Retrieved from http://dictionary.reference.com/browse/ambivalence

Andersen, A. (1990). *Males with eating disorders.* Philadelphia, PA: Brunner/Mazel.

Andersen, A., Cohn, L., & Holbrook, T. (2000). *Making weight: Men's conflicts with food, weight, shape, and appearance.* Carlsbad, CA: Gurze Books.

Aria. (n.d.). Retrieved from http://dictionary.reference.com/browse/aria

Arnold, B. T. (2003). *The NIV 1 & 2 Samuel application commentary.* Grand Rapids, MI: Zondervan.

Austin, L., & Kortum, J. (2004). Self-injury: The secret language of pain for teenagers. *Education, 124*(3), 517-527.

Babiker, G., & Arnold, L. (1997). *The language of injury: Comprehending self-mutilation.* Leicester, United Kingdom: British Psychological Society.

Bass, E., & Davis, L. (1988). *The courage to heal: A guide for women survivors of child sexual abuse.* New York, NY: Harper & Row.

Bell, R. (2007). *Sex God: Exploring the endless connections between sexuality and spirituality.* Grand Rapids, MI: Zondervan.

Bender, L., Mosier, S., Smith, K., Weinstein, B., Weinstein, H. (Producers), & Sant, G. V. (Director). (1997). *Good will hunting* [Motion picture]. United States: A Band Apart and Lawrence Bender Productions.

Berendzen, R., & Palmer, L. (1993). *Come here: A man overcomes the tragic aftermath of childhood sexual abuse.* New York, NY: Villard Books.

Blue Letter Bible. (1996-2008a). Dictionary and Word Search for aphiemi (Strong's 863). Retrieved from http://cf.blueletterbible.org/lang/lexicon/lexicon.cfm?

Blue Letter Bible. (1996-2008b). Dictionary and Word Search for *dynatos (Strong's 1415).* Retrieved from http://cf.blueletterbible.org/lang/lexicon/lexicon.cfm?Strongs=G1415&t=KJV

Blue Letter Bible. (1996-2008c). Dictionary and Word Search for ektenēs (Strong,s 1618). Retrieved from http://www.blueletter-bible.org/lang/lexicon/lexicon.cfm?Strongs=G1618&t=KJV

Blue Letter Bible. (1996-2008d). Dictionary and Word Search for *kathairesis (Strong's 2506)*. Retrieved from http://cf.blueletterbible.org/lang/lexicon/lexicon.cfm?Strongs=G2506&t=KJV

Blue Letter Bible. (1996-2008e). Dictionary and Word Search for *ochyrōma (Strong,s 3794)*. Retrieved from http://cf.blueletterbible.org/lang/lexicon/lexicon.cfm?Strongs=G3794&t=KJV

Blue Letter Bible. (1996-2008f). Dictionary and Word Search for Tamar (Strong's 08559). Retrieved from http://www.blueletterbible.org/search/translationResults.cfm?Criteria=Tamar&t=NIV&sf=5

Blue Letter Bible. (1996-2008g). Strong's G1 – *alpha*. Retrieved from http://www.blueletterbible.org/lang/lexicon/lexicon.cfm?Strongs=G622&t=KJV

Blue Letter Bible. (1996-2008h). Strong's G639 – *aporeō*. Retrieved from http://www.blueletterbible.org/lang/lexicon/lexicon.cfm?Strongs=G639&t=KJV

Blue Letter Bible. (1996-2008i). Strong's G1820 – *exaporeō*. Retrieved from http://www.blueletterbible.org/lang/lexicon/lexicon.cfm?Strongs=G1820&t=KJV

Blue Letter Bible. (1996-2008j). Strong's G5438- *charizomai*. Revrieved from http://www.blueletterbible.org/lang/lexicon/lexicon.cfm?Strongs=G5483&t=NIV

Blue Letter Bible. (1996-2009a). Dictionary and Word Search for tachath (Strong's 8478). Retrieved from http://www.blueletter-bible.org/lang/lexicon/lexicon.cfm?Strongs=H8478&t=NIV

Blue Letter Bible. (1996-2009b). Dictionary and Word Search for *plēroō (Strong,s 4137)*. Retrieved from http://www.blueletter-bible.org/lang/lexicon/lexicon.cfm?Strongs=G4137&t=KJV

Blue Letter Bible. (1996-2011). NIV Concordance for your trust. Retrieved from http://www.blueletterbible.org/search/translationResults.cfm?Criteria=%22your+trust%22&t=NIV

Birth. (2009). In *Collins essential English dictionary online.* Retrieved from http://dictionary.reference.com/browse/birth

Bramon-Bosch, E., Troop, N. A., & Treasure, J. L. (2000). Eating disorders in males: A comparison with female patients. *European Eating Disorders Review, 8*(4), 321-328.

Bremner, J. D., & Narayan, M. (1998). The effects of stress on memory and the hippocampus throughout the life cycle: Implications for childhood development and aging. *Development and Psychopathology, 10*(4), 871-886.

Bremner J. D., Scott, T. M., Delaney, R. C., Southwick, S. M., Mason, J. W., Johnson, D. R., . . . Charney, D. S. (1993). Deficits in short-term memory in post-traumatic stress disorder. *American Journal of Psychiatry, 150*(7), 1015-1019.

Briere, J. (1996). *Therapy for adults molested as children: Beyond survival.* New York, NY: Springer Publishing Company.

Briere, J., & Elliot, D. M. (2003). Prevalence and psychological sequelae of self-reported childhood physical and sexual abuse in a general population sample of men and women. *Child Abuse and Neglect, 27*(10), 1205-1222.

Briere, J. & Lanktree, C.B. (2012). Treating complex trauma in adolescents and young adults. Los Angeles, CA: SAGE.

Brinkley, J. (2010, August 29). Afghanistan's dirty little secret. *San Francisco Chronicle*, p. E-8.

Brown, L. S. (2009). Cultural Competence. In Courtois, C.A., & Ford, J.D. (Eds.), Treating complex traumatic stress disorders: An evidence-based guide (166-182). New York, NY: The Guilford Press.

Browne, A., & Finkelhor, D. (1986). Impact of child sexual abuse: A review of the research. *Psychological Bulletin, 99*(1), 66-77.

Bruce, F. (1952). *Lexicon results*. Retrieved from http://cf.blueletterbible.org/lang/lexicon/lexicon.cfm?Strongs=G3340&t=kjv

Burroughs, A. (2004). *Dry: A memoir*. New York, NY: Picador.

Burton, M., & Burton, R. (1969). *The international wildlife encyclopedia*. New York, NY: Marshall Cavendish Corporation.

Bury the hatchet. (n.d.). In *Cambridge international dictionary of idioms*. Retrieved July 24, 2008, from The Free Dictionary: http://idioms.thefreedictionary.com/bury+the+hatchet

Bury your head in the sand. (n.d.). In *Cambridge international dictionary of idioms*. Retrieved July 24, 2008, from The Free Dictionary: http://idioms.thefreedictionary.com/bury+head+in+the+sand

Card, M. (2005). *A sacred sorrow*. Colorado Springs, CO: NavPress.

Cavatina. (n.d.). Retrieved from http://dictionary.reference.com/browse/cavatina

Chambers, O. (1995). *Christian disciplines*. Grand Rapids, MI: Discovery House.

Chu, J. A. (1998). *Rebuilding shattered lives: The responsible treatment of complex post-traumatic and dissociative disorders*. New York, NY: John Wiley & Sons.

Church, T. M. (1905). Come, Thou Fount of Ev'ry Blessing. Nashville: Publishing House of the M.E. Church.

Clark, K. (2009). Institutional child sexual abuse—Not just a Catholic thing. *William Mitchell Law Review*, *36*(1), 220-240.

Cohn, L. (1996). From sexual abuse to empowerment. In M. F. Schwartz & L. Cohn, *Sexual abuse and eating disorders*. New York, NY: Brunner-Routledge.

Conte, J. B. (1993). Self-reported amnesia for abuse in adults molested as children. *Journal of Traumatic Stress, 6*(1), 21-31.

Conterio, K., Lader, W., & Bloom, J. K. (1998). *Bodily harm: The breakthrough healing program for self-injurers.* New York, NY: Hyperion.

Corbin, W. R., Bernat, J. A., Calhoun, K. S., McNair, L. D., & Seals, K. L. (2001). The role of alcohol expectancies and alcohol consumption among sexually victimized and nonvictimized college women. *Journal of Interpersonal Violence, 16*(4), 297-311.

Corcoran, J. (2005). *Building strengths and skills: A collaborative approach to working with clients.* New York, NY: Oxford University Press.

Corey, G. (2009). *Theory and practice of counseling and psychotherapy.* Belmont, CA: Thomson Brooks/Cole.

Costin, C. (2007). *The eating disorder sourcebook: A comprehensive guide to the causes, treatments, and prevention of eating disorders.* New York, NY: McGraw-Hill.

Courtois, C. A. (1996). *Healing the incest wound: Adult survivors in therapy.* New York, NY: Norton.

Courtois, C. A., Ford, J.D., & Cloitre, M. (2009). Best practices in psychotherapy for adults. In C. A. Courtois & J.D. Ford (Eds.), *Treating complex stress disorders: An evidence-based guide* (pp. 82-103). New York, NY: The Guilford Press.

Crabb, L. (2001). *Shattered dreams.* Colorado Springs, CO: WaterBrook Press.

Dalenberg, C. J. (2000). *Countertransference and the treatment of trauma.* Washington, DC: American Psychological Association.

Darwish, N. (2008). *Cruel and usual punishment.* Nashville, TN: Thomas Nelson.

Dawn, M. J. (1998). *I'm lonely, LORD—How long?* Grand Rapids, MI: Eerdmans.

Dearman, J. A. (2002). *The NIV Jeremiah/Lamentations application commentary.* Grand Rapids, MI: Zondervan.

DeSalvo, L. A. (1989). *Virginia Woolf: The impact of childhood sexual abuse on her life and work*. Boston, MA: Beacon Press.

Dewey, A., Hahn, D., McArthur, S., Schumacher, T. (Producers), & Allers, R., & Minkoff, R. (Directors). (1994). *The lion king* [Motion picture]. United States: Walt Disney Motion Pictures.

Doctor, R. M., & Shiromoto, F. N. (2010). *The encyclopedia of trauma and traumatic stress disorders*. New York, NY: Facts on File.

Doka, K. J. (1989). *Disenfranchised grief*. Lexington: Lexington Books. As quoted in C. J. Sofka (1999), For the butterflies I never chased, I grieve: Incorporating grief and loss issues in treatment with survivors of childhood sexual abuse. *Journal of Personal & Interpersonal Loss, 4*(2), 125-144.

D'Onofrio, A. A. (2007). *Adolescent self-injury: A comprehensive guide for counselors and health care professionals*. New York, NY: Springer Publishers.

Drisdelle, R. (n.d.). *Suite 101.com*. Retrieved from http://rosemary-drisdelle.suite101.com/how-do-penguins-keep-warm--a9817

Dube, S. R., Anda, R. F., Whitfield, C. L., Brown, D. W., Felitti, V. J., Dong, M., & Giles, W. H. (2005). Long-term consequences of childhood sexual abuse by gender of victim. *American Journal of Preventative Medicine, 28*(5), 430-438.

Duncan, K. A. (2005). The relationship between posttraumatic stress disorder and substance abuse in women with a history of childhood sexual abuse trauma. In G. R. Walz & R. K. Yep (Eds.), VISTAS: Compelling perspectives on counseling. Alexandria, VA: American Counseling Association.

Dworkin, A. (1997). Prostitution and male supremacy. In A. Dworkin, *Life and death*. New York, NY: Free Press. Quoted in Prostitution factsheet on human rights violations. Retrieved from http://www.prostitutionresearch.com/factsheet.html

Eager, G. B. (1913). Ashes. In J. Orr (Ed.), *International Standard Bible Encyclopaedia.* (2007, April 1 ed.). Retrieved from http://www.blueletterbible.org/search/Dictionary/viewTopic.cfm?type=GetTopic&Topic=Ashes&DictList=4#ISBE

Ekhart, A., Lorenz, C. (Producers), & Stern, J. M. (Director). (2005). *Neverwas* [Motion picture]. United States: Miramax Home Entertainment and Sidney Kimmel Entertainment.

Eldredge, J. (2007). *Desire: The journey we must take to find the life God offers.* Nashville, TN: Thomas Nelson.

Elliot, D. M., & Briere, J. (1992). Sexual abuse trauma among professional women: Validating the trauma symptom checklist 40 (TSC-40). *Child Abuse and Neglect, 16*(3), 391-398.

Elliott, D. M. (1997). Traumatic events: Prevalence and delayed recall in the general population. *Journal of Counseling and Clinical Psychology, 65*(5) 811-820.

Enns, P. (2000). *The NIV Exodus application commentary.* Grand Rapids, MI: Zondervan.

Farber, B. A. (2006). *Self-disclosure in psychotherapy.* New York, NY: The Guilford Press.

Featherman, J. M. (1995). Jews and sexual child abuse. In L. A. Fontes, *Sexual abuse in nine North American cultures: Treatment and prevention.* Thousand Oaks, CA: Sage Publications.

Feiring, C., Taska, L., & Lewis, M. (2002). Adjustment following sexual abuse discovery: The role of shame and attributional style. *Developmental Psychology, 38*(1), 79-92.

Fine, D., Head, S., Wilson, S., & Sharp, I. (1998). *Tess of the D'Urbervilles.* United Kingdom: London Weekend Television & A&E Television Networks.

Finkelhor, D. (1979). *Sexually victimized children.* New York, NY: Free Press.

Finkelhor, D., & Browne, A. (1985). The traumatic impact of child sexual abuse: A conceptualization. *American Journal of Orthopsychiatry, 55*(4), 530-541.

Fisher, A. Q., & Rivas, M. E. (2001). *Finding fish: A memoir.* New York, NY: Morrow.

Follette, V., Polusny, M., & Milbeck, K. (1994). Mental health and law enforcement professionals: Trauma history, psychological symptoms, and impact of providing services to child sexual abuse survivors. *Professional Psychology: Research and Practice, 25*(3), 275-282.

Fontes, L. A. (2005). *Child abuse and culture: Working with diverse families.* New York, NY: Guilford Press.

Foote, C. J. (1994). *Survivor prayers: Talking with God about childhood sexual abuse.* Louisville, KY: Westminster/John Knox Press.

Ford, J.D., & Courtois, C.A. (2009). Defining and understanding complex trauma and complex traumatic stress disorders. In Courtois, C.A., & Ford, J.D. (Eds.), Treating complex traumatic stress disorders: An evidence-based guide (13-30). New York, NY: The Guilford Press.

Foster, R. (1992). *Prayer: Finding the heart's true home.* New York, NY: HarperSanFrancisco.

Frawley O'Dea, M. G., & Golder, V. (Eds.). (2007). *Predatory priests, silenced victims: The sexual abuse crisis and the Catholic church.* New York, NY: Routledge.

Freedman, S. R., & Enright, D. R. (1996). Forgiveness as an intervention goal with incest survivors. *Journal of Consulting and Clinical Psychology, 64*(5), 983-992.

French, R. (2007, June 14). Three insurers shed light on Protestant church sex abuse. *The Houston Chronicle.* Retrieved from http://stopbaptistpredators.org/article07/three_insurers_shed_light.html

Freyd, J. J. (1997). *Betrayal trauma: The logic of forgetting childhood abuse.* Cambridge, MA: Harvard University Press.

Frisbie, A. Y., Berner, F., Myers, M. (Producers), & Sharzer, J. (Director). (2004). *Speak* [Motion picture]. United States: Showtime Independent Films.

Froeschle, J., & Moyer, M. (2004). Just cut it out: Legal and ethical challenges in counseling students who self-mutilate. *Professional School Counseling, 7*(4), 231-235.

Fung, G. & Fung, C. (2009, May). What do prayer studies prove? *Christianity Today, 53*, 43-44.

Galloway, J. (2005). *Run injury free with Jeff Galloway*. Retrieved from http://www.jeffgalloway.com/training/walk_breaks.html.

Gartner, R. B. (2004). Predatory priests: Sexually abusing fathers. *Studies in Gender and Sexuality, 5*(1), 31-56.

Gartner, R. B. (2007). Failed "fathers," boys betrayed. In M.G. Frawley-O'Dea & V. Goldner, (Eds.), *Predatory Priests, Silenced Victims*. Hillsdale, NJ: The Analytic Press, Inc.

Gary. (2006). Justice partners. In P. Yancey, *Prayer: Does it make any difference?* (p.110). Grand Rapids, MI: Zondervan.

Geisel, T. S. (1949). *Bartholomew and the Oobleck*. New York, NY: Random House.

Gilligan, P. & Akhtar, S. (2006). Cultural barriers to the disclosures of child sexual abuse in Asian communities: Listening to what women say. *British Journal of Social Work, 36*, 1361-1377.

Glover, N. M., Janikowski, T. P., & Benshoff, J. J. (1995). The incidence of incest histories among clients receiving substance abuse treatment. *Journal of Counseling and Development, 73*(4), 475-480.

Grant, B., & Hudlin, C.L. (Eds.). (2007). *Hands that heal: International curriculum to train caregivers of trafficking survivors*, Springfield, MO: Life Publishers.

Gupton-Pruett, R. (2009). *Be a part of the modern abolitionist movement*. Retrieved from http://rondagp.wordpress.com/category/modern-slavery-human-trafficking-abolitionist/

Guthrie, N. (2005). *The one year book of hope*. Wheaton, IL: Tyndale House.

Guy, J. D. (1987). *The personal life of the psychotherapist*. New York, NY: Wiley.

Haines, J., & Williams, C. (2003). Coping and problem solving of self-mutilators. *Journal of Clinical Psychology, 59*(10), 1097-1106.

Hallesby, O. (1994). *Prayer*. Minneapolis, MN: Augsburg Fortress.

Hallman, J. (2008). *The heart of female same-sex attraction: A comprehensive counseling resource*. Downers Grove, IL: InterVarsity Press.

Hammel-Zabin, A. (2003). *Conversations with a pedophile*. Fort Lee, NJ: Barricade Books.

Hardy, T. (1891). *Tess of the D'Urbervilles*. Boston, MA: The Riverside Press.

Harrison, K. (1998). In Strong, M., *A bright red scream: Self-mutilation and the language of pain*. (p. 17). New York, NY: Penguin Group.

Hemingway, E. (1929). *A farewell to arms*. New York, NY: SCRIBNER.

Herman, J. (1997). *Trauma and recovery*. New York, NY: Basic Books.

Himelein, M., & McElrath, J. (1996). Resilient child sexual abuse survivors: Cognitive coping and illusion. *Child Abuse and Neglect, 20*(8), 747-758.

Hinduism gods. (2011). Retrieved from http://www.allaboutreligion.org/hinduism-gods-faq.htm.

Holeman, V. T., & Myers, R. W. (1997). Effects of forgiveness of perpetrators on marital adjustment for survivors of sexual abuse. *The Family Journal: Counseling and Therapy for Couples and Families, 6*(3), 182-188.

Hope. (2003). In *The American heritage dictionary*. Retrieved November 15, 2008, from http://www.thefreedictionary.com/hope

Hopper, J. (2011). *Jim Hopper, Ph.D.*.Retrieved from http://www.jimhopper.com/memory/

Hubbard, D. A., & Wiseman, D. J. (Eds.). (1989). *Tyndale Old Testament commentaries: Hosea*. Downers Grove, IL: InterVarsity Press.

Hugo, V. (1862). *Les misérables*. New York, NY: Random House.

Human Rights Watch. (1999). Retrieved August 21, 2008 from: http://www.hrw.org/reports/1999/rwanda/Geno1-3-04.htm

Hunter, M. (1990). *Abused boys: The neglected victims of sexual abuse*. New York, NY: Fawcett Columbine.

Hunter, M., & Gerber, P. N. (1990). Use of the term victim and survivor in the grief stages commonly seen during recovery from sexual abuse. In M. Hunter (Ed.), *The sexually abused male: Application of treatment strategies* (pp. 79-89). Lexington, KY: Lexington Books.

iloveindia.com. (n.d.). Retrieved June 25, 2009, from Benefits of Dates: http://lifestyle.iloveindia.com/lounge/benefits-of-dates-1962.html

International Society for the Study of Dissociation (ISSD). (2005). Guidelines for treating dissociative identity disorder in adults. *Journal of Trauma and Disscociation, 6*(4), 69-149.

James, C. C. (2008). *The Gospel of Ruth: Loving God enough to break the rules*. Grand Rapids, MI: Zondervan.

Jamieson, R., Faussct, A. R., & Brown, D. (2000). The book of the prophet Ezekiel. *Commentary critical and explanatory on the whole Bible*. Blue Letter Bible. Retrieved from http://www.blueletterbible.org/commentaries/comm_view.cfm?AuthorID=7&contentID=2726&commInfo=6&topic=Ezekiel

Jantz, G. L. (1995). *Hope, help, and healing for eating disorders*. Colorado Springs, CO: Shaw Books.

Jars of Clay (2005). God will lift up your head [recorded by Jars of Clay]. On *Redemption Songs* [CD]. Franklin, TN: Essential Records.

Judean date palm. (n.d.). In *Wikipedia, The Free Encyclopedia.* Retrieved from http://en.wikipedia.org/w/index. php?title=Judean_date_palm&oldid=287990651.

Kalman, M. (2005, June 12). *San Francisco Chronicle, Foreign Service.* Retrieved from http://www.sfgate.com/cgi-bin/article. cgi?f=/c/a/2005/06/12/MNGJND7G5T1.DTL

Kane, D., Cheston, S. E., & Greer, J. (1993). Perceptions of God by survivors of childhood sexual abuse: An exploratory study in an underresearched area. *Journal of Psychology and Theology, 21*(3), 228-237.

Kang, S., et al. (1999). Adverse effect of child abuse victimization among substance-using women in treatment. *Journal of Interpersonal Violence, 14*(6), 657-670.

Kardam, F. (2005). *The dynamics of honor killing in Turkey.* Ankara: United Nations Development Program.

Kellemen, R. W. (2007). *Soul physicians: A theology of soul care and spiritual direction.* Winona Lake, IN: BMH Books.

Keller, W. P. (1986). *Phillip Keller: The inspirational writings.* New York, NY: Inspirational Press.

Kennedy, D., Howsam, G., Bloye, C. (Producers), & Curtis, D. (Producer and Director). (2005). *Our fathers* [Motion Picture]. United States: Showtime.

Kettlewell, C. (1999). *Skin game.* New York, NY: St. Martin's Press.

Kidd, S.M. (2002). *The secret life of bees.* New York, NY: Penguin Books.

Kinzie, J. D. (1983). Posttraumatic effects and their treatment among Southeast Asian refugees. In J.P. Wilson & B. Raphael (Eds.), *International handbook of traumatic stress syndromes* (pp. 311-319). New York, NY: Plenum Press.

Klonsky, E. D., & Muehlenkamp, J. J. (2007). Self-injury: A research review for the practitioner. *Journal of Clinical Psychology, 63*(11), 1045-1056.

Kluft, R. P. (1990). On the apparent invisibility of incest: A personal reflection on things known and forgotten. In R.P. Kluft (Ed.), *Incest related syndromes of adult psychopathology* (pp. 11-34). Washington, DC: American Psychiatric Press.

Knapp, C. (1996). *Drinking.* New York, NY: Dell Publishing.

Kristof, N.K., & WuDunn, S. (2009). *Half the sky.* New York, NY: Random House, Inc.

Lambeth, M. (2009, January 16). *Waste management.* Retrieved from http://worcestershire.whub.org.uk/home/wcc-waste-composting-how-it-works

Lament. (2011). In *Collins essential English dictionary online.* Retrieved from http://www.collinslanguage.com/results.asp x?context=3&reversed=False&action=define&homonym=-1&text=lament

Lamott, A. (1999). *Traveling mercies.* New York, NY: Anchor Books.

Langberg, D. (2003). *Counseling survivors of sexual abuse.* Longwood, FL: Xulon Press.

Larson, C. C. (2008). *Charting a route to restoration.* Retrieved from http://www.prisonfellowship.org/component/content/article/48-stories-of-transformation/341-charting-a-route-to-restoration

Larson, C. C. (2009). *As we forgive: Stories of reconciliation from Rwanda.* Grand Rapids, MI: Zondervan.

Lawson, R., Drebing, C., Berge, G., Mincellett, A., & Penk, W. (1998). The long-term impact of child abuse on religious behavior and spirituality in men. *Child Abuse and Neglect, 22*(5), 1245-1254.

Lee, J. (1989). "Our hearts are collectively breaking": Teaching survivors of violence. *Gender and Society, 3*(4), 541-548.

Lewis, C. S. (1964). *Letters to Malcolm: Chiefly on prayer.* New York, NY: Harcourt, Brace, and World.

Lewis, C. S. (1978). *Prince Caspian.* (pp. 123-124). London, United Kingdom: Puffin Books.

Lewis, C. S. (2001a). *The chronicles of Narnia.* New York, NY: HarperCollins.

Lewis, C. S. (2001b). *Mere Christianity: A revised and amplified edition, with a new introduction, of the three books, broadcast talks, Christian behavior, and beyond personality.* San Francisco, CA: HarperSanFrancisco.

Linde, D. (1999). Goodbye Earl [Recorded by The Dixie Chicks]. On *Fly* [CD]. New York, NY: Sony.

Lisak, D. (1994). The psychological impact of sexual abuse: Content analysis of interviews with male survivors. *Journal of Traumatic Stress, 7*(4), 525-548.

Loftus, E. F. (1993). *The reality of repressed memories. American Psychologist, 48*(5), 518-537.

Loftus, E., & Ketcham, K. (1994). *The myth of repressed memory: False memories and allegations of sexual abuse.* New York, NY: St. Martin's Griffin

Lotz, A. G. (2005). *Heaven: My Father's House.* Nashville, TN: Thomas Nelson.

Lovett, B. B. (2004). Child sexual abuse disclosure: Maternal response and other variables impacting the victim. *Child and Adolescent Social Work Journal, 21*(4), 355-371.

Macy, H. (1999). *Rhythms of the inner life: Yearning for closeness with God.* Colorado Springs, CO: Victor Publishing.

Madakasira, S. & O'Brien, K. (1987). Acute Posttraumatic Stress Disorder in Victims of a Natural Disaster. *Journal of Nervous and Mental Disease, 175*(5), 286-290.

Mahoney, M. J. (1991). *Human change processes: The scientific foundations of psychotherapy.* New York, NY: Basic Books.

Malchiodi, C. A. (2003). *Handbook of art therapy.* New York, NY: Guilford Press.

Manning, B. (1999). *The ragamuffin Gospel*. Sisters, OR: Multnomah Publishers.

Manning, B. (2009). *The furious longing of God*. Colorado Springs, CO: David C. Cook.

Martinez-Taboas, A. (1996). Repressed memories: Some clinical data contributing toward its elucidation. *American Journal of Psychotherapy, 50*(2), 217-230.

Marvin, N. (Producer), & Darabont, F. (Director). (1994). *The Shawshank redemption* [Motion picture]. United States: Castle Rock Entertainment.

Matchan, L. (1992, June 8). Ex-priests' accusers tell of the damage. *Boston Globe*. Retrieved from http://www.boston.com/globe/spotlight/abuse/archives/060892_porter.htm

May, G. G. (1988). *Addiction and grace*. New York, NY: HarperCollins.

Mcalinden, A. (2006). 'Setting 'em up': Personal, familial, and institutional grooming in the sexual abuse of children. *Social Legal Studies, 15,* 339-362.

McCammon, S. L. (1999). Painful pedagogy: Teaching about trauma in academic and training settings. In B. H. Stamm (Ed.), *Secondary traumatic stress: Self-care issues for clinicians, researchers, and educators*. Lutherville, MD: Sidran Press.

McKinley, R. (2005). *Jesus in the margins*. Sisters, OR: Multnomah Publishers.

McMillen, C., Zuravin, S., & Rideout, G. (1995). Perceived benefit from child sexual abuse. *Journal of Consulting and Clinical Psychology, 63*(6), 1037-1043.

Merton, T. (1999). *The seven storey mountain*. San Diego, CA: Harcourt Trade Publishers.

Milchan, A., Grisham, J., Nathansham, M., Lowry, H. (Producers), & Schumacher, J. (Director). (1996). *A time to kill* [Motion picture]. United States: Regency Enterprises.

Miller, A. (1991). *Breaking down the wall of silence: The liberating experience of facing painful truth.* New York, NY: E. P. Dutton.

Miller, D. (2004). *Searching for God knows what.* Nashville, TN: Thomas Nelson.

Moncrieff, J., et al. (1996). Sexual abuse in people with alcohol problems: A study of the prevalence of sexual abuse and its relationship to drinking behavior. *British Journal of Psychiatry, 169*(3), 355-360.

Moody, D. L. (1994). Blessed hope. In W. W. Wiersbe, *Classic sermons on hope* (p. 63). Peabody, MA: Hendrickson Publishers.

Moore, B. (1999). *Breaking free: Making liberty in Christ a reality in life.* Nashville, TN: LifeWay Press.

Mosaic. (2005). In *The American Heritage New Dictionary of Cultural Literacy.* (3rd ed.). Houghton Mifflin. Retrieved from http://dictionary.reference.com/browse/mosaic.

Murphy, J. (Ed.). (2005). *Art therapy with young survivors of sexual abuse: Lost for words.* Philadelphia, PA: Taylor & Francis Inc.

Neumann, D. A., & Gamble, S. J. (1995). Issues in the professional development of psychotherapists: Countertransference and vicarious traumatization in the new trauma therapist. *Psychotherapy, 32*(2), 341-347.

Newton, M. (2007). Father James Porter. *Sexual predators.* Retrieved from http://www.trutv.com/library/crime/serial_killers/predators/porter/justice_7.html

North, J. (1987). Wrongdoing and Forgiveness. *Philosophy, 62,* 502.

Nouwen, H. J. M. (1993). *The return of the prodigal son: A story of homecoming.* New York, NY: Image.

Nouwen, H. J. M. (1995). *The Genesee diary: Report from a Trappist monastery.* London, United Kingdom: Darton, Longman and Todd.

Osborne, B., Sanders, T., Walsh, F. (Producers), & Jackson, P. (Producer and Director). (2001). *The lord of the rings: The fellowship of the ring* [Motion picture]. United States: WingNut Films and The Saul Zaentz Company.

Oswalt, J. N. (2003). *The NIV Isaiah application commentary.* Grand Rapids, MI: Zondervan.

Parker, S. & Thomas, R. (2009). Psychological differences in shame vs. guilt: Implications for mental health counselors. *Journal of Mental Health Counseling, 31*(3), 213-224.

Parkinson, P. (1997). *Child sexual abuse and the churches.* London, United Kingdom: Hodder and Stoughton.

Parkinson, P. (2003). *Child sexual abuse and the churches.* Sydney, Australia: Aquila Press.

Pearlman, L. A., & Mac Ian, P. S. (1995). Vicarious traumatization: An empirical study of the effects of trauma work on trauma therapists. *Professional Psychology: Research and Practice, 26*(6), 558-565.

Pearlman, L. A., & Mac Ian, P. S. (1999). Vicarious traumatization among trauma therapists: Empirical findings on self care. *Traumatic Stress Points: News for the International Society for Traumatic Stress Studies, 26,* 558-565.

Peterson, E. (2005). Foreword. In M. Card, *A sacred sorrow* (p. 11). Colorado Springs, CO: NavPress.

Peugh, R., & Schultz, T. (2005). *Transformed in His presence: The need for prayer in counseling.* Winona Lake, IN: BMH Books.

Piper, J. (1982). Call me husband, not Baal. Retrieved from http://www.desiringgod.org/ResourceLibrary/Sermons/ByScripture/41/372_Call_Me_Husband_Not_Baal/

Polemic. (2003). *The American heritage dictionary of the English language* (4th ed.). Boston, MA: Houghton Mifflin Company.

Ponton, L., & Goldstein, D. (2004). Sexual abuse of boys by clergy. *Adolescent Psychiatry, 28,* 209-229.

Putnam, F. W. (2003, March). Ten-year research update review: Child sexual abuse. *Journal of American Academy of Child Adolescent Psychiatry, 42*(3), 269-278.

Qobil, R. (2010, September 7). The sexually abused dancing boys of Afghanistan. *BBC World Service*. Retrieved from http://www.bbc.co.uk/news/world-south-asia-11217772

Quinn, P. E. (1994). *From victim to victory: Prescriptions from a child abuse survivor*. Nashville, TN: Abingdon Press.

Rivers, F. (1997). *Redeeming love*. Colorado Springs, CO: Multnomah Books.

Romano, E., & De Luca, R. V. (2001). Male sexual abuse: A review of effects, abuse characteristics, and links with later psychological functioning. *Aggression and Violent Behavior, 6*(1), 55-78.

Ropelato, J. (2008). Internet pornography statistics. Retrieved from http://internet-filter-review.toptenreviews.com/internet-pornography-statistics.html

Rosenthal, A. M. (1999). *Thirty-eight witnesses: The Kitty Genovese case*. Berkeley, CA: University of California Press.

Rossetti, S. J. (1995). The impact of child sexual abuse on attitudes toward God and the Catholic church. *Child Abuse and Neglect, 19*(12), 1469-1481.

Roy, A. C (2003, January 27). Confronting Empire. *World Social Forum*, Porto Allegre, Brazil.

Rucyahana, J. (2007). *The bishop of Rwanda*. Nashville, TN: Thomas Nelson.

Russell, D.E.H. (1999). *The secret trauma: Incest in the lives of girls and women*. New York, NY: Basic Books.

Saakvitne, K. W. (1995). *Trauma and the therapist: Countertransference and vicarious traumatization in psychotherapy with incest survivors*. New York, NY: Norton.

Saakvitne, K. W., & Pearlman, L. A. (1996). *Transforming the pain: A workbook on vicarious traumatization for helping professionals who work with traumatized clients*. New York, NY: Norton.

Salter, A. C. (1995). *Transforming trauma: A guide to understanding and treating adult survivors of child sexual abuse*. Thousand Oaks, NY: Sage Publications.

Salter, A. C. (2003). *Predators: Pedophiles, rapists, and other sex of-fenders.* New York, NY: Basic Books.

Sanderson, C. (2006). *Counselling adult survivors of child sexual abuse* (3rd ed.). London, United Kingdom: Jessica Kingsley Publishers.

Schauben, L. J., & Frazier, P. A. (1995). Vicarious trauma: The ef-fects on female counselors of working with sexual violence sur-vivors. *Psychology of Women Quarterly, 19*(1), 49-64.

Schneider, W. (Producer and Director). (2007). *Cut: Teens and self-injury.* [Motion picture]. United States: Coney Island Studios.

Schulkind, J. (Ed.). (1985). *Moments of being* (2nd ed.). New York, NY: Harcourt Brace.

Schultz, T. (2000, August). Memory recall among individuals re-porting child sexual abuse: The role of suggestibility, dissocia-tion, and closeness with the perpetrator. *Dissertation Abstracts International, 62,* 1-146.

Schultz, T., Passmore, L., & Yoder, C. Y. (2003). Emotional close-ness with perpetrators and amnesia for child sexual abuse. *Journal of Child Sexual Abuse, 12*(1), 67-88.

Seibold, M. (2001). When the wounding runs deep: Encouragement for those on the road to forgiveness. In M. R. McMinn & T. R. Phillips (Eds.), *Care for the soul.* Downers Grove, IL: InterVarsity Press.

Sgroi, S. M. (1982). *Handbook of clinical intervention in child sexual abuse.* Lexington, KY: Lexington Books.

Sheff, D. (2008). *Beautiful boy.* Boston, MA: Houghton Mifflin.

Sheinberg, M., & Fraenkel, P. (1999, May/June). Loyalty violated. *Family Therapy Networker—Vienna, 63*-78.

Shelley, S. W., & Stoecker, L. I. (2005). *Human traffic and transna-tional crime: Eurasian and American perspectives.* Lanham, MD: Rowman and Littlefield.

Shults, F. L., & Sandage, S. J. (2003). *The faces of forgiveness: Searching for wholeness and salvation.* Grand Rapids, MI: Baker Academic.

Seibold, M. (2001) When the wounding runs deep: Encouragement for those on the road to forgiveness. In M.R. McMinn & T. R. Phillips (Eds.) *Care for the soul.* (p. 295) Downers Grove, IL: InterVarsity Press.

Shonnenberg, S. M. & Blank, A. S. (1985). *The trauma of war: Stress and recovery in Viet Nam veterans.* Washington, D.C.: American Psychiatric Press.

Silverman, S. W. (1999). *Because I remember terror, Father, I remember you.* Athens, GA: The University of Georgia Press.

Sittser, J. (2003). *When God doesn't answer your prayer.* Grand Rapids, MI: Zondervan.

Smiley, J. (1991). *A thousand acres.* New York, NY: Knopf.

Smith, E. M. (2002). *Healing life's hurts through theophostic prayer.* Royal Oak, MI: New Creation Publishing, Inc.

Smith, E. M. (2008). *A "theophostic" moment in the life of Simon Peter.* Retrieved from http://www.swrcb.ca.gov/water_issues/ programs/swamp/docs/cwt/guidance/3159.pdf

Smith, M. D. (2004). *Encyclopedia of rape.* Westport, CT: Greenwood Press.

Solnit, R. (2006). *Hope in the dark.* New York, NY: Nation Books.

Spitzer, B., & Avis, J. M. (2006). Recounting graphic sexual abuse memories in therapy: The impact on women's healing. *Journal of Family Violence, 21*(3), 173-184.

State Water Resources Control Board Clean Water Team. (n.d.). Color of water fact sheet. Retrieved from http://www.swrcb.ca.gov/ water_issues/programs/swamp/docs/cwt/guidance/3159.pdf

Steele, K., & van der Hart, O. (2009). Treating dissociation. In C. A. Courtois & J.D. Ford (Eds.), *Treating complex stress disor-*

ders: An evidence-based guide (pp. 145-165). New York, NY: The Guilford Press.

Steele, K., & van der Hart, O., & Nijenhuis, E.R.S. (2005). Phase-oriented treatment of structural dissociation in complex traumatization. *Journal of Trauma and Dissociation, 6*(3), 11-53.

Summit, R. (1983). Child sexual abuse accommodation syndrome. *Child Abuse and Neglect, 7*(2), 177-193.

Surgereons, A. A. (2007, October). *Your orthopaedic connection.* Retrieved from http://orthoinfo.aaos.org/topic.cfm?topic=a00097

Sunstone, P. (2008, May 6). The metaphors of heaven and hell. *Café Philos: An internet cafe.* Retrieved from http://cafephilos.wordpress.com/2008/05/06/the-metaphors-of-heaven-and-hell

Teacher, J. B. (Ed.), & Powell, J. (1994). *Women of words: A personal introduction to thirty-five important writers.* Philadelphia, PA: Courage Books.

Ten Boom, C., Sherrill, J. L., & Sherrill, E. (1971). *The hiding place.* Washington Depot, CT: Chosen Books.

Terr, L. C. (1990). Who's afraid of Virginia Woolf? Clues to early sexual abuse in literature. *The Psychoanalytic Study of the Child, 45.* 539-540.

Terr, L. (1991). Childhood traumas. *American Journal of Psychiatry, 148,* 10-20.

The 'monsters' among us. [Editorial]. (2012, May). *Christianity Today,* 47.

Tiegreen, C. (2007). *Creative prayer.* Colorado Springs, CO: Multnomah Books.

Tozer, A. (1961). *The knowledge of the holy.* New York, NY: HarperCollins.

Tracy, S. R. (1999). Sexual abuse and forgiveness. *Journal of Psychology and Theology, 27*(3), 219-229.

Tracy, S. R. (2005). *Mending the soul: Understanding and healing abuse.* Grand Rapids, MI: Zondervan.

Trippany, R. L., Wilcoxon, S. A., & Satcher, J. F. (2003). Factors influencing vicarious traumatization for therapists of survivors of sexual victimization. *Journal of Trauma Practice, 2*(1), 47-60.

Trippany, R. L., Kress, V. E. W., & Wilcoxon, S. A. (2004). Preventing vicarious trauma: What counselors should know when working with trauma survivors. *Journal of Counseling and Development, 82*(1), 31-37.

U2. (1987). Still haven't found what I'm looking for [Recorded by U2]. On *Joshua tree* [CD]. London: Island Records.

United Nations Children's Fund Innocenti Research Centre. (2001). Early marriage: Child spouses. *Innocenti Digest, 7.* Retrieved from http://www.unicef-irc.org/publications/pdf/digest7e.pdf

van der Kolk, B. (1997). Posttraumatic stress disorder and memory. *Psychiatric Times, 14*, 2.

van der Kolk, B. A., McFarlane, A. C., & Weisaeth, L. (1996). *Traumatic stress: The effects of overwhelming experience on mind, body, and society.* New York, NY: The Guilford Press.

van der Kolk, B. A. (2007). The complexity of adaptation to trauma self-regulation, stimulus discrimination, and characterological development. In B. A. van der Kolk, A. C. McFarlane, & L. Weisaeth (Eds.), *Traumatic stress: The effects of overwhelming experience on mind, body, and society* (pp. 303-327). New York, NY: Guilford Press.

Veenstra, G. J. (1992). Psychological concepts of forgiveness. *Journal of Psychology and Christianity, 11*(2), 160-169.

Volf, M. (2006). *The end of memory: Remembering rightly in a violent world.* Grand Rapids, MI: William B. Eerdmans Publishing Company.

Wardle, T. (2001). *Healing care healing prayer: Helping the broken find wholeness in Christ.* Orange, CA: New Leaf Books.

White, E. B. (1980). *Charlotte's web*. New York, NY: HarperCollins Publishers.

White, V., Trepal-Wollenzier, H., & Nolan, J. (2002). College students and self-injury: Intervention strategies for counselors. *Journal of College Counseling, 5*(2), 105-113.

Widom, C. S., & Hiller-Sturmhofel, S. (2001). Alcohol abuse as a risk factor for and consequence of child abuse. *Alcohol Research and Health: The Journal of the National Institute on Alcohol Abuse and Alcoholism, 25*(1), 52-57.

Wilkinson, C. B. (1983). Aftermath of a disaster: The collapse of the Hyatt Regency Hotel Skywalks. *American Journal of Psychiatry, 140*(9), 1134-1139.

Wilsnack, S. C., Vogeltanz, N. D., Klassen, A. D., & Harris, T. R. (1997). Childhood sexual abuse and women's substance abuse: National survey findings. *Journal of Studies on Alcohol, 58*(3), 264-271.

Wolff, C. G. (1988). Emily Dickinson. *Radcliffe biography series*. Reading, MA: Addison-Wesley.

Wright, M., Crawford, E., & Sebastian, K. (2007). Positive resolution of childhood sexual abuse experiences: The role of coping, benefit-finding and meaning-making. *Journal of Family Violence, 22*(7), 597-608.

Yancey, P. (1988). *Disappointment with God*. Grand Rapids, MI: Zondervan.

Yancey, P. (2000). *Reaching for the invisible God*. Grand Rapids, MI: Zondervan.

Yancey, P. (2006). *Prayer: Does it make any difference?* Grand Rapids, MI: Zondervan.

Yapko, M. D. (1994). Suggestibility and repressed memories of abuse: A survey of psychotherapist's beliefs. *American Journal of Clinical Hypnosis, 36*(3), 163-171.

Yuan, C., & Yuan, A. (2011). *Out of a far country: A gay son's journey to God: A broken mother's search for hope.* Colorado Springs, CO: Waterbrook Press.

Yuksel, S. (2000). Collusion and denial of childhood sexual trauma in traditional societies. In A. Y. Shalev, R. Yehud, & A. C. McFarlane (Eds.), *International Handbook of Human Response to Trauma* (pp.153-162). New York, NY: Kluwer.

Zacharias, R. (1994). *Can man live without God.* Dallas, TX: Word Publishing.

Zarra III, E. J. (1997). *It should never happen here: A guide for minimizing the risk of child abuse in ministry.* Grand Rapids, MI: Baker Books.

Zuk, R. J., & Wetmore, A. A. (1993). Teaching the incest narrative: Problems and possibilities. *Feminist Teacher, 7*(3), 21-26.

how to use this book

If *Beyond Desolate* inspires you to do something beyond,
here are possibilities:

1. Let the work happen in your own life. Read it again, and be sure
    to ponder and respond to the questions at the end of each chapter.
    If you are a survivor, share your story of abuse with a trusted
    friend or mentor. Consider Christian counseling. Allow God to
    break the chains of abuse.

2. If you are a caregiver, invite your client to read *Beyond Desolate*
    and respond.

3. Suggest *Beyond Desolate* to a friend, family member, colleague,
    pastor, professor, book club, women's group, church group,
    counseling center, high school, university or graduate school.
    Or anyone else we didn't think of!

4. Contact your church pastor about what resources are currently
    available to members suffering with this type of trauma.
    Encourage your pastor to read this book as a possible additional
    resource.

6. Consider hosting a speaking engagement for the authors of
    Beyond Desolate at your church, school, or counseling center.
    Contact Tammy Schultz at *schulttm@grace.edu*

7. Pray – for survivors of abuse everywhere, for perpetrators, too.
    And pray for the ministry of *Beyond Desolate* to extend *beyond*
    what we authors could ask or imagine!

8. Write a *Beyond Desolate* review for Amazon.com. Your comments help!

9. Consider volunteering for or donating to organizations that work to help victims of abuse or trafficking. There are many, but some that we know of and love are:
   - Love 146 (international trafficking)
   - IJM (international slavery in general)
   - Not for Sale (trafficking)
   - Generate Hope (domestic trafficking – San Diego)
   - Amani Ya Juu (hosting a jewelry party to benefit refugees in Kenya)
   - Asia's Hope (building orphanages for children in Cambodia, Thailand, and India to help prevent trafficking of children)

10. If you are blessed with money, consider paying for counseling for just one survivor of abuse. Contact your nearest Christian counseling center for ways to do this.

11. Look up the legal consequences of sexual perpetration in your state. Consider writing to your state official regarding these (generally soft) consequences.

12. Check to see whether *Beyond Desolate* is in your local library. If not, consider donating a copy or suggest to the library to add *Beyond Desolate* to their collection.

13. Encourage your local independent or chain bookstore to carry this book.

14. Ask the book editor of your local newspaper or radio to consider reviewing the book.

about the authors

TAMMY SCHULTZ, PH.D., is a professor, speaker, and counselor. She has passionately taught about sexual abuse in the U.S., Nicaragua, Canada, South Korea, Central Asia, and the Ukraine. Her publications include *Transformed in His Presence: The Need for Prayer in Counseling* (BMH Books) and articles on sexual abuse, prayer, and ethics. She was awarded the 2010 Indiana Counselor of the Year by the Indiana Counseling Association.

HANNAH ESTABROOK, M.A., received her Master's in Counseling from Grace College in 2007 and since then has been able to utilize her skills in community mental health, home-based therapy, and pastoral counseling. Hannah is the co-founder of AVAH! Ministries, an organization that provides seminars for women on a variety of topics such as body image, sexuality, prayer, and friendship. She is passionate about her work counseling survivors of sexual abuse and sex-trafficking. She currently lives in Columbus, Ohio, with her husband, Brian.